High-Risk Infants

High-Risk Infants:
Identification, Assessment, and Intervention

Louis M. Rossetti, Ph.D.
Associate Professor of Speech Pathology
Northeast Missouri State University
Kirksville, Missouri

A College-Hill Publication
Little, Brown and Company
Boston/Toronto/San Diego

College-Hill Press
A Division of
Little, Brown and Company (Inc.)
34 Beacon Street
Boston, Massachusetts 02108

Library of Congress Cataloging-in-Publication Data

Rossetti, Louis Michael.
    High risk infants: Identification, Assessment, and Intervention

    Includes bibliographies and index.
    1. Infants—Diseases—Complications and sequelae.
2. Infants—Development. 3. Developmental disabilities.
I. Title. [DNLM: 1. Child Development Disorders—
diagnosis. 2. Child Development Disorders—prevention &
control. WS 350.6 R829h]
RJ135.R67 1986   618.92   86-17139
ISBN 0–316–75757–8

Printed in the United States of America

This text is affectionately dedicated to the five most important women in my life: Elizabeth, Robyn, Nicole, Jennifer, and their mother, Ruth, without whose encouragement and support it would never have been completed.

CONTENTS

ACKNOWLEDGMENTS

Although the completion of this volume was a time-consuming and serious task, attempting to recall and adequately acknowledge those who helped make it possible is an equally serious endeavor.

I have found College-Hill Press to be a dream publisher, and one that authors from a variety of disciplines should use to a greater degree. Their encouragement and support for a relatively "unknown author" has made the whole process a pleasant one. They are interested in quality publications, and it shows in their products.

No single-authored text can be completed without the aid of an editor. Lee Snyder-McLean of Parsons Research Center, Bureau of Child Research, University of Kansas, has been a superlative one. Her breadth of knowledge relative to child development and associated topics is nothing short of astounding. Her understanding of the authoring process, trials and tribulations included, made her the ideal editor for this work. I deeply appreciate her encouragement, patience, insight, energy, and personal friendship as she provided consistently helpful suggestions throughout the completion of the text.

I would also like to express appreciation to my colleagues in the Speech Pathology Department at Northeast Missouri State University. They have been most patient with me for the past 18 months during the completion of this work. In particular I would like to thank Bill McClelland, my Department Chair, for creating an atmosphere within the department that allowed me the freedom to devote increased time to writing. I have received support from the entire university community, both faculty and administration, and for this I am truly grateful.

The Department of Pediatrics at Kirksville Osteopathic Medical Center, in particular Drs. Kline, Department Head, and Marshall, neonatologist, afforded me unlimited access to patients toward whom clinical interest and activity was directed. Without access of this nature many of the insights provided in this text would not have been possible.

The bulk of manuscript typing and word processing was provided by a steady stream of talented and bright graduate students in speech pathology and audiology. Tracy Engel in particular deserves special recognition.

Finally, many friends who knew little about the topic this work was addressing provided helpful encouragement. Their support, encouragement, and, most importantly, prayers, are greatly appreciated.

FOREWORD

Because the phenomenon of human gestation and birth is associated with so many complex medical, legal, and ethical issues, it enjoys an unprecedented prominence in the collective consciousness and conscience of society in the 1980s. Thus, it seems ironic that, as yet, relatively little public attention or policy is directed towards what happens to the infant, and its family, following that gestation and birth. This is ironic because we have increasing evidence that the quality of familial, medical, therapeutic, and educational care that are provided to the child in the hours, months, and years immediately following birth will greatly influence the ultimate quality of that child's life and the child's family. For no population is this more true than for that of infants identified as being at risk and their parents.

Among professionals growing realization of the critical importance of these early influences on the lives of high-risk infants and their families has paralleled the medical advances that are allowing more and more high-risk infants to survive infancy. Together these forces have resulted in the emergence of the relatively new field of early intervention for high-risk infants that is the focus of this book. The data bases and literature that undergird and are critical to this field have proliferated over the past 2 decades in the journals and edited compendia of many different disciplines. There is an entire literature devoted to the medical sequelae and developmental prognoses associated with different prenatal and perinatal risk factors and another that deals with the processes of bonding and attachment, as well as the consequences of disrupting those processes. Likewise, research outlining the course of early cognitive, motor, social, and language development is found in the child development literature; whereas research on the emotional and practical impact of an at-risk infant on its family will be found in the literature from such disciplines as psychology, family counseling, and social work. Finally, of course, there has emerged a literature devoted to the practice of early intervention—including descriptions of specific assessment procedures and treatment techniques and research reports documenting the absolute and relative effectiveness of different approaches to early intervention. The task of accessing and digesting all of this information can be truly overwhelming for the practitioner interested in early intervention for at-risk infants and their families.

In this volume, Dr. Rossetti has provided a concise, and yet comprehensive, overview of the information and issues associated with intervention for high-risk infants and their families. The early chapters review and interpret medical and developmental literature to provide the reader with a summary of current knowledge about both normal and high-risk infant development, including current outcome data for infants in different risk categories, with and without early intervention. The chapter on parental concerns is particularly powerful in presenting the parents' point of view and in providing information on specific intervention procedures and issues associated with meeting the needs of parents with high-risk infants. The last three chapters and the appendices contain a wealth of information on the early intervention process. There are concise descriptions of different models for delivering early intervention in various service settings and a discussion of transdisciplinary team makeup and functioning required for such a program. Different approaches to infant assessment and the issues associated with these are described. Finally, the author draws upon his own experience and provides specific suggestions regarding practical problems such as how to "sell" an early intervention program to a community or how to read infant hospital discharge reports. In all of these chapters the author has summarized and condensed a great deal of current information and made this information readily available to the interested reader.

I have had the opportunity to interact with Dr. Rossetti throughout the writing of this book and, from the first, I have been struck by two special qualities that he brought to this project. The first is Dr. Rossetti's firsthand knowledge of his subject matter, as he has drawn from his own experience as the speech-language pathologist on a transdisciplinary hospital-based early intervention team serving high-risk infants and their families. In addition to this direct clinical commitment, Dr. Rossetti is involved in numerous research and teaching activities related to this topic. I was equally struck by Dr. Rossetti's unflagging enthusiasm for his subject matter—enthusiasm nurtured by both his professional interest and his experience as a parent who has suffered through a high-risk pregnancy and the loss of an infant. Clearly, this book was a labor of love for Dr. Rossetti, and I am grateful to him for both the labor and the love he has invested in it—I know it is a book that will be used and cited often. And, perhaps we can hope that society at large will soon begin to expand its concern beyond the birth process, to include a serious concern with, and commitment to, the futures of these infants and their families.

Lee K. Snyder-McLean, PhD
University of Kansas
Bureau of Child Research

PREFACE

Interest in the unique needs of high-risk infants has been increasing in recent years. This interest is evidenced in numerous fields of study. Medical technology has made possible the survival of an increasing number of infants who previously would not have survived a precarious neonatal period. With the advent of neonatal intensive care nursery facilities internationally serious questions arise about the developmental status of these infants. Medical personnel have become interested in methodologies to reduce potential contributing factors to developmental delay while children are still in the nursery. Early childhood educators are expressing interest in detecting the presence of developmental delay at as early an age as possible. Special education personnel are concerned about the possible link between risk factors and later academic and school difficulties. Speech-language pathologists have become interested in the speech and language performance of children of younger and younger ages, including the at-risk population. Throughout the remainder of this text the terms practitioner and clinician-educator will be used to designate the increasing number of professionals who are currently or who will be increasingly involved with the provision of services to the at-risk population.

In any area of study descriptive data and information usually precede comparative research endeavors. We are indebted to a number of pioneers, who over the years have provided an increasingly sophisticated picture of the capabilities of infants. Data relative to normal infant development are readily available to those so interested. The visual, motor, auditory, tactile, cognitive, language, and sensory capabilities of infants have been the subject of increasing research. The research undertaken with this unique population has become increasingly sophisticated and has revealed much previously unknown about the tremendous inborn capabilities of very young children. With a new awareness of the infant's ability, it was only natural that important questions about the capabilities of stressed infants would arise. One important concept to keep in mind is that anything that interferes with a child's ability to interact with the environment in a normal manner is a potential source of or contributing factor to the presence of developmental delay. Certainly the high-risk population has been subjected to a potent list of factors that may increase the risk of later developmental problems.

Speech-language pathologists, special education personnel, early childhood educators, and developmental psychologists are at present in a unique position to aid in the ongoing evolution of services to at-risk infants. Although only a minority of clinician-educators are currently involved in providing services to this population, interest is clearly growing as an increasing number of states are mandating services to younger and younger children. In addition, personnel in hospital settings are being asked with increasing frequency to participate in clinical services, joint research efforts, education of parents and other professionals, and developmental follow-up activity with at-risk infants. The academic preparation provided for current students in training is often lacking in material directed specifically to the high-risk population. Those clinician-educators who are involved in service provision have had to overcome in many instances their lack of preparation in efforts to equip themselves to perform adequately with this population of clients.

The purpose of this text is to provide both the student in training and the practitioner in the field with a resource that can be used to increase their understanding of the high-risk population. Chapters include information relative to defining the at-risk population, incidence of high-risk infants, terminology specific to the population, an overview of infant development research, infant assessment data and materials, predictive ability of infant assessment results, relationship between high-risk factors and later developmental status, effectiveness of and need for early intervention, working with the parents of high-risk infants, and the overall role of professional personnel who work with this unique population of clients.

Historically, speech pathology, special education, and developmental psychology as professions have demonstrated a consistent desire to initiate new avenues of service provision. They are again in this position as it relates to the high-risk infant. The opportunity exists to demonstrate the high level of performance and service to which clients have become accustomed. In the years ahead, as more and more is learned about the capability and unique needs of infants, in particular sick infants, the opportunity to provide leadership and demonstrate continued excellence will be presented. This text is directed toward that goal.

Chapter 1

What Is a High-Risk Infant?

DEFINITION

The term *high-risk infant* has been seen much more frequently in the medical, developmental psychology, educational, special education, and speech pathology literature in the past 15 years. To each area of expertise the term may have various meanings. The physician is primarily concerned with mortality and morbidity factors when serving high-risk infants. Other professionals are interested in developmental performance, family concerns, speech and language development, and later school achievement. Although the chances of being born alive and surviving the first year of life have steadily improved, the well-being of an infant born today is by no means assured. For example, in 1979, in the United States alone, 241,000 infants were born weighing less than 2,500 g (5.5 lb), and 44,200 infants died before reaching 1 year of age (McAnarney, 1982).

To facilitate enhanced communication between professionals currently involved in the provision of services to the at-risk population, a clear and concise definition of the term *at-risk* must be agreed upon. Although a variety of systems have been used to classify an infant as being at risk, in this book the term is applied to that class of infants who have been exposed to any one of a number of medical factors that may contribute to later developmental delay. These are infants who have been subjected to a potent array of potentially debilitating conditions. Furthermore, the use of birth weight and gestational age as barometers for developmental risk is a most helpful tool and provides an objective means of establishing risk status. Thus, the high-risk infant is an infant who because of low birth weight, prematurity, or the presence of serious medical complications associated with or independent from birth weight or prematurity, has a greater than normal chance of displaying developmental delay or later cognitive or motor deficits or a combination of these that can be linked with the high-risk status present in the neonatal or postnatal period. Known mental retardation syndromes (Down's syndrome and others) are assumed to be accompanied by relatively predictable patterns of developmental performance. Thus, the presence of the syndrome eliminates doubt about the presence of developmental delay. These children are not included as part of the high-risk population as described in this text. Although psychosocial status and socioeconomic status (SES) are not discussed in detail as separate contributors to risk status, their presence in high-risk populations as defined is acknowledged. The relationship between SES and increased medical risk relative to childbearing is well established. Subsequent chapters discuss the relationship between SES and developmental outcome for high-risk infants. Whereas the term high-risk was used initially to describe children at risk for poor academic performance due to lower SES (the Head Start Program in the United States is an example of a federal attempt to deal with the increased risk for this population), it now applies more readily to medical risk related to neonatal history as defined here.

Because of the tremendous advances in medical technology, and the emergence of neonatology as a medical specialty, many children who previously would not have lived through a precarious neonatal period are now surviving. Hence, the developmental status of these children is of great concern to a wide range of professionals. Many factors, which were initially important to the infant's survival, are now considered important relative to developmental status. The relationship between several factors in the neonatal period and subsequent developmental status is discussed in greater detail in later chapters. It must be recalled, however, that anything that interferes with an infant's ability to interact normally with its environment is a potential source of developmental delay. The factors that contribute to the at-risk label being applied to an infant certainly constitute a potent list of hindrances to normal environmental interaction. Hence, the increased risk of developmental delay.

Many changes in public education have taken place since 1975 when the Education For All Handicapped Children Act was passed by the United States Congress. This law, which guarantees a free, appropriate public education for all handicapped children 3 to 21 years of age, has led to the view that special services are the right of every child. The passage of this piece of legislation has served to involve an increasing number of professionals with the high-risk population. Many states, and the number is increasing, have lowered to birth the age for which public education is mandated for handicapped children. The result is that special educators, school psychologists, developmental psychologists, early childhood educators, and speech and language pathologists are dealing with a new category of special children. Professionals from each of these disciplines are involved in the direct and indirect provision of services in a variety of professional contexts. These include public education settings, private agencies, federally funded child development and demonstration centers, university clinics, and private and public hospitals. Each of these avenues of service provision is discussed in greater detail in later chapters. Research interest in the developmental outcome (quality of life) of neonatal intensive care survivors has been evident for decades. However, regardless of the setting—school, home, or hospital—practitioners are being asked to an increasing degree to provide a variety of services to the at-risk population.

HIGH-RISK FACTORS

Factors that are known to contribute to greater perinatal loss and greater risk of developmental delay for those surviving infants have been presented in a variety of formats. Until recently, birth weight alone was the single most important parameter considered when identifying infants with a higher risk of morbidity, and for those surviving infants, of developmental delay. Although maturity was known to be an important determinant of risk, methods for the accurate assessment of gestational age had yet to be developed. Previous attempts were based on calculations relative to the mother's last normal menstrual period. However, it was not until gestational age could be reliably measured from birth, based on the infant's physical characteristics, prenatal information, and neurological status, that gestational age could be used in the classification of all newborn infants. Thus, birth weight and gestational age together provide a much more accurate means of determining an infant's risk status. In addition, many if not most of the medical complications that place an infant in the at-risk category are closely associated with prematurity and low birth weight. A more detailed discussion of the relationship between prematurity, birth weight and developmental status is presented in Chapter 3.

Determination of gestational age for an infant can proceed along various lines. Overall methodologies for assessing gestational age were presented by Lubchenco (1976). (If greater detail is desired, see the initial description provided by Lubchenco.) Methods include the following:

1. Obstetric history: The primary tool used to determine gestational age remains the obstetric history.
2. Ultrasound: Fetal size and maturity progress together; thus, size can be equated with gestational age in the normal fetus.
3. Radiological examination: Although radiological examination for fetal size and maturity is not recommended, x-ray findings may be helpful in judging fetal maturity in cases in which information is required through the use of this method.
4. Amniotic fluid: Amniocentesis has become a well-established tool for determining gestational age prenatally as well as for establishing lung maturity for infants suspected of having intrauterine growth retardation or who will be premature because of complications due to pregnancy.
5. Physical characteristics of the infant: A variety of physical characteristics have been used to assess gestational age. These include examination of the skin vernix, sole creases, skin color and texture, hair, eyes, ear form and cartilage, breast development, genitalia, skull firmness, and various neurological measurements. The latter include muscle tone, both passive and active, joint mobility, and primitive reflexes.

A variety of scoring systems have been devised to assess gestational age based on these criteria. However, as was previously indicated, the combination of birth weight and gestational age is the most frequently used system for determining overall risk status. Preterm birth is separated from full-term birth at 37 weeks gestational age, according to the World Health Organization recommendations. Guidelines provided by WHO identify preterm low birth weight and preterm high birth weight infants as those who weigh more or less than 2,500 g at birth. Thus, the determinant factor of 2,500 g is important when assessing birth weight relative to risk status. One final comment is needed at this point. Risk status may vary, depending on whether an infant's birth weight is appropriate or inappropriate for gestational age. Morbidity varies greatly, depending on appropriate versus inappropriate for gestational age birth weight status. Survival rates and the prevalence of later neurodevelopmental sequelae depend in part on the degree of intrauterine growth retardation experienced by the infant. This is reflected in whether the infant's weight is appropriate for gestational age at birth or not.

The terms *appropriate for gestational age* (AGA), *small for gestational age* (SGA) and *very low birth weight* (VLBW) are seen frequently in the literature. In addition, specific medical and obstetric factors are used to identify subpopulations within the high-risk group, and these contribute to the heterogeneity seen in the high-risk category of infants. Each of these subpopulations is reviewed in greater detail in later chapters.

As will be seen, developmental outcome varies relative to the AGA, SGA, or VLBW designation. Postmaturity and large-for-gestational-age infants are recognized as distinct categories of infants and present unique medical management problems. Prolonged gestation is not fully understood. Large-for-gestational-age infants are usually the result of maternal factors, such as diabetes. Neither of these categories of infants is the focus of the discussions that follow. Table 1–1 provides data on average weight and length at various gestational ages. This information should be useful for more accurately determining developmental risk status. Table 1–2 is a chart for converting birth weights from pounds to grams or vice versa.

Interested professionals often may not have access to high-risk data relative to the child's hospital course and specific medical complications while in the intensive care nursery. Risk data (hospital discharge summaries and other medical data) most likely are not available to many practitioners outside a hospital setting. Although information of this type can be quite difficult for the nonphysician to understand, familiarity with the medical course of an infant can give the practitioner a better "feel" for the unique circumstances surrounding each child served. Appendix B presents sample data from several discharge summaries and follow-up evaluation data for representative infants. In lieu of hospital discharge summary information Oberman (1975) presented criteria that may be more readily useful when considering high-risk potential for a particular infant. The criteria, which are broken down into five major categories, are presented in the following sections.

Maternal Factors

A variety of maternal factors are significant in determining risk potential for a particular infant. Certainly, historical data are important, and a family history of mental retardation or neurological handicaps should be considered. Other important data include a maternal history of premature births, repeated miscarriage, cervical incompetence, stillbirth, placental abnormalities, intrauterine growth retardation, blood group problems, unexplained fetal or neonatal deaths, and genetic disease or chromosomal disorders. Age is also a critical consideration; women less

Table 1–1. Average Fetal Weight and Size by Gestational Age

Week (postconception)	Weight (g)	Length (cm)
8	1	4.0
9	2	4.0
10	4	6.5
11	7	6.5
12	14	9.0
13	25	9.0
14	45	12.5
15	70	12.5
16	100	16.0
17	140	16.0
18	190	20.5
19	240	20.5
20	300	25.0
21	360	25.0
22	430	27.5
23	501	27.5
24	600	30.0
25	700	30.0
26	800	32.5
27	900	32.5
28	1,001	35.0
29	1,175	35.0
30	1,350	37.5
31	1,501	37.5
32	1,675	40.0
33	1,825	40.0
34	2,001	42.5
35	2,160	42.5
36	2,340	45.0
37	2,501	45.0
38	2,775	47.5
39	3,001	47.5
40	3,250	50.0
41	3,501	50.0
42	4,001	52.5
43	4,501	52.5

than 16 years or more than 36 years have greater risk potential. A variety of infections during the first trimester of pregnancy can be critical. Rubella is the one most commonly thought of, but recent discussions also have centered on the presence of influenza as a potentially dangerous consideration. Toxemia of pregnancy, threatened spontaneous abortion during the second or third trimester, unexplained bleeding, premature rupture of membranes, and maternal diabetes or mental retardation are all important considerations. The presence of any one of the aforementioned factors may in and of itself lead to higher risk potential. However, two or more of these factors increase the risk potential of a particular infant to a greater degree.

Table 1-2. Conversion, Pounds to Grams

POUNDS	\ OUNCES → 0	1	2	3	4	5	6	7	8	9	10	11	12	13	14	15
0	—	28	57	85	113	142	170	198	227	255	283	312	340	369	397	425
1	454	482	510	539	567	595	624	652	680	709	737	765	794	822	850	879
2	907	936	964	992	1021	1049	1077	1106	1134	1162	1191	1219	1247	1276	1304	1332
3	1361	1389	1417	1446	1474	1503	1531	1559	1588	1616	1644	1673	1701	1729	1758	1786
4	1814	1843	1871	1899	1928	1956	1984	2013	2041	2070	2098	2126	2155	2183	2211	2240
5	2268	2296	2325	2353	2381	2410	2438	2466	2495	2523	2551	2580	2608	2637	2665	2693
6	2722	2750	2778	2807	2835	2863	2892	2920	2948	2977	3005	3033	3062	3090	3118	3147
7	3175	3203	3232	3260	3289	3317	3345	3374	3402	3430	3459	3487	3515	3544	3572	3600
8	3629	3657	3685	3714	3742	3770	3799	3827	3856	3884	3912	3941	3969	3997	4026	4054
9	4082	4111	4139	4167	4196	4224	4252	4281	4309	4337	4366	4394	4423	4451	4479	4508
10	4536	4564	4593	4621	4649	4678	4706	4734	4763	4791	4819	4848	4876	4904	4933	4961
11	4990	5018	5046	5075	5103	5131	5160	5188	5216	5245	5273	5301	5330	5358	5386	5415
12	5443	5471	5500	5528	5557	5585	5613	5642	5670	5698	5727	5755	5783	5812	5840	5868
13	5897	5925	5953	5982	6010	6038	6067	6095	6123	6152	6180	6209	6237	6265	6294	6322
14	6350	6379	6407	6435	6464	6492	6520	6549	6577	6605	6634	6662	6690	6719	6747	6776
15	6804	6832	6860	6889	6917	6945	6973	7002	7030	7059	7087	7115	7144	7172	7201	7228
16	7257	7286	7313	7342	7371	7399	7427	7456	7484	7512	7541	7569	7597	7626	7654	7682
17	7711	7739	7768	7796	7824	7853	7881	7909	7938	7966	7994	8023	8051	8079	8108	8136
18	8165	8192	8221	8249	8278	8306	8335	8363	8391	8420	8448	8476	8504	8533	8561	8590
19	8618	8646	8675	8703	8731	8760	8788	8816	8845	8873	8902	8930	8958	8987	9015	9043
20	9072	9100	9128	9157	9185	9213	9242	9270	9298	9327	9355	9383	9412	9440	9469	9497
21	9525	9554	9582	9610	9639	9667	9695	9724	9752	9780	9809	9837	9865	9894	9922	9950
22	9979	10007	10036	10064	10092	10120	10149	10177	10206	10234	10262	10291	10319	10347	10376	10404

Social and Psychological Factors

Several considerations relative to social and psychological factors should be kept in mind when determining risk status for a particular infant. Certainly, socioeconomic factors are important. At lower incomes the potential for nutritional problems arises. Also, lower family income is associated with less frequent and, in some cases, a lack of prenatal care. Maternal psychological status during pregnancy can be a concern. An unwanted pregnancy, an out-of-wedlock pregnancy, and maternal psychiatric disorders all influence risk potential. Although social and psychological concerns may not in and of themselves be of primary importance when considering risk status, they are certainly correlated with previously mentioned factors that are of primary importance.

Factors Related to Labor and Delivery

Concerns related to labor and delivery are often the first factors thought of when risk potential is mentioned. Their connection to infant health is obvious and cannot be dismissed. Length of labor is a significant concern. Labor that lasts longer than 18 hours in primagravida women (initial pregnancy) and longer than 8 hours in multigravida women (subsequent pregnancies) should be considered potentially significant. Labor duration that exceeds these norms is classified as prolonged. From the fetal standpoint, however, this method of defining normal labor may not be as reliable as expected. If the fetus is already compromised because of maternal medical complications of pregnancy, it may not be able to tolerate the stress of even a few minutes of labor. Normal labor, therefore, is better defined as that degree of labor that does not endanger the fetus if medical complications are present. A precipitate or uncontrolled delivery, an abnormal presentation, and prolonged forceps application may be relevant concerns. A history of fetal distress, in particular fetal heart rate greater than 160 or less than 100 beats per minute for 30 seconds or more, can indicate significant fetal risk that may result in a variety of neonatal complications. Fetal distress may necessitate a cesarean delivery, which can be a risk factor in and of itself. The presence of any of these factors alone may not indicate excessive risk. However, two or more of these concerns may indicate serious risk potential.

Neonatal Syndromes

A variety of factors that are first detected in the neonatal period certainly contribute to developmental risk. Some of these are closely aligned to the maternal factors previously discussed. However, it is entirely possible that significant risk results from the presence of neonatal considerations that were not suspected in the prenatal period. Birth weight and gestational age are relevant and are most reliably assessed shortly after birth. Methods for determining gestational age were discussed previously, as was the relationship between birth weight and gestational age. Hyperbilirubinemia is an important factor to consider as more serious conditions can develop in the presence of elevated bilirubin levels (see Appendix A). Meconium staining is also an important factor and contributes to respiratory difficulties. Central nervous system disorders, hypertonia, asymmetry of tone, abnormal head size, convulsions, excess irritability, and abnormal reflex patterns may be negative and serious signs. Respiratory distress, usually associated with prematurity and characterized by grunting respirations, marked retraction of the chest during respiration, cyanosis, and fetal asphyxia are serious concerns. A more complete discussion of respiratory distress is presented in Appendix A. Gastrointestinal difficulties, poor sucking or swallowing, repeated regurgitation, poor weight gain, and abdominal distension may be indicative of factors that will result in developmental delay. Serious neonatal infection, generalized edema or gross cerebral hemorrhage, the presence of major congenital anomalies, and an Apgar score of 6 or less may also point to enhanced risk status.

Postnatal Conditions and Syndromes

The final broad category of risk factors presented by Oberman (1975) includes those factors that become apparent after birth. These include serious injury or illness; any clinical manifestation of a previously unrecognized anomaly; inattention to sound or visual stimulus (lack of environmental awareness); delayed pattern of overall development in motor, social, speech and language, or adaptive behaviors; and general failure to thrive and develop normally. Generally, the parents are the first to suspect delay in any of these areas and readily report their concerns to their pediatrician. Professional evaluation and verification of delay often come at a much later date.

The clinician-educator should make it a point to obtain detailed historical data on a particular infant when assessing overall risk status. The concepts presented here should be readily understood by nonmedical personnel and should be of great value in interpreting diagnostic data and in formulating prognostic impressions.

INCIDENCE OF HIGH-RISK INFANTS

The most commonly used method for determining the risk status of an infant relies on birth weight and gestational age as a gauge. With this in mind, the following information will serve to alert interested professionals to the numbers of children that are classified as being at risk for potential developmental delay.

Before the advent of neonatal intensive care the risk of neonatal death (death within 4 weeks of birth) was 30 times greater for the low birth weight infant (Chase, 1969). Between 1958 and 1968 the neonatal mortality rate was 23 deaths per 1,000 births. Between 1970 and 1973 the rate reflected advances in neonatal medicine and dropped to 15 deaths per 1,000 births. Infant death rate for those less than 1 year old in the United States in 1978 was 13.6 per 1,000 live births. This was a decline from the previous year's rate of 14 deaths per 1,000 live births. Current statistics indicate the infant mortality rate is 10 deaths per 1,000 live births. Tables 1–3 to 1–7 present mortality statistics from several perinatal centers as well as data amplifying the effectiveness in reducing infant mortality as a result of neonatal intensive care.

There is also a marked difference between the neonatal death rate (the first 28 days of life) and the postneonatal death rate (from 28 days to 11 months). There are about three times as many deaths in the neonatal period as in the postneonatal period. The highest number of deaths occur on the first day, and a high percentage of neonatal deaths occur during the first week (Haynes, 1980). Very low birth weight infants (less than 1,500 g) accounted for nearly 50 percent of all neonatal deaths in Victoria, Australia, as reported by Kitchen and colleagues (1980). Fitzhardinge and colleagues (1976) reported a very high incidence of serious neurological sequelae in low birth weight infants who had received ventilator therapy. Fitzhardinge, Ashley, and Pape also reported that intercranial hemorrhage in a population of very low birth weight infants also carried an unfavorable prognosis for long-term developmental status (1974). However, as the survival rate for low birth weight infants increased so did the percentage of infants with handicapping conditions. Kierscht and Meuwissen (1979) pointed out that "neonatal intensive care may also be contributing to saving an increased number of infants with handicaps" (p. 130).

The classification of high-risk infants includes a number of diagnostic factors. Komich and colleagues (1973) pointed out that a higher incidence of physical and mental deficits is found in the high-risk population and that the overall high-risk group may make up from 5 to 15 percent of all newborns. Reynold (1976) reported that 9 percent of the babies in his follow-up group who weighed 1,500 g or less at birth

Table 1–3. University of Colorado Mortality Statistics for 1979

Birth Weight	Mortality Rate
600–700 grams	70%
700–800 grams	63%
800–900 grams	64%
900–1000 grams	32%

Note: *From Infants at Risk for Developmental Dysfunction* (p. 78) by D. Parson and L. Eisenberg (Eds.), 1982, Washington, D.C.: National Academy Press. Copyright 1982 by National Academy Press. Reprinted by permission.

displayed handicapping conditions. He further stated that "as far as can be determined perinatal and neonatal intensive care is associated not just with increased survival, but with a low incidence of major mental and physical handicaps" (p. 292). In a regional study designed to assess the reduction in neonatal morbidity due to the initiation of an intensive care nursery, Miller and Bush (1982) provided frequency data on the number of infants admitted to the intensive care nursery. Birth weight-specific survival rates over 3 years were 10 percent for infants less than 1,000 g, 68 percent for infants between 1,001 and 1,500 g, and 96.5 percent for infants between 1,501 and 2,500 g. They further reported that 6.4 percent of the total live-born infants in their region were admitted to the intensive care nursery. Overall survival rate for these infants was 89 percent.

Lubchenco (1976) reported on the relationship between birth weight, gestational age, and congenital anomalies in 10,000 live-born infants born between 1962 and 1968 at the University of Colorado Medical Center. These data indicated that when birth weight is viewed, the incidence of congenital anomalies ranges from 1.9 percent for those infants who weighed between 3,500 and 4,000 g to 25.6 percent for infants who weighed between 1,000 to 1,500 g. Data on gestational age indicated an incidence of congenital anomalies between 2.3 percent for infants of 40 to 41 weeks gestational age and 30 percent for infants of 28 to 29 weeks gestational age. The type and degree of anomaly were not specified. The fact that these anomalies were congenital precludes the effects of low birth weight and prematurity alone on developmental status. The potential exists that developmental delay, not immediately observable at birth, was not recognized until a later date.

An additional system for the classification of and incidence of data for at risk infants was described by Usher (1981). He divided premature infants into three categories based on the degree of prematurity:

1. Borderline prematurity (37 to 38 weeks): These infants are usually of normal birth weight but may manifest excessive jaundice or

Table 1-4. Infants Born at the University of California at San Francisco, 1965-1981, with Birth Weights Less than 1,500 Grams

	1965-69	1970-75	1976-81	Total
Born	100	128	289	517
Died, neonatal	52	46	62	188
Died, post-discharge	3	6	8	17
Survived	45	76	219	340
percent survived	45	59	75	65

Note: From "Learning Disabilities in Children With Birth Weights Less Than 1,500 Grams." by J. Hunt, W. Tooley, and D. Harvin, 1982, *Seminars in Perinatology*, *6*, p. 282. Copyright 1982 by Grune & Stratton, Inc. Reprinted by permission.

slowness to feed. They may develop life-threatening respiratory distress syndrome. Infants of 37 to 38 weeks gestation usually weigh 2,500 to 3,250 g at birth and make up 10 percent of all live births.

2. Moderately premature infants (31 to 36 weeks): Infants of 31 to 36 weeks gestation make up 6 to 7 percent of all newborn infants. Although premature, many (more than 50 percent) have birth weights greater than 2,500 g. The smallest infants in this category have birth weights close to 1,500 g. Modern therapeutic techniques deal effectively with the physiological problems of this category of infants. Death is a result of specific disease (respiratory distress syndrome or severe infection).

3. Extremely premature infants (24 to 30 weeks): These infants are at the borderline of viability. Until recently few survived, and then often with impaired physical or neurological function. Infants in the 28 to 30-week range did better than those in the 24 to 27-week range. Infants of 24 to 30 weeks gestation (usually 500 to 1,500 g) make up only 0.8 percent of the live-born population but account for almost all neonatal deaths and neurologic sequelae.

As is readily evident from the incidence studies, no strong consensus exists regarding a definitive definition of the at-risk infant. Although a definition was presented at the beginning of the chapter, definitive incidence data is difficult to agree upon. Inclusion in the at-risk category may vary, depending on the particular definition used by an individual investigator.

SUMMARY

The high-risk infant is one who, because of various factors surrounding prenatal, natal, and postnatal history, has a greater than normal risk of

Table 1-5. Survival by Birth Weight (BW) Categories for Three Time Periods

BW/Years	Born	Survived	% Survived
<750 g			
1965–69	8	0	0
1970–75	12	1	8.3
1976–81	27	6	22.2
750–1000 g			
1965–69	26	7	26.9
1970–75	24	6	25.0
1976–81	77	46	59.7
1001–1250 g			
1965–69	31	17	54.8
1970–75	41	29	70.7
1976–81	81	70	86.4
1251–1500 g			
1965–69	35	21	60.0
1970–75	51	41	80.4
1976–81	104	97	93.3

Note: From "Learning Disabilities in Children With Birth Weights Less Than 1500 Grams" by J. Hunt, W. Tooley, and D. Harvin, 1982, *Seminars in Perinatology, 6,* p. 280. Copyright 1982 by Grune & Stratton, Inc. Reprinted by permission.

displaying developmental delay and later potential developmental problems. The initial concern for this population is survival. Approximately 5 to 15 percent of all live-born infants can be classified as at risk. The number of these infants who will ultimately display some form of developmental deviance, cognitive deficit, school difficulty, or behavioral differences ranging from mild to severe falls in the 30 to 50 percent and above range. With this in mind, an aggressive posture toward early identification of those infants who do display developmental delay, coupled with early intervention, is crucial for ensuring optimal developmental outcome. Birth weight and gestational age are the main determinants of overall risk status. A determination of whether an infant's birth weight is appropriate or inappropriate for gestational age is helpful in further assessing risk status. In most cases factors that indicate an infant is at risk deny the infant the opportunity for normal environmental interaction. Hence, the potential for delayed development in one or more areas is enhanced. Stuart (1981) indicated that low birth weight infants are usually

> Potentially normal at birth, particularly if their obstetric management has been optimal, but they are at risk from a wide variety of hazards resulting from immaturity of the structure and function of many organs, which

Table 1-6. Impact of Intensive Care (IC)

	Hospital	Before IC	After IC
Stillbirth rate*	St. Boniface	8.8	3.5 (1973)
	St. Joseph's	10.4	7.3 (1969)
	Women's College	—	8.3 (1978)
	Royal Victoria	—	6.9 (1972)
	Queens	20.8	12.0 (1968)
Neonatal mortality 0-6 days*	St. Boniface	5.0	3.5 (1973)
	Women's College	10.6	6.2 (1971)
	Jewish General	7.6	6.4 (1973)
	Queens	17.0	9.9 (1968)
Perinatal mortality†	St. Boniface	13.9	7.0 (1973)
	St. Joseph's	21.6	19.0 (1969)
	Women's College	20.5	14.8 (1971)
	Royal Victoria	19.1	15.2 (1972)
	Jewish General	20.9	14.9 (1973)
	Grace	12.5	7.7 (1975)

*Per 1,000 births.
† Per 1,000 live births.
Adapted from Sawyer (1981).

Table 1-7. Perinatal Deaths per 1,000 Live Births—International Comparison

Country	Late Fetal Mortality	Neonatal Mortality	Perinatal Mortality
Canada	7.9	10.0	16.6 (1974)
Sweden			
1974	6.7	7.5	13.3
1975	5.8	6.4	11.3
1976	5.5	6.3	10.7
1977	5.1	5.8	10.2
Denmark	6.6	7.3	12.7 (1976)
Switzerland	7.2	7.4	13.5 (1975)
Finland	6.6	8.6	13.9 (1974)
Netherlands	7.7	7.6	14.0 (1975)
Norway	8.1	7.3	14.2 (1975)
New Zealand	8.3	9.6	16.5 (1975)
Japan	8.3	9.6	16.5 (1975)
England and Wales	9.8	9.7	17.9 (1976)
Australia	10.4	10.0	19.2 (1975)
France	11.7	9.9	19.5 (1977)
Poland	7.6	12.0	19.6 (1975)
Belgium	9.5	11.8	19.7 (1975)
USA	10.7	11.6	20.7 (1975)
Italy	11.0	16.0	24.1 (1975)
Hungary	8.3	26.7	31.6 (1975)

Adapted from Sawyer (1981).

may cause death or permanent damage. The objective of intensive care is to protect the infant from these hazards for the first days or weeks of life. If this objective is achieved, the infant should survive as a normal member of society (p. 1038).

The role of a variety of professionals who provide services to this population of children is greatly expanding. Enhanced communication between those interested in developmental performance and other professionals (developmental pediatricians, neonatologists, developmental psychologists, and special educators) will serve to increase the effectiveness of intervention and identification capabilities.

REFERENCES

Chase, H. C. (1969). Infant mortality and weight at birth: 1960 United States birth cohort. *American Public Health, 59,* 1618.

Fitzhardinge, P., Ashley, S., and Pape, K. (1974). Present status of the infant of very low birth weight treated in a referral neonatal intensive care unit in 1974. *Ciba Foundation Symposium, 59,* 226.

Fitzhardinge, P., Pape, K., Arstikaitis, M., Boyle, M., Ashley, S., Rowley, A., Netley, C., and Sawyer, P. (1976). Mechanical ventilation of infants of less than 1500 grams at birth: Health growth and neurological sequelae. *Journal of Pedatrics, 88,* 531.

Haynes, U. (1980). A developmental approach to casefinding among infants and young children (DHEW Publication No. HSA 79-5210). Rockville, MD: U.S. Department of Health Education and Welfare.

Hunt, J., Tooley, W., and Harvin, D. (1982). Learning disabilities in children with birth weights less than 1500 grams. *Seminars in Perinatology, 6,* 280.

Kierscht, M., and Meuwissen, J. (1979). Follow-up of preschool age survivors of neonatal intensive care. *The Journal of Psychology, 101,* 129.

Kitchen, W., Ryan, M., Rickards, A., McDougal, A., Billson, F., Kier, E., and Naylor, F. (1980). A longitudinal study of very low birth weight infants: An overview of performance at eight years of age. *Developmental Medicine and Child Neurology, 22,* 172.

Komich, P., Lansford, A., Lord, L., and Tireney, A. (1973). The sequential development of infants of low birth weight. *American Journal of Occupational Therapy, 27,* 396.

Lubchenco, L. (1981). Gestational age, birth weight and the high risk infant. In C. Brown (Ed.), *Infants at risk.* Johnson & Johnson Baby Products.

McAnarney, E. (1982). Low birthweight infants: Health and behavior (a research agenda interim report No. 4). In D. Parron and L. Eisenberg (Eds.), *Infants at risk for developmental dysfunction.* Washington D.C.: National Academy Press.

Miller, T., and Bush, B. (1982). Infants surviving neonatal intensive care. *Illinois Medical Journal, 162,* 95.

Oberman, W. (1975). Factors contributing to perinatal loss and risk status. In U. Haynes (Ed.), *A developmental approach to case finding.* Washington, D.C.: U.S. Department of Health Education and Welfare.

Reynolds, E. (1976). The low birth weight infant: A follow-up. *Arizona Medicine, 33,* 290.

Stuart, A., Reynolds, E., and Lipscomb, A. (1981). Outcome for infants of very low birth weight: Survey of world literature. *Lancet, 5,* 1038.

Sawyer, P. (1981). The organization of perinatal care with particular reference to the newborn. In G. Avery (Ed.), *Neonatology, pathophysiology and management of the newborn.* Philadelphia: J.B. Lippincott.

Usher, R. (1981). The special problems of the premature infant. In G. Avery (Ed.), *Neonatology, pathophysiology and management of the newborn.* Philadelphia: J.B. Lippincott.

Chapter 2

Overview of Infant Development

Students of normal infant development have observed an increasingly sophisticated picture of infant capabilities evolve over the past 75 years. Researchers have explored the visual, auditory, cognitive, learning, social, language, motor, sensory, and psychological development of infants. They have used a variety of methodologies and have incorporated samples of children from diverse cultural and racial backgrounds. As a result of this intense scrutiny a comprehensive and sometimes surprising picture of the inborn capabilities of the infant has emerged.

Students in training often are not exposed to information designed to provide a comprehensive understanding of normal infant development even though this is a valuable data base upon which service to the at-risk population depends. Diagnosis, intervention, and communication with parents are only a few of the areas that require a thorough understanding of infant development. The purpose of this chapter, therefore, is to provide an overview of infant development for students in training as well as for clinician-educators who are presently providing services to high-risk infants. A complete and comprehensive coverage is outside the scope of this text. However, a fuller appreciation of and familiarity with the amazing capabilities of the newborn will allow for more effective service to the at-risk population.

The present chapter views infant development as something greater than a list of changes and advances that take place over time. Developmental principles and generalization are active across developmental domains; hence, skill acquisition is interdependent, and developmental progress across all modalities is influenced to a greater or lesser degree by delays in any single area of maturation. Owens (1984) listed five developmental principles that are important to keep in mind when viewing infant development:

1. Development is predictable.
2. Developmental milestones are attained at about the same age in most children.
3. Developmental opportunity is needed.
4. Children go through developmental changes or periods.
5. Individuals differ greatly.

The following material is divided into six major areas, and selected literature within each area is reviewed in an attempt to provide an overview of current knowledge about infant performance.

VISUAL ABILITY

Infant visual perception has been studied by means of a variety of methodologies. What emerges is a paradigm of visual skills quite unlike the limited ability initially ascribed to the infant. The fact that the newborn is able to visually track stimuli is well documented. Table 2–1 presents data about visual acuity at various ages and points to the fact that infants do display appropriate visual acuity that enables them to demonstrate the scanning and gazing behavior described by a variety of investigators.

As early as 1913 researchers were presenting various objects to infants in an attempt to gauge infant preference for color. Since these early investigations increasingly sophisticated physiological and behavioral measures of infant responses have been made. The basic logic behind these measures is the inference that if an infant behaves differently for different stimuli, the child is able to discriminate between them (Cohen, DeLoache, and Strauss, 1979). Subsequent studies on infant visual skills have examined color perception, categorical perception, form perception, visual complexity, and shape constancy.

Fantz (1961) provided some of the most innovative and impressive data. He initially demonstrated what was referred to as an "innate visual preference" for human faces among human infants. Subjects between 4 days and 6 months of age were presented with all possible pairs from three stimuli sources:

1. A schematic representation of a human face, with the features drawn in black on a pink background

Table 2-1. Visual Acuity and Age Norms

Visual Acuity	Age	Author
At birth, demonstrates poor visual acuity, at least 20/150 vision in newborns	Neonate	Dayton, 1964
Demonstrates varying acuity range (20/400, 20/800) depending on testing procedures and amount of illumination	Neonate	Fantz, 1962
Shows visual acuity of 20/670	Neonate	Gorman, 1962
Shows visual acuity of 20/500	2 mo.	Salapatek, 1975
Shows visual acuity of 20/200 or better	4 mo.	Fantz, 1962
Shows acuity of 20/150	4 mo.	Salapatek, 1975
Shows indications of increased acuity (20/100, 20/70) according to pattern fixation test results	6 mo.	Fantz, 1962
Adult capacity to distinguish shapes and patterns improves greatly but does not reach adult capacity till 10 years of age.		Bee, 1975

Note: From *The Developmental Resource: Behavioral Sequencing for Assessment and Programming Planning* (p. 53) by M. Cohen and P. Gross, 1979, New York: Grune & Stratton. Copyright 1979 Grune & Stratton. Reprinted by permission.

2. A form with the same detail as the first but with the facial features randomly scrambled
3. A similar form to the two others but with a solid patch of black at the top equal in area to that occupied by the features in the two other stimuli

Results indicated that at all age levels infants looked more at the real face than at the scrambled face and that they mostly ignored the control pattern. Lewis (1969) hypothesized that the most realistic facial schema would elicit more interest in the earlier months of life and that the least realistic would elicit interest in the later months. Results of his study revealed that although facial stimulus elicited significantly less fixation time as a function of age, with the older children fixating less, the same stimuli elicited significantly greater vocalizations and smiling in the older infants. Goren, Sartz, and Wye (1975) supported Fantz's initial findings by demonstrating that immediately after birth a human neonate not only would visually fix on a drawing that resembled a human face but also would follow it, with both eyes and head turning. A scrambled face did not demand the same kind of attention, nor did the infant completely follow the distorted face with head and eye movement. The implications of these results are that a primitive and unlearned preference for human faces exists in the infant. Although additional studies designed to replicate these findings have yielded mixed results, even at an early age the human infant demonstrates a preference for viewing certain objects over other objects.

Visual scanning by newborns has received considerable research interest in an effort to further define the innate visual ability present in human infants (Brennan, Ames, and Moore, 1966; Greenman, 1963; Haith, 1973; Salapatek and Kessen, 1973). What has emerged from this work is a comprehensive description that attributes to the infant extensive visual scanning ability at a very young age. During the first month of life the infant fixates on a single feature of an object. By 2 months of age scanning tends to be broader and attention is paid to figures and patterns. Specific memory for visual data does not appear to evolve, even though extensive gaze time for objects is noted at 1 month of age and below, until approximately 8 to 10 weeks of age.

Form perception and attention to pattern in infancy has been approached from a variety of methodological and theoretical viewpoints, but disagreement about a definition of the term form makes statements about infant form perception somewhat more difficult. The very young infant gives little indication of memory for shape and pattern. As a result, researchers have used a strategy of visual preference to assess the visual discriminative capabilities of the very young infant. One major strategy has been the measurement of infant gaze time through the use of corneal reflection apparatus. This method simply allows the researcher to measure how long an infant will gaze at a stimulus by observing the reflected image of that stimulus on the cornea of the infant. Results of studies using this strategy have revealed that infants have fairly acute pattern vision during the early months of life, that they show greater preference for patterns than for plain colors, that they differentiate among patterns of similar complexity and that they show visual interest in patterns similar to that of the human face (Fantz and Miranda, 1975; Haith, 1976; Kessen, Salapatek, and Haith, 1972; Salapatek, 1975). These results have been replicated by a variety of researchers.

MOTOR DEVELOPMENT

Motor development in infancy (from birth to 12 months) may be described as a broad, general pattern in which postural control precedes efforts at locomotion, effort precedes success at locomotion, and some form of locomotion precedes walking. There are many stages and, with rare exceptions, all babies pass through each stage. There are, however, minor differences in the sequence of stages from baby to baby. A rapid progression of developmental milestones may be observed in the healthy infant during the first 12 months of life. The infant's motor system, which is initially characterized by reflexive responses over which the infant has little or no voluntary control, slowly evolves. The result is an increase in the amount and variety of purposeful and voluntary motor movements.

Motor Reflexes

During the first 12 months certain reflexive patterns disappear as the motor system evolves and others appear. These changes reflect an evolving motor system and increased control of motor responses.

Signs That Disappear

Moro Reflex.   The Moro reflex is a reflexive response characterized by sudden abduction of the arms, extension of the legs, and flexion of the hips when the position of the head is changed abruptly in relationship to the body. It is present in all healthy full-term infants and usually disappears by 4 to 5 months of age.

Tonic Neck Reflex.   When the infant is in the supine position, turning the infant's head to one side results in extension of the arm and leg on that side, with flexion of the other arm. This has also been called the fencing position. The tonic neck reflex usually is not present in the newborn but appears at about 2 to 3 weeks of age. It is most prominent during the second month of life. It is rarely present after 5 to 6 months of age, and if it is observed after that age abnormal neurological development may be suspected.

Reflexes and Signs That Appear

Neck Righting Reflex.   When the infant is in the supine position, turning the infant's head to one side results in a turning of the shoulders and trunk to the same side. It usually appears when the tonic neck reflex disappears, usually when the baby begins to roll over. All healthy infants should display a neck righting reflex until they are 8 to 10 months of age; after that time it becomes part of voluntary activity.

Hand Grasp.   Reflexive hand grasp is generally present at birth. Voluntary hand grasp appears later. An infant is able to reach and grasp with the whole hand by 4 to 5 months of age. Thumb and finger (pincer) grasp begins at 6 to 7 months and is fully present in healthy infants by 1 year of age. Transferring objects from one hand to the other begins at 7 to 8 months. Table 2–2 presents in greater detail reflexes and signs during the first year of life.

Maturational Changes

A concise and easy to understand description of motor development and maturational changes in infancy has been presented by Shirley (1959). Maturational changes are described as a series of advances presented as first through fifth order skills. These advances are not random or haphazard but follow an orderly plan. First, the baby gains postural control of the upper trunk; second, postural control moves downward to include the entire trunk region and in addition exhibits activity directed toward locomotion; third, active and rigorous effort at locomotion is observed; fourth, postural control of the entire body becomes complete; and fifth, postural control and coordination are combined as the child reaches the goal of walking sometime around 12 months of age. A summary of these stages is presented in Table 2–3.

Abnormal development of motor skills during early and later infancy may be indicative of neurological problems and should be closely monitored. Once walking is achieved the child's overall development is enhanced as independent locomotion affords the child the opportunity to explore new environmental territory. Thus, the progressive development of motor functioning may be thought of as a most important process that has an impact on the overall developmental integrity of the child during the first years of life and beyond.

LANGUAGE DEVELOPMENT

Language acquisition is clearly a systematic and rule-governed process that is initiated shortly after birth and that results in meaningful speech appearing at approximately 12 months of age. Both receptive (comprehension) and expressive (production) aspects of language continue to develop through the early months and years of life. Social contact, environmental exposure, and an intact maturational system are all needed for adequate development.

Since the completion of early investigations designed to chronicle vocabulary growth, a large and impressive body of literature on language development has evolved. Consequently, information is available on all aspects of this phenomenon: phonology, the sounds of language; morphology, the study of the smallest units of meaning in a language; syn-

Table 2-2. Reflexes and Signs During the First Year

Reflex	Appears	Disappears
Moro	Birth	4-5 mo
Stepping and Placing	Newborn	Persists as standing
Positive supporting	Newborn-3 mo	Persists voluntarily
Tonic neck	2-3 wk	4-6 mo
Neck righting	4-6 mo	Persists voluntarily
Grasp		
Palmar (reflexive)	Birth	3-4 mo
Palmar grasp (whole hand)	Persists voluntarily after 4 mo	
Pincer grasp	Persists voluntarily after 6-7 mo	

tax, the rules of combining words and phrases into sentences; semantics, the acquisition of vocabulary and of the meanings associated with words; and pragmatics, the social rules for language usage. A complete discussion of each of these areas is not possible in an overview chapter. However, a general discussion of language development and, more specifically, the importance of the period of infancy (birth to 12 months) is presented.

Phonological Development

In the first year of life, the sounds that the infant makes change from simple crying in the newborn to complex babbling in the period just before the onset of speech (Sachs, 1985). A variety of descriptive paradigms have been presented in an effort to delineate changes in sound production during the infant's first year. Stark (1979) however, presented a format that is easily understood by persons interested in greater detail about early language development. The series of five stages described by Stark are presented here in modified form. The stages generally overlap and thus they should not be viewed as independent from each other.

Stage 1

Stage 1 consists of reflexive crying and vegetative sounds. This stage is present from birth to 8 weeks of age. The initial sounds that the infant can produce are restricted by physiological limitations. Voluntary control of the speech mechanism is limited to movements that serve biological purposes. Greater control of the speech mechanism, which results in purposeful sound production, does not take place until later in

Table 2-3. Median Age of Acquisition of Motor Skills by Stages

Stage	Median Age (wk)
First-Order Skills	
On stomach, chin up	3.0
On stomach, chest up	9.0
Held erect, stepping	13.0
On back, tense for lifting	15.0
Held erect, knees straight	15.0
Sit on lap, support at lower ribs	
Complete head control	18.5
Second-Order Skills	
Sit alone momentarily	25.0
On stomach, knee push or swim	25.0
On back rolling	29.0
Held erect, stand firmly with help	29.5
Sit alone 1 minute	31.0
Third-Order Skills	
On stomach, some progress	37.0
On stomach, scoot backwards	39.5
Fourth-Order Skills	
Stand holding to furniture	42.0
Creep	44.5
Walk when led	45.0
Pull to stand by furniture	47.0
Fifth-Order Skills	
Stand alone	62.0
Walk alone	64.0

the developmental sequence. Thus, newborn infants are quite limited in the sounds they can produce. Vegetative noises are common and include burps, coughs, and sneezes. Crying is the preponderant sound produced by the newborn.

Stage 2

Stage 2 is characterized by cooing and laughing and is present in infants 8 to 20 weeks of age. During this stage the infant begins to make an increased amount of pleasant sounds during social interactions. These sounds are called cooing. Crying tends to become less frequent and more variable in sound. Different types of cries (discomfort, call, and request) were reported by D'Odorico (1984).

Stage 3

Stage 3 is vocal play. It is characterized by prolonged single syllable utterances and is a transitional stage that lies between cooing and babbling. The change in vocal production probably reflects changes in both the articulatory structure and the central nervous system. This stage is present between 16 to 30 weeks of age.

Stage 4

Reduplicated babbling is first evidenced between 25 to 50 weeks of age. During this stage consonant vowel combinations are repeated. Previous utterances by the infant were more likely to be in response to social stimuli and interaction. The babbling present in this stage is likely to take place when the infant is not communicating with others. The presence of babbling reflects the infant's increased control over the articulatory mechanism.

Stage 5

Stage 5 is characterized by increased babbling and expressive jargon and is present at 36 to 72 weeks of age. Babbling now becomes more complex, and the variety of consonant vowel utterances displayed by the child increase considerably. Strings of sounds are uttered with a variety of stress and intonation patterns. This stage usually precedes true speech production. Subsequent phonological development—the acquisition of the sounds of a language—takes place simultaneously with the progression of language comprehension and usage.

Language Comprehension and Cognitive Development

Up to this point the discussion of language development has focused on the productive aspects of an infant's early vocalizations. Infant receptive language (language comprehension) is also developing during the first months of life. Any discussion of language comprehension must also address cognitive development as it relates to language learning. The exact relationship between thought (cognition) and language is unknown. Several investigators have presented theoretical models to describe the relationship between thought and language (see Chomsky, 1968; Schlesinger, 1977; Vygotsky, 1962; Whorf, 1956). Lindsay and Norman (1977) concluded that the available information on thought and language indicated that "as his capacity to communicate symbolically develops, language and thought become so inextricably intermixed it becomes almost impossible to separate them" (p. 437). A more complete discussion of cognitive development is presented later in this chapter.

Slobin (1973) contended that the "pacesetter in linguistic growth is the child's cognitive growth as opposed to autonomous linguistic development which can reflect back on cognition" (p. 184). The infant, even from the earliest days of life, is not wholly passive but is increasingly active and engaged in the world. The infant is building a "vocabulary of sense experiences and forming abilities on which later learning depends; paying attention and developing specific, controlled sequences of action" (Caplan, 1973, p. 79). Even very young children understand much of what is being said to them. Through shared experiences with the mother (see the next section on social development) communication by the infant, although not in the form of speech, has already taken place by 12 months of age. These interactive forms of communication include gestures, facial expressions, body movements, and vocalizations. The social context in which these events take place is centrally important to the development of language comprehension and later production. As the infant's behavioral repertoire expands, and the infant becomes increasingly interested in objects rather than people, the mother makes increasing reference to objects. Thus, the symbolic aspect of language, the realization that a spoken utterance refers to an item in the infant's sensory experience, is acquired by the infant. It is clear that young children first acquire meaning in a very controlled manner. Children learn to associate the meanings of words with the words and phrases they hear as part of their normal daily routine. The words they hear regularly are thus associated with the event that accompanies them, and the result is the beginning of language comprehension (McNamara, 1972).

For a comprehensive discussion of language development in infancy and later years, see the following texts: Berko-Gleason, 1985; Dale, 1976; Gratch, 1979; McClowery, Guilford, and Richardson, 1982; McLean and Snyder-McLean, 1978; Owens, 1984; and Schiefelbusch and Lloyd, 1974.

SOCIAL DEVELOPMENT

Social and language development are so interdependent, in particular during the first year of life, that one cannot be discussed apart from the other. Table 2–4 presents a description of cognitive, social, and language development during the first 24 months of life.

Currently, there are basically two schools of thought on the origins of social responsiveness in humans. One, which has been termed the social learning theory, states that humans learn social response patterns from specific encounters with the natural environment. For example, by 6 weeks of age nearly all babies have begun to smile at human faces. Supporters of the social learning theory would state that babies smile

Table 2-4. Cognitive, Social, Language Development—Birth to 24 Months

Age (mo)	Cognitive Development (Piaget Stages)	Social and Language Development
0-1	Variations of reflex activity First primitive schemes	Initial impressions of others Beginning of preferential responses to caretakers
1-4	Primary circular reactions Exploration of own body senses	Establishment of reciprocal interactions with caregivers Vocalizing with parents and mutual interaction
4-10	Secondary circular reactions Object permanence Intentional repetition of originally spontaneous activities	Initiation of social exchanges, engages in social games, makes an effort to elicit social responses
10-12	Coordination of secondary schemes Switch from exploration of own body to exploration of objects, purposeful manipulation	First word uttered Expanded exploration of environment
12-18	Tertiary circular reactions Rapidly developing ability to walk and talk lead to greatly increased exploration	Telegraphic speech, groping patterns in combining words More self-assertive as fear of separation and strangers lessens
18-24	Beginning of thought The child now beginning to engage in both mental and physical manipulation	In use of language, increasing ability to convey deep structures (what is meant) Greater awareness of self and sense of separateness and self-assertion

Adapted from Biehler (1981).

because they have learned to associate faces with pleasurable stimulation or with relief from the discomfort of being cold, wet, hungry, or thirsty.

Others hold that social responsiveness develops in a biologically predetermined manner as a result of an innate predisposition to interact in predictable ways to social stimuli. Those who hold this view claim that smiling is an innate response that is genetically predetermined to appear at a predictable time. Support for this view is gathered from the observation that all babies begin to smile on a remarkably similar schedule, regardless of how much time they may have had to associate faces with pleasure or freedom from discomfort. A complete discussion of each of these opposing views is not possible in this chapter. However, a description of the symbiotic relationship between mother and infant as it relates to social alertness and responsiveness is presented.

The supposition that it is the development of language that lets children become communicative beings does not reflect the actual behavior of infants. Children communicate before they have language (Bruner, 1978). Language has been described as a subset of communication skills, the development of language depending upon the prior development of communication itself (Kaye, 1979). Both the nature of communication and the process of communication are affected by the social interaction afforded the infant. Another way of stating these concepts is to say that language represents only a portion of a larger interactional pattern that reflects the manner in which human infants are both exposed to and react to their environment.

Temperament

Individual differences in infant temperament may also have consequences on subsequent social development. Many of the temperamental differences that distinguish young infants from one another have social implications in infancy as well as later in childhood. A highly active child will initiate and conduct different sorts of social interactions with parents and peers than will a less active child. However much a child's distinctive temperament establishes a basis for uniqueness and individuality, the ultimate significance of these temperamental characteristics to the child, as an individual and as a member of society, will be determined by the ways in which these characteristics influence the child's interactions with other persons.

Thomas, Chess, and Birch (1970) and Thomas and Chess (1977) followed the temperamental development of 18 infants from the time the infants were born through the elementary school years. They focused on nine aspects of temperament that can be observed in very young infants: (1) activity level, (2) rhythmicity or regularity of behavior, (3) distractability, (4) approach or withdrawal when confronted by a new experience, (5) adaptability to change, (6) attention span or persistence, (7) intensity of reaction to stimuli, (8) threshold of responsiveness, and (9) quality of mood. The researchers concluded that the original characteristics of temperament tend to persist in many children over the years. The effects on overall social development in early infancy and later childhood are obvious.

Mother-Infant Interactions

How adults speak to young children has been of interest to students of social and language development for many years. The unique pattern of interaction between a mother and her infant represents a sociocommunicative process that is sensitively attuned to the mother-infant relationship. The child sets the level of the exchange because of its limited abilities. The initial infant responses are rigid and fixed. Only gradually does the infant acquire additional behaviors. On the other hand, the mother controls the exchanges by providing an appropriate framework and by adjusting her behavior. For example, when the newborn cries, the mother will usually offer breast or bottle and usually the infant will suck. Later in infancy additional responses by the mother will follow cries. Mothers learn to differentiate between cries due to hunger and those due to other causes. Thus, maternal responses are adjusted to meet the mother's perceptions of the infant's needs. Maternal responses to the infant rest heavily on the expanding social repertoire of the infant. A chronology of infant behaviors and maternal responses in the context of social interaction is described in the following paragraphs.

Birth to 6 Months

Shortly after birth the infant becomes an active participant in the interactive process that takes place between mother and child. By 1 month of age, and quite spontaneously, the infant engages in exchanges that include soft vocalizations when face to face with the mother. The child likewise displays keen sensitivity to the mother's vocalizations and movements. The child is quite attentive to the mother's face, to the exclusion of many other stimuli. Gross hand gestures, tongue protrusions, and mouth opening are imitated by the infant during the first weeks of life and are quite reflective of the child's social awareness. Trevathen (1979) has indicated that by 1 month of age the infant may approximate imitations of the mother's pitch and duration of speech sounds. The infant will turn toward an adult and gaze intently at the adult's face and mouth. At about 3 weeks of age the first social smile may be observed. It is at this time that the infant begins to smile in response to external stimuli. As the child gains increased control over voluntary movements, the human face alone does not keep the child's attention. At this point the mother uses exaggerated facial expressions as well as vocalizations. The mother at this point controls the amount of stimulation afforded the child, thus avoiding excitation and disinterest. Overall handling decreases, and dialogue between mother and child increases by the third month. Mother-infant dialogues of this nature have been termed *turn-taking* and suggest that the mother in part perceives her role as that of replier to the infant's vocalizations (Schaffer, Collins, and Parsons, 1977). It is at this time that an increased use of smiles, head movements, and gestures are observed. In addition, by 3 to 4 months of age additional response patterns such as game playing are likely to emerge.

Daily routine, including feeding and changing, provide predictable patterns of behavior and speech experience. During these times the infant is able to display cooperative and pleasurable responses that are reinforced by the mother's participation and response to infant behaviors. Both partners are active participants in these exchanges. By 5 months the infant shows more deliberate imitation of movements and vocalizations. By 6 to 8 months hand and nonspeech imitation become more frequent. Vocalizations that accompany different attitudes are noted in the 5-month-old infant. Infant emotions are summarized in Table 2–5. As the child nears 6 months of age interest in objects increases. A shift away from people and toward objects is evident. Reaching, grasping, and manipulating are noted at this time as eye-hand coordination matures.

7 to 12 Months

As the developing child approaches 6 months of age, the child displays an increased amount of control over relationships with the mother. Intentions are communicated more clearly and with better response on the part of the mother. Gestural and vocal patterns are the primary mode of expression at this stage. The daily routine activities of the mother and child are providing a rich range of experiences upon which later language learning depends. The mother can be observed during this period to regulate her speech to enhance the child's acquisition of language. The mother's language is child-sensitive relative to complexity, and geared toward the child's level of comprehension. Maternal language at this time also tends to be redundant. Her communication is geared toward explanation of, clarification of, and comments about shared experiences.

Several researchers have observed that by 7 months of age the infant begins to respond differently to the interactional partner. As the child is better able to play with objects, the mother makes increasing reference to objects. The infant then begins to associate verbal labels with specific objects. Simple motor behaviors are also now imitated by the infant at 9 to 10 months of age. Requests to wave bye-bye may now be followed. Mothers tend to monitor infant vocalizations more accurately and are better able to identify intentional messages (Ricks, 1979). Although vocalizations of the mother and infant tend initially to overlap, as the child approaches 1 year of age less vocal overlap is noted and turn-taking is in full effect. Intentionality emerges at 8 to 9 months of age and is expressed initially by gesture. (For a more com-

Table 2-5.   Infant Emotions

Emotions	Description	Age
interest	brows knit or raised, mouth rounded, lips pursed	birth
distress	eyes closed tightly, mouth square and angular	birth
disgust	nose wrinkled, upper lip elevated, tongue protruded	birth
smile	corners of mouth raised, cheeks lifted, eyes twinkle	4-6 weeks
fear	brows level but drawn in and up, eyes widened, mouth retracted	5-7 weeks
anger	brows together and lifted downward, eyes set, mouth square	12-16 weeks
sadness	inner corners of brows raised, mouth turns down in corners, pout	12-16 weeks
surprise	brows raised, eyes widened, oval shaped mouth	12-16 weeks

Note: From "Baby Face" by R. Trotter, April 1983, *Psychology Today,* p. 14. Copyright 1983 by *Psychology Today.* Reprinted with permission.

plete discussion of the stages present in the development of early communication functions see Bates, Camaioni, and Volterra, 1975).

It is during the second 6 months of life that the infant develops functional communication, first gesturally and then verbally. All of the rich social interactions between mother and infant result in spoken meaningful speech that emerges at approximately 12 months of age for most children. From this point on rapid changes are observed in syntax, grammar, vocabulary, and phonology. The importance of the unique interplay of social behaviors between mother and infant cannot be underestimated relative to their role in the formulation of one of humanity's most basic and essential skills, spoken language.

COGNITIVE DEVELOPMENT

A comprehensive and detailed discussion of cognitive development is clearly outside the scope of this chapter. The sheer amount of information available amounts to thousands of pages of discussion that present several major theoretical frameworks describing cognitive development. The purpose of the present discussion is to examine early cognitive development and to provide an overview of the importance of early experience from which later skill acquisition emerges.

The infant is not a passive creature but instead is actively engaged in its environment from birth. The child is busy building a repertoire of experiences, based on normal environmental interaction opportunities, and forming abilities and skills on which later learning depends. The child is paying attention and developing specific and controlled sequences of action (Caplan, 1973). Experiences are organized by the infant into general classes and larger concepts. The individual learns to use and understand in relation to (or as a representation of) the ideas or mental concepts that have been formed through experience (Bloom and Lahey, 1978). Several general statements relative to cognitive development will aid in interpreting the discussion to follow (Lichtenberg and Norton, 1970):

1. Inherent characteristics affect cognitive development.
2 Cognitive development involves a maturational process of hierarchical stages that incorporate characteristics from previous stages.
3. Cognitive growth occurs through the motivation to master the new and more difficult.
4. Autonomous thinking is based on definite internal cognitive organization that permits the child to interact with the external world.

A definite balance between innate biological characteristics and environmental opportunity is seen in the cognitive growth of the infant from birth to 12 months of age. For any given child physical growth and development follow a certain growth rate that is relatively resistant to external environmental variations. Even when unusual circumstances interfere with the normal pace of growth, the child's normal growth rate is resumed as soon as the interfering circumstances are removed. As mentioned previously, the human infant does possess many abilities, observed shortly after birth, that support the supposition that the child does possess a remarkable array of abilities that are biologically innate and that enable the child to process and interact with the environment in ways not previously thought possible. Thus, biological integrity as well as environmental opportunity and exposure are primary prerequisites for the process of developmental skill acquisition to begin and for cognitive development and organization to proceed normally.

The concept of internal cognitive organization has been the subject of much interest. How exactly does the infant organize and ultimately make sense of the world around it? What specific stages does the infant pass through that allow for the incorporation of previously learned skills and information into the hierarchical acquisition of new abilities? These are not easy questions to address, and the answers have enormous implications for the understanding of infant development.

One of the foremost influences on modern cognitive development theory has been Jean Piaget. In general, Piaget viewed cognitive development not as a quantitative accumulation of facts and ideas but as qualitative changes in the process of thought. This view allows for the supposition that as an individual matures, material is organized and stored in different ways that are reflected in different qualities of thought.

An important consideration is the notion that these changes occur through the individual's active involvement with the environment. Hence environmental exposure is fundamental to cognitive growth. The individual is thus internally motivated for change and learning. It is this internal motivation that pushes the individual, even in infancy, to explore new sensory experiences and attempt to make sense of the surrounding world. Piaget's four broad periods of cognitive development are (1) sensorimotor, 0 to 2 years, (2) preoperational, 2 to 7 years, (3) concrete operational, 7 to 11 years, and (4) formal, 11 plus years (Owens, 1984). During the sensorimotor period of development tremendous cognitive growth is taking place. It is during this period that the early structures of intelligence begin to evolve. The infant displays action-oriented responses to people and objects that are quite predictable, thus indicating recognition and familiarity. Table 2–6 presents six stages that Piaget describes as being part of the sensorimotor period of development. The process of cognitive development, as has been pointed out, is clearly dependent on sufficient learning opportunity (environmental exposure). The product of this exposure during the first year of life is a remarkably organized and coherent expansion of the infant's ability to make sense of the world around it.

Although Piaget's work and that of his followers form the largest single body of work on this topic, no comprehensive understanding of cognitive development can be based on this approach alone. Piaget's work has stimulated numerous research projects, and not all of the results have been in total agreement. Part of the discussion that has disagreed with Piaget's initial theory was motivated by interest in the relationship between cognition and language. Piaget has presented no specific model of language development. He has ascribed to language its function as the primary symbolic communication mode, but not the only mode of communication available to the individual. Hence, children learn object functions through manipulation and then use these functional characteristics to relate to classes of objects. These common features may form the semantic basis for early words. Piaget's theory of cognitive development has had great appeal because of its broad-based approach.

Table 2-6. Six Stages of the Sensorimotor Period

Stage	Characteristics
Stage 1 **Birth to** **1 Month**	Stage 1 is largely a reflexive stage during which certain reflexes present at birth (sucking, eye movement, and some movement of the head and arms) undergo developmental changes as a function of repeated practice. These reflexes, the infant's first means of dealing with the environment, are rapidly perfected and changed with repeated application to external events and objects and are seen as initial components for human cognitive growth.
Stage 2 **1 to 4 Months**	Stage 2 is marked by continued development and perfection of the abilities present at birth as well as by the addition of two additional events. First, visual and auditory skills increase, and the infant gains an expanded ability to turn its head and eyes in the direction of a sound source. The initial ability to visually fixate on the infant's own hand, within the first 2 months, results in the desire to reach and grasp objects in view somewhere around the fourth month. Second, the infant engages in continued repetition of previously learned response routines. If accidental contact is made with a toy, the infant will attempt to repeat the motor pattern that brought the toy into contact initially. No concept of object permanence is seen at this point. Once an object is out of visual contact, it ceases to exist for the infant.
Stage 3 **4 to 8 Months**	During stage 3 the infant continues to practice and expand motor movements but with new variations that require greater visual-motor coordination. The infant may play with toys that make noise for the pleasure of hearing the results (noise). The infant is intensely interested in objects and explores them freely. The infant also begins to imitate what it sees to a greater degree. The first signs of the concept of object permanence begin to appear. Rudimentary search behavior is noted when an object is only partially in view. The infant will not as yet search for an object that is totally out of view.
Stage 4 **8 to 12 Months**	The infant's behavior is characterized by increased intentional behavior designed to achieve a desired end. The child's behavior appears to have a definite goal or purpose. The child may push at an adult's hand, encouraging the adult to continue a desired activity. The infant now engages in active search for objects that are hidden and may display distress if the desired object is not located. Increased sophistication of independent locomotion is also evident during this stage.
Stage 5 **12 to 18 Months**	The infant is now able to walk and explore the environment much more actively, thus encountering a much wider range of experiences. The examination of objects is increased as more objects are available as a result of the child walking. Problem-solving strategies are mostly trial and error. Hidden objects are conceptualized; however, if not found where they usually are, the child will not search and explore alternative placements for desired objects.
Stage 6 **18 to 24 Months**	Problem-solving ability increased greatly as the child is able to form internal representations of objects, thus understanding to a greater degree the effects of personal, immediate actions upon an object. The sensorimotor period ends for the most part when the child is able to solve problems by inventing new means and not by having to take a trial-and-error approach, able to search successfully for objects even when alternative placements must be considered, and able to imitate concepts not immediately demonstrated for the child.

Reformulation of Piaget's initial theory has been accomplished by a variety of investigators. Case (1978) described a theoretical view of cognitive development that supports individual skill criteria as the basis of cognitive growth rather than developmental stages. Moore and Meltzoff (1978) likewise offered a reformulation of Piaget's initial paradigm of cognitive development by stating that object identity, those objects and experiences to which the infant is exposed, are the organizing principles of cognitive development. Additional contributions to cognitive development theory have been made by Bruner (1964); Bruner, Oliver, and Greenfield (1966); Flavell (1977, 1982); and Lindsay and Norman (1977).

PARENT-INFANT BONDING AND ATTACHMENT AND CAREGIVING

Social, language, and cognitive development are highly interrelated activities that have immense influence on one another. An additional area that is crucially important to the child's short- and long-term development, and that has enormous impact on the areas of language, cognitive, and social maturation, is the forming of adequate attachment between infant and mother or primary caregiver. A variety of terms have been used to describe this important area, two of which are *attachment* and *bonding*. Bonding and attachment are more clearly described in Chapter 4 in the context of the negative impact of a lack of their proper formation. They are defined as a unique relationship that lasts over time, and although they are difficult to quantify, a variety of activities such as touch, gazing, and fondling by the mother have been used.

Perhaps the best way in which to describe the tremendous shift in thought about the importance of proper parent-child relationships is to describe current pediatric practice in comparision to past practices. In the 1940s parents were allowed to visit their hospitalized children for only 1 or 2 hours each week. Currently, the majority of pediatric units allow unlimited parental visitation and encourage parents to live in with their young children, thus acknowledging the importance of the child's attachment to the parents (Kennell, Voos, and Klaus, 1979). The manner in which a mother and her infant relate is extremely important and has been shown to be related to the child's emotional, cognitive, and motor development. The goals of professional perinatal care should be (1) to maximize the strengths of the mother's ability for and sensitivity to the caretaking of her child, (2) to produce a child who is maximally capable of signaling needs and responding to the mother, and (3) to provide the setting in which the initial bonding between mother and infant can take place (Sameroff, 1981).

The information that follows is an examination of various aspects of the parent-infant relationship as well as attachment and caregiving. It is not exhaustive but is designed to provide the practitioner with an understanding of the importance of the first hours, days, and weeks of life relative to normal infant development and attachment with mother.

Early Infant-Mother Contact

Various investigations have been conducted to ascertain the importance of the first few hours of maternal-infant contact. These studies are quite revealing about later mother-infant interactions. Perhaps one of the most informative was conducted by Kennell and colleagues (1974). Normal full-term infants were allowed various amounts and schedules of contact with their mothers. The schedules varied from 1 hour of exposure within 2 hours of birth (early contact group) to visits of 20 to 30 minutes every 4 hours for feeding purposes starting 6 to 8 hours after birth (late contact group). Significant differences in the general style of maternal caregiving were observed between the groups of mothers at follow-up visits 1 month later. For example, the early contact mothers stood near their infants and watched more closely during stressful physical examinations. The early contact mothers soothed their crying infants more and participated in more eye-to-eye contact during feeding. They were also more reluctant to leave their babies with someone else. Follow-up 1 year later revealed some of the same patterns of interaction. Follow-up at 2 years revealed significant differences between early and late contact groups with regard to language behavior. Kennell concluded that an extra 16 hours of contact in the first 3 days of life appeared to have affected maternal behavior for 2 years.

Additional studies designed to assess the long- and short-term impact on early mother-infant contact have been conducted by other investigators. Results have strongly supported the value to the overall mother-infant relationship of early and prolonged contact (de Chateau, 1976; Greenberg, Rosenberg, and Lind, 1973; Leifer, Liederman, Barnett, and Williams, 1972; Sousa, et al., 1974; Winters, 1973). This early period following birth when attachment opportunity is at its optimum has been termed the *sensitive period*. Thus, the very early postpartum period (sensitive period) is especially significant for the development of parental attachment and has consequences relative to maternal caregiving style.

Patterns of Attachment

Ainsworth (1982) in a discussion of early caregiving and later patterns of attachment described several patterns of maternal behavior relative to caregiving. These observations provide valuable insight on maternal behavior and its importance in a variety of caregiving situations. The variety of caregiving situations and the observations made by Ainsworth are as follows:

Maternal Behavior Relevant to Feeding

The extent to which the mother showed sensitive responsiveness to the baby's signals, either gearing her behavior to the baby's signals or dominating the interaction herself, was rated. Mothers whose responsiveness was low in the first 3 months of the infant's life had babies whose feedings were characterized as unhappy throughout the first year. Infants characterized as securely attached to their mothers at 12 months of age had mothers who had been most sensitive to the infant's signals during the first three months.

Maternal Responsiveness to Infant Crying

Infant crying was measured in terms of the frequency of crying episodes as well as maternal response to it. The amount of early crying was shown to have no correlation to the amount of later crying. The degree of maternal responsiveness to crying was consistent throughout the first year. Mothers who tended to be unresponsive to crying had babies who cried relatively more later on. Prompt response to crying was more effective in reducing the amount of crying as the baby matured.

Maternal Behavior in Face-to-Face Situations

From 6 to 15 weeks of age positive infant behavior (vocalizing and smiling) were associated with playful and contingent maternal behavior. Mothers who initiated interactions silently or who sustained a matter-of-fact expression while face to face with their babies had babies who tended merely to look at them.

Behavior in Everyday Separation and Reunion Situations

Frequent protests by the infant in the presence of maternal separation at 1 year of age were associated with the mother's unresponsiveness to crying and general insensitivity to infant signals. Mothers who responded more readily to infant crying and who were judged to be accepting and cooperative tended to have babies who responded more favorably to their return after a brief separation.

Maternal Behavior Relevant to Close Body Contact

Maternal behavior throughout the first year of life tended to be relatively consistent relative to bodily contact (maternal picking up and holding of her baby). Maternal behavior tended to range from tender or careful and affectionate attentions to inept holding and interfering behavior. Frequent picking up of the baby was associated with inept and interfering behavior. Mothers who picked their babies up often also tended to put them down again quickly. Positive infant responses throughout the first year were associated not with the length of time they were held but rather with how the mother held them (tender or careful quality). Thus, mothers who are tender and careful early on, gearing their behavior to the baby's cues, tend to evoke a positive response in the baby, which carries over into later in the first year. In addition, mothers who displayed tender or careful patterns of holding in the first 3 months of life had babies who were securely attached to them at 1 year of age. Mothers who handled their babies ineptly tended to have anxiously attached babies later on.

CONCLUSIONS

Each of the areas of infant development discussed in this chapter have portrayed the newborn as a remarkably alert and active organism. Many areas of sensory function are involved in the processing of complex environmental stimuli, thus making the newborn an active observer and, as time progresses, an active participant in its world. The importance of early stimulation and developmental opportunity to the initiation of the normal progression of skill acquisition is evident. Data such as this have salient implications for those infants who, because of prematurity or any one of a host of potent conditions, are not afforded the opportunity to participate normally in the world around them.

Recall a statement made in the introduction to this text: "Anything that interferes with a child's ability to interact with the environment in a normal manner is a potential source or contributing factor to the presence of developmental delay. Certainly the at-risk infant has been subjected to a potent list of factors that may increase the risk of later developmental problems." Although the presence of developmental delay will not be seen in all high-risk infants, the delicate balance of circumstances necessary for developmental adequacy are certainly affected by neonatal complications that lead to significant illness early in life. That is not to say that catch-up growth, the ability to overcome early risk conditions, is not possible. In fact, as will be discussed later, remarkable catch-up growth is possible with proper intervention when needed. The clinician-educator is in a unique position to facilitate greater understanding between medical, educational, and parental interests relative to developmental skill acquisition for the high-risk infant. However, only a thorough understanding of and familiarity with normal child development in the areas discussed in this chapter will allow the clinician-educator the opportunity to perform this function and to perform it well.

REFERENCES

Ainsworth, M. (1982). Early caregiving and later attachment problems. In M. Klaus (Ed.), *Birth-interaction and attachment* (Johnson and Johnson Pediatric Round Table No. 6, p. 35). Johnson and Johnson Baby Products.

Bates, E., Camaioni, L., Volterra, V. (1975). The acquisition of performatives prior to speech. *Merill-Palmer Quarterly, 21,* 205.

Berko-Gleason, J. (1985). *The development of language.* Columbus, OH: Charles E. Merrill.

Biehler, R. (1981). *Child development: An introduction.* Boston: Houghton-Mifflin.

Bloom, L., and Lahey, M. (1978). *Language development and language disorders.* New York: John Wiley & Sons.

Brennan, W., Ames, E., and Moore, R. (1966). Age differences in infant's attention to patterns of different complexities. *Science, 151,* 354.

Bruner, J. (1964). The course of cognitive growth. *American Psychologist, 19,* 1.

Bruner, J. (1978). Learning how to do things with words. In J. Bruner and A. Gurton (Eds.), *Human growth and development.* Oxford: Oxford University Press.

Bruner, J., Oliver, R., and Greenfield, P. (1966). *Studies in cognitive growth.* New York: John Wiley & Sons.

Caplan, F. (1973). *The first 12 months of life.* New York: Grosset & Dunlap.

Case, R. (1978). Intellectual development from birth to adulthood: A neo-Piagetian interpretation. In R. Sieglar (Ed.), *Children's thinking: What develops?* Hillsdale, NJ: Lawerence Erlbaum Associates.

Chomsky, N. (1968). *Language and mind.* New York: Harcourt, Brace and World.

Cohen, L., DeLoache, J., and Strauss, M. (1979). Infant visual perception. In J. Osofsky (Ed.), *Handbook of infant development.* New York: John Wiley & Sons.

Cohen, M., and Gross, P. (1979). *The developmental resource: Behavior sequencing for assessment and programming planning.* New York: Grune & Stratton.

Dale, P. (1976). *Language development (2nd ed.).* New York: Holt, Rinehart & Winston.

de Chateau, P. (1976). *Neonatal care routines: Influences on maternal and infant behavior and breastfeeding* (Medical Dissertations, N.S. No.20). Umea, Sweden. Umea University.

D'Odorico, L. (1984). Nonsegmental features in prelinguistic communication: An analysis of some types of infant cry and non-cry vocalizations. *Journal of Child Language, 11,* 17.

Fantz, R. (1961). The origin of form perception. *Scientific American, 204,* 66.

Fantz, R., and Miranda, S. (1975). Newborn infant attention to form of contour. *Child Development, 46,* 224.

Flavell, J. (1977). *Cognitive development.* Englewood Cliffs, NJ: Prentice-Hall.

Flavell, J. (1982). On cognitive development. *Child Development, 53,* 1.

Goren, C., Sartz, M., and Wye, P. (1975). Visual following and pattern discrimination by newborn infants. *Pediatrics, 56,* 544.

Gratch, G. (1979). The development of thought and language in infancy. In J. Osofsky (Ed.), *Handbook of infant development.* New York: John Wiley & Sons.

Greenberg, M., Rosenberg, I., and Lind, J. (1973). First mothers rooming in with their newborns: Its impact upon the mother. *American Journal of Orthopsychiatry, 43,* 783.

Greenman, G. (1963). Visual behavior of newborn infants. In D. Solnit and S. Provence (Eds.), *Modern perspectives in child development.* New York: Hallmark.

Haith, M. (1973). Visual scanning in infants. In J. Stone, H. Smith, and L. Murphy (Eds.), *The competent infant.* New York: Basic Books.

Haith, M. (1976). *Organization of visual behavior at birth.* Paper presented in a symposium on Perception in Infancy at the XXI International Congress of Psychology, Paris.

Kaye, K. (1979). Thickening thin data: The maternal role in developing communication and language. In M. Bullowa (Ed.), *Before speech.* New York: Cambridge University Press.

Kennell, J. Jerauld, R., Wolfe, H., Chesler, D., Kreger, N., McAlpine, W., Steffa, N., and Klaus, M. (1974). Maternal behavior one year after early and extended post partum contact. *Developmental Medicine and Child Neurology, 16,* 172.

Kennell, J., Voos, D., and Klaus, M. (1979). Parent infant bonding. In J. Osofosky (Ed.), *Handbook of infant development.* New York: John Wiley & Sons.

Kessen, W., Salapatek, P., and Haith, M. (1972). The visual response of the human newborn to linear contour. *Journal of Experimental Child Psychology, 13,* 9.

Leifer, A., Liederman, P., Barnett, C., and Williams, J. (1972). Effects of mother-infant separation on maternal attachment behavior. *Child Development, 43,* 1203.

Lewis, M. (1969). Infant's response to facial stimuli during the first year of life. *Developmental Psychology, 1,* 75.

Lichtenberg, P., and Norton, D. (1970). *Cognitive and mental development in the first five years of life* (publication no. 2057). Rockville, MD: National Institute of Mental Health.

Lindsay, P., and Norman, D. (1977). *Human information processing (2nd ed.).* New York: Academic Press.

McClowery, D., Guilford, A., and Richardson, S. (1982). *Infant communication development, assessment and intervention.* New York: Grune & Stratton.

McLean, J., and Synder-McLean, L. (1978). *A transactional approach to early language training.* Columbus, OH: Charles E. Merrill.

McNamara, L. (1972). Cognitive basis of language learning in infants. *Psychological Review, 79,* 1.

Moore, K., and Meltzoff, A. (1978). Object permanence, imitation and language development in infancy: Toward a neo-Piagetian perspective on communication development. In F. Minifie and L. Lloyd (Eds.), *Communicative and cognitive abilities: Early behavioral assessment.* Baltimore: University Park Press.

Owens, R. (1984). *Language Development: An introduction.* Columbus, OH: Charles E. Merrill.

Ricks, D. (1979). Making sense of experience to make sensible sounds. In M. Bullowa (Ed.), *Before Speech.* New York: Cambridge University Press.

Sachs, J. (1985). Prelinguistic development. In J. Gleason (Ed.), *The development of language.* Columbus, OH: Charles E. Merrill.

Salapatek, P. (1975). Pattern perception in early infancy. In L. B. Cohen and P. Salapatek (Eds.), *Infant perception: From sensation to cognition: Basic visual processes.* New York: Academic Press.

Salapatek, P., and Kessen, W. (1973). Prolonged investigation of a plane geometric triangle by the human newborn. *Journal of Exceptional Child Psychology, 15,* 22.

Sameroff, A. (1981). Psychological needs of the mother in early mother-infant interaction. In G. Avey (Ed.), *Neonatology, pathophysiology and management of the newborn.* Philadelphia: J. B. Lippincott.

Schaffer, H., Collis, C., and Parsons, G. (1977). Vocal interchange and visual regard in verbal and preverbal children. In H. Schaffer (Ed.), *Studies in mother-infant interaction.* New York: Academic Press.

Schiefelbusch, R., and Lloyd, L. (1974). *Language perspective: Acquisition, retardation, and intervention.* Baltimore: University Park Press.

Schlesinger, I. (1977). The role of cognitive development and linguistic input in language acquisition. *Journal of Child Language, 4,* 153.

Shirley, M. (1959). *The first two years: A study of 25 babies.* Minneapolis: University of Minnesota Press.

Slobin, D. (1973). Cognitive prerequisites for the development of grammar. In C. Ferguson and D. Slobin (Eds.), *Studies of child language development.* New York: Holt, Rinehart & Winston.

Sousa, P., Bamos, F., Gazalle, R., Begeres, R., Pinheirie, G., Menezea, S., and Amuda, L. (1974). *Attachment and Lactation,* Fifteenth International Congress of Pediatrics, Buenos Aires.

Stark, R. (1979). Prespeech segmental feature development. In P. Fletcher and M. Garman (Eds.), *Language acquisition.* New York: Holt, Rinehart & Winston.

Trevathen, C. (1979). Communication and cooperation in early infancy: A description of primary intersubjectivity. In M. Bullowa (Ed.), *Before speech.* New York: Cambridge University Press.

Thomas, A., and Chess, S. (1977). *Temperament and development.* New York: Bruner-Mazel.

Thomas, A., Chess, S., and Birch, H. (1970). The origin of personality. *Scientific American, 223,* 102.

Trotter, R. (1983, April). Baby face. *Psychology Today,* p. 14.

Vygotsky, L. (1962). *Thought and language.* Cambridge: MIT Press. (Original work published 1934.)

Whorf, B. (1956). *Language, thought and reality.* New York: John Wiley & Sons.

Winters, M, (1973). *The relationship of time of initial feeding to success of breastfeeding.* Unpublished masters thesis, University of Washington.

Chapter 3

The Developmental Outcome of High-Risk Infants

Current literature on the developmental outcome of high-risk infants has shown that at-risk infants display increased susceptibility to a variety of physical and developmental deficits. These infants later on face an increased incidence of behavioral abnormalities, abuse and neglect, developmental delay, educational difficulties, and deficient parent-infant bonding and relationships. It must be mentioned at this juncture that certainly not all high-risk infants display subsequent neurodevelopmental sequelae and that many do ultimately display normal developmental patterns. The preterm low birth weight infant, however, is clearly at greater risk for the later manifestation of both subtle and more obvious developmental deviations. These deviations are observed in the neonatal period as well as in later school years.

The vulnerability of the stressed infant must be viewed in part relative to what is lost both to the individual and to society if that person does not survive as a productive human being. Or, if the high-risk infant survives but is biologically damaged, what is the loss to the person, the family, and society as a whole? These concerns have become increasingly relevant in recent years as an expanding number of professionals have become involved in the provision of services to the developmentally delayed. Legislative initiative, state and private funding, research endeavors, and educational preparation of professionals are all affected by the presence of a substantial developmentally delayed population.

With the tremendous successes seen in keeping high-risk infants alive, more at-risk infants live today than ever before. This category of children is most vulnerable to biological damage and resultant developmental delay, and although the incidence of prematurity and low birth weight have not changed dramatically, survival is increasing. Thus, the living population of at-risk infants is expanding.

The majority of follow-up studies on the high-risk population have viewed specific subpopulations (populations determined by birth weight, gestational age, or specific neonatal medical complications). Studies that examined birth-weight-specific populations tended to view low birth weight infants in one of two ways: infants born prematurely—less than 38 weeks gestation and weighing less than 2,500 g—or full term infants weighing less than 2,500 g who were referred to as small for gestational age (SGA). The term low birth weight is not a pure one and includes several categories of infants with various etiologies and reasons for their inclusion. The low birth weight infant may be born too soon (preterm), too small (SGA), or too soon and too small. Differences exist in the long-term prognosis for each of these categories.

Preterm denotes an infant born after less than 38 weeks of gestation, regardless of its weight. Low birth weight, as previously discussed, signifies an infant of less than 2,500 g at birth regardless of the length of gestation. Low birth weight relates to how well fed the infant was in utero and may also be related to how well the infant's systems function at birth. If, therefore, 2,500 g is used as the upper limit for describing low birth weight infants, approximately 80,000 low birth weight infants are born per million births in the United States each year (Rosen, 1982).

Data on developmental follow-up of SGA term infants are readily available and indicate that these infants (1) display IQ scores that are similar to all term infants, (2) display an incidence of major neurological deficits similar to all SGA infants, (3) display an increased incidence of school problems that require special placement, and (4) tend to remain underweight and small for their age (Babson, 1970; Babson and Kangas, 1973; Fitzhardinge and Stevens, 1972; Rubin, Rosenblatt, and Balow, 1973).

The preterm SGA infant, however, displays a different picture. In particular, very low birth weight (VLBW) infants, either term or preterm, present a variety of sequelae that demand special attention. These are discussed in greater detail in later sections. Advances in neonatal medicine have lowered the birth weight for which a significant increase in sequelae are expected. At present, the outcome for babies who weigh

1,500 to 2,500 g at birth is generally good; they usually survive and have a satisfactory neurological development. The outcome for babies who weigh less than 1,500 g, however, is different from that for those who weigh more than 1,500 g.

The present chapter is designed to provide the practitioner with an understanding of what is currently known about the behavioral and physical expectations of those infants who survive a precarious neonatal period. Rosen (1982) stated that the low birth weight (high-risk) infant is one of the major biomedical problems of the 1980s. Clearly, professionals from a variety of disciplines are focusing with increasing frequency on the developmental outcome of high-risk infants. It is imperative that special education personnel, speech-language pathologists, developmental psychologists, and early childhood education specialists be familiar with the developmental performance and unique needs of these infants.

PHYSICAL DEVELOPMENT

Regular follow-up of physical development is common practice in light of what has been learned in the last 20 years of neonatal and postnatal care of the at-risk infant. Serial measurements of length, weight, and head circumference can be sensitive reflections of health or disease. Aberrations in these growth parameters have different causes and prognostic significance for both the high- and low-risk infant. In the high-risk population of infants close monitoring of overall growth provides an indication of the continuing well-being of a previously sick infant.

Growth Patterns

In low-risk healthy infants weight increases an average of 208 g/wk from the 28th week of gestation through the 6th month of extrauterine life. Length increases 1.1 cm/wk from 28 to 40 weeks of gestation. Increases in head circumference average 0.75 cm/wk through the last trimester of pregnancy. The actual growth patterns of infants born at 28 to 32 weeks gestation who survive the neonatal period display obvious differences from the growth patterns of term infants (Maisels and Marks, 1981).

General Patterns

Manser (1984) has described the aberrant pattern of growth present in high-risk infants. The growth of these infants may be divided into four arbitrary phases that will vary in duration. Each of these phases may last from days to weeks, depending on several factors. Further data on growth patterns related to specific subpopulations of high-risk infants are also available. The four growth patterns presented by Manser are presented in modified form in the following sections and in Table 3–1.

Growth Delay.   The first phase of growth in the high-risk infant has been termed the period of growth delay. A variety of dynamic physical changes occur that result in decreases in weight and even head circumference. This is somewhat comparable to the pattern seen in the first several days of life in a healthy infant who also has a mild weight loss. In the sick or premature infant massive fluid losses are superimposed upon the normal physiological changes. Thus, the weight of the sick or premature infant must be closely monitored. The presence of severe illness or prolonged nutritional restrictions will also contribute to the initial growth delay.

Transition.   As the overall physical well-being of the infant improves, specifically, fluid intake and medical status, general caloric intake is increased and becomes easier to achieve. As general caloric intake increases and exceeds the infant's needs for maintenance, slow growth begins, thus marking the transition from the phase of growth delay to the phase of catch-up growth. As weight loss ends, there is initially a slow increase in head circumference paralleled by a slow increase in length.

Catch-Up Growth.   The third phase of growth is characterized by increases in head circumference, length, and weight at rates exceeding those found in healthy infants. Intrauterine growth retarded infants may display quite marked head growth at this time. Accelerated increases in length should occur within 4 to 10 days of onset of rapid head growth. Under normal circumstances an increase in weight also takes place. Slower catch-up growth will be observed in those babies who have experienced prolonged growth delay or who have continuing illness. The presence of increased environmental stimulation also has been observed to affect the magnitude of catch-up growth (Kramer and Pierpoint, 1976). The ultimate outcome for improving the long-term potential for high-risk infants depends in part on providing environmental and nutritional adequacy during this stage. The overall length of this phase will vary, depending on the circumstances surrounding each infant relative to prematurity, birth weight, and medical condition. In quite small, premature, and sick infants catch-up growth may be observed for up to 3 years.

Homeorrhesis.   The final phase of growth is characterized by patterns that closely resemble growth described by normal growth

Table 3-1. Characteristic Growth Phases in High-Risk Infants

Initial Growth Delay

  Increases with decreasing gestational age
  May be shorter or nonexistent in SGA infants
  Correlates directly with severity and duration of medical illness
  Correlates directly with degree of nutritional restrictions

Transition to Catch-Up Growth

  Head growth most prominent
  SGA infants may show increases in head growth greater than AGA infants
  Head growth paralleled by increases in length

Catch-Up Growth

  Velocity
    low with nutritional restrictions
    low with continued medical compromise
    low with longest growth delay
    may surpass well baby population
    enhanced by environmental stimulation
  Duration
    May last 3 years in AGA infants
    Is limited in SGA infants

Homeorrhesis

  Lowest growth percentiles reached in infants
    With prolonged growth delay
    With limited catch-up growth
    At high risk for subsequent neurodevelopmental handicaps

charts. This phase begins when accelerated catch-up growth has ceased.

Patterns in Subpopulations

Various subpopulations within the high-risk group display variety in overall growth patterns. However, the phases of growth presented in the previous sections appear to be equally applicable.

Infants born between 27 and 33 weeks gestation who are not subjected to prolonged or severe neonatal disease display the greatest catch-up growth between 36 to 44 weeks postconception (Brandt, 1978; Cruise, 1973). Subnormal growth has been reported in preterm infants who survived more severe neonatal diseases with catch-up growth displayed at later ages. Follow-up of AGA infants with birth weights of less that 1,000 g and with no long-term or medical compromise showed that at 3 years of age 15 percent of the children were below the 5th percentile for body weight, and 20 percent of the children displayed head circumference below the 5th percentile for age (Kimble, Ariagno, and Stevenson, 1982). Pape, Buncie, and Ashley (1978) conducted a 2-year follow-up study in Toronto of 43 infants who weighed less that 1,000 g at birth. Results indicated that the infants displayed aberrant growth patterns; height at 2 years fell between the 10th and 25th percentiles for normal growth and weight between the 3rd and 10th percentiles. Fitzhardinge and Stevens (1972) also presented data on the later growth patterns of SGA infants who were followed for 4 years. At 4 years of age the groups of infants studied fell between the 10th and 25th percentiles for normal growth; 33 percent were below the 3rd percentile on measures of weight.

Other researchers have followed groups of SGA infants through adolescence (13 to 19 years of age). Measures have been made on physical growth and neurological development. Significant differences in height, weight, and head circumference were found between SGA and AGA infants. These differences were present even after statistical control for socioeconomic status and parental height were implemented. These results indicated that SGA infants have impaired potential for physical growth through adolescence (Westwood, Kramer, Munz, Lovett, and Watters, 1983).

It is apparent from these and other studies that the general physical growth of the high-risk infant, in particular the SGA infant with or without long-term medical compromise, differs from that of the full-term or AGA infant. However, poor growth does not always indicate poor neurodevelopmental outcome, thus pointing out the need for regular follow-up and evaluation.

Neurodevelopmental Performance

Routine examination and follow-up of high-risk infants most certainly includes the assessment of overall neurological status. The relationship between aberrant neurological functioning in infancy and later delayed neurodevelopmental performance is well established and is present to an increased degree in the high-risk population. The concept that children with moderate-to-severe neurologic abnormalities in infancy have an increased incidence of mental retardation at preschool or early school years is well documented. For example, Michaelsson, Yliner, and Donner, (1981) devised an overall risk scale based on a neurodevelopmental screening administered to a population of Finnish children at 5 years of age who had been placed in the high-risk category in the newborn period. Point values were assigned to various test items, which included scoring on visual acuity, gross motor performance, fine motor performance, coordination and balance, involuntary movements when standing, articulation skills, language skills, perception, concentration, and behavior. The mean score of 19.7 for the risk group, compared with 9.0 for the control group, indicated that children who were at risk in the newborn period had significantly more divergent neurodevelopmental behavior than control children. The results also showed differences according to the dominant risk factor, and especially high scores were present when the children had several risk factors simultaneously. It is evident that neurodevelopmental deviations at the age of 5 years can result from disorders in the neonatal period. The following information is designed to present an overview of neurological functioning in the high-risk population.

Common Abnormalities

The most common finding in infants in a neonatal intensive care unit (NICU) is hypotonia (less than normal muscle tone), including delayed head control. Spasticity is usually not observed; however, by 3 months of age some infants will display signs of spasticity. It must be pointed out, however, that the detection of mild and moderate neurological deficits in children less than 3 months of age is quite difficult. The major types of abnormalities seen in high-risk infants have been presented in excellent fashion by Ellison (1984) and are summarized here:

Cerebral Palsy. Cerebral palsy has been defined as a nonprogressive, chronic disability characterized by aberrant control of movement and posture appearing early in life. Abnormal movement and posture during infancy are not difficult to detect; however, some infants outgrow this abnormality, most in late infancy and some in preschool years, leaving only a remnant of chronic disability at 7 years of age.

Motor Dysfunction in Infancy. Motor dysfunction in infancy is an umbrella term that refers to four types or categories of dysfunction. It covers abnormalities that remain, as well as those that eventually disappear. It differs from cerebral palsy in that the specific muscles involved may be mixed, and the type of involvement among muscle groups likewise may be mixed. These four categories are characterized by the following:

1. An involvement of all four limbs that is different from that characterized by abnormal tension of the muscles (hypertonia). The infant may have hypotonia of the arms and spasticity of the legs or a dyskinetic quality to arm movement and posture and spasticity of the legs.
2. A one-sided involvement with generally more involvement of the arm than the leg.
3. Bilateral leg involvement (with lesser involvement of the arms) often manifested as some delayed or clumsy fine motor control rather than spasticity.

4. A delay in head control, sitting with rounded back, delay in independent sitting, and delay in leg control with delayed pulling to standing, cruising, and independent walking.

Transient Abnormality of Infancy. Transient abnormalities fall between the abnormal and the normal. These are observations relative to abnormal function that appear and disappear at different ages of infancy. The recurrent theme is that of neurological abnormality that disappears by late infancy.

Determination of Infants at Risk

The determination in the NICU of which infants are more likely to display neurological dysfunction later on is not an easy one to make. Advances in neonatal intensive care have resulted in a decrease in the survivable birth weight from 1,500 g to 1,000 g for which neurological handicaps are present with greater frequency. The percentage of infants who display neurological abnormalities ranged from 9 to 13 percent in studies conducted by Ellison, Browning, and Trostmiller (1982). Davis and Tizard (1975) in London reported an incidence rate of 10.3 percent in a population of 170 children with birth weights of less than 1,500 g. They were specifically interested in the presence of spastic dyplegia. Additional studies described the presence of "weak neurological responses" when preterm and full-term infants were compared. Preterm infants of lowest birth weight at all gestational ages showed the greatest number of weak responses (Howard, Parmalee, Koop, and Littman, 1976). These differences were detected when the preterm infants were tested at their expected date of birth (40 weeks conceptual age).

Specific categories of infants who are at greater risk for neurological disability have been described by Ellison, Horn, and Browning (1983). Babies with a birth weight of less than 750 g, intracranial hemorrhage, or hydrocephalus were at greatest risk. Other variables that increased risk for neurological abnormality included the presence of apnea, the use of a respirator, maternal bleeding, respiratory distress syndrome, pneumothorax, the need to provide oxygenation at a level above 60 percent, low Apgar scores, neonatal seizures, and intubation. De Souza and Richards (1978) likewise examined factors that placed infants at greater risk for neurological difficulties. In their follow-up group in Manchester, England, babies with a history of severe neurological abnormality were followed for between 2 and 5 years. Considerable improvement in function was noted in many children. However, those babies that exhibited apathy initially but subsequently displayed hyperexcitability and extensor hypertonia had the worst prognosis. Comparison studies between infants weighing less than 1,000 g at birth and receiving assisted ventilation and those not receiving assisted ventilation indicated marked differences between the groups. The assisted ventilation group scored significantly poorer on measures of neurological status and developmental performance. The authors concluded that the requirement for assisted ventilation in this study was associated with increased morbidity and sequelae (Rothberg et al., 1983).

The presence of neurological disability for the term but SGA infant reveals that the incidence of disability is similar to that of all SGA infants (Rubin, et al., 1973). Preterm SGA infants follow a different course, however, with as many as 49 percent displaying neurological damage. These handicaps appear to be related to CNS depression at the time of birth (Fitzhardinge and Stevens, 1972).

These data demonstrate that the high-risk infant, in particular the SGA infant, is more susceptible to neurological handicaps. When handicap is defined as the presence of a major or minor neurological abnormality, it is found in 18 to 44 percent of babies weighing less than 1,500 g (Davies, 1976). Clearly, the preterm infant, and in particular the SGA infant, is in need of systematic and ongoing evaluation to detect the presence of neurological abnormalities.

PRESCHOOL PERFORMANCE OF HIGH-RISK INFANTS

Developmental follow-up of high-risk infants has been undertaken in a variety of ways. Specific skill areas such as vision, speech, and hearing have been examined as well as overall developmental performance. A vast amount of literature is available concerning the follow-up of these infants during the preschool years. The information given here addresses the general developmental expectations of high-risk infants during the preschool years (birth to 5 years of age). Specific skill areas are addressed when applicable and in the context of overall development.

Neonatal Neurobehavioral Performance

Recent investigations have pointed to measurable differences between the behavioral performance of preterm infants at 40 weeks postconception and of full-term infants. Similar findings were presented for preterm infants less than 40 weeks postconceptual age as well. These observations included measures on muscle tone, neurological responses, increased asymmetrical responses, and an increased extensor tone of the lower limbs. Preterm infants displayed a decreased capacity to stay alert, and this was accompanied by over-excitation. They were emotionally labile, irritable, and hard to console, with increased fragility of emotional and autonomic regulation with shorter periods of alertness. Crying among preterm infants also appeared to be less frequent and robust (Di Vitto and Goldberg, 1979; Hatcher, 1977; Howard et al., 1976; Lester and Zeskind, 1979).

Kurtzburg and colleagues (1979) used the Neonatal Behavioral Assessment Scale (Brazelton, 1973) to study preterm and full-term infants at 40 weeks postconception. They compared the neurobehavioral status of 118 low birth weight (LBW) infants with that of 76 normal full-term infants. Differences were present between the groups in the areas of visual following and auditory orienting, with the at-risk infants scoring lower on each of these measures. The LBW infants scored significantly lower on tasks that measured the infants' ability to visually follow a face and a bull's-eye pattern. Ninety-nine percent of the full-term infants had total bull's-eye following scores greater than 12 out of a possible 24. Only 32 percent of the LBW infants achieved a score of 12 or better. Face and voice following revealed a similar pattern: 96 percent of the full-term infants scored greater than 12 and only 31 percent of the LBW infants scored 12 or better. The LBW infants also scored lower in responsivity to auditory stimuli (bell, rattle, and human voice). Ninety-six percent of the full-term infants achieved total scores greater than 12 (18 maximum) for orienting to a rattle, compared with 21 percent for the LBW group. Orienting for the bell and human voice revealed similar differences between the two groups: 96 percent versus 37 percent for the bell, and 96 percent versus 32 percent for the human voice. Patterns of performance in the two groups studied were also of interest. The full-term infants scored well on both modalities (auditory and visual); their scores were slightly higher for auditory orienting than for visual following. In contrast, the LBW infants did not display a modality preference; their scores were widely scattered.

Other researchers who examined the visual and auditory performance of LBW infants at postconceptual ages between 33 and 37 weeks discovered that the LBW infants displayed orienting behavior less adequate than that of full-term infants (Scarr and Williams, 1971). Neurobehavioral performance of the LBW infants in the study by Kurtzburg and colleagues also differed for the LBW infants in the areas of lateral head position preference, active mobility, reflexive responses (optic blink, acoustic blink), rooting, sucking, grasp, tonic neck reflexes, and general muscle tone. Differences between LBW infants and normal birth weight infants were also detected by Rubin and colleagues (1973) on Apgar measures as well as the overall number of diagnosed abnormalities such as neurological deficits.

Ferrari, Grosoli, Fontance, and Cauazzuti (1983) used the Brazelton Neonatal Behavioral Assessment Scale to examine 20 low-risk preterm infants in Modena, Italy. The infants were examined at their expected date of birth (38 to 41 weeks postconception). Results indicated that low gestational age at birth, even after relatively normal intrauterine development and with good perinatal and neonatal condition, was associated with different and often poorer behavioral organization when the expected term of pregnancy was reached.

These results clearly point to consistent differences in the LBW infant during the early neonatal period. The high-risk infant's inability to fully process and take advantage of the environmental stimulation afforded it, in conjunction with the tremendous effort it exerted toward survival, of necessity relegates the infant to a late start toward developmental adequacy.

Preschool Mastery of Developmental Skills

Acquisition of developmental skills passes through many stages during the preschool years. Motor performance, cognitive development, social awareness and language functioning are only a few of the skills that are developed and modified during this period. The performance of the high-risk infant during the neonatal period was shown in the previous section to differ significantly from that of full-term and healthy infants. What observations can be made about the neurobehavioral performance of high-risk preschoolers when compared to healthy full-term preschoolers with no neonatal risk history? Differences, if they exist, would appear to have an effect on later stages of performance when the child is expected to grasp preacademic concepts in preparation for starting school.

The present section examines what is currently known about the developmental performance of high-risk infants during the preschool years. Emphasis is given to studies of VLBW infant. Literature on this subject can be divided into several categories. Information has been obtained through longitudinal study on populations, through measures on specific skill areas, as well as through examining the effect of specific medical conditions experienced in infancy.

Very low birth weight infants, those with a weight of 1,500 g or less at birth, constitute about 1 percent of all deliveries. Yet, nearly 50 percent of all neonatal deaths reported by Kitchen and colleagues (1980) in Victoria, Australia, were infants who weighed less than 1,500 g at birth. At present the outcome for babies born in the 1,500 to 2,500 g range is generally good; they usually survive and have a satisfactory neurobehavioral developmental profile during the preschool years. The outcome for babies who weigh less than 1,500 g at birth, however, varies from that for babies who weigh more than 1,500 g. Although the survival prospects for the VLBW infant have increased, apprehension remains regarding the long-term prognosis for these children. Reports on surviving VLBW infants born in the 1950s and 1960s indicated a high incidence of serious handicaps (Drillen, 1964; Lubchenco, 1976; Wright et al., 1972). The outcome of VLBW infants born in the late 1960s and early 1970s has improved considerably. However, there are still reports of serious neurological sequelae (Fitzhardinge et al., 1976). Infants of birth weights less that 1,500 g are at greatest risk for higher mortality and morbidity. At present they comprise a large portion of the infants in the NICU. Incidence rates for neurological and developmental delay range from 18 to 80 percent, depending on the assessment measures used and on additional variables included in particular follow-up studies (Knobloch, Malone, Ellison, Stevens, and Zdeb, 1982; Paz et al., 1981; Rothberg et al., 1983).

Siegel (1982) followed a group of VLBW infants from birth through 60 months of age. In general the VLBW infants were inferior in perceptual skills, memory, and motor abilities in comparison to control infants. No differences were observed between the small for gestational age and appropriate for gestational age VLBW infants. Other researchers have followed and measured the visual skills, hearing, speech development, and intellectual status of VLBW infants. A discussion of each of these areas follows:

Hearing

Prior to 1960 severe hearing loss was reported in 10 percent of VLBW survivors. The incidence in the 1960s dropped to between 1 and 2 percent. However, studies on current survivors have reported clinically significant sensorineural hearing loss in the range of 8 to 9 percent (Abramowich, Gregory, Slemuk, and Stewart, 1979; Drillen, 1967; Fitzhardinge and Ramsey, 1973). At highest risk for hearing loss are infants who sustained severe asphyxia or recurrent apnea in the neonatal period. Fitzhardinge and Pape (1981) reviewed the hearing status of 62 surviving VLBW infants who had received ventilatory assistance as neonates. Clinical hearing loss was diagnosed in 30 percent of those with major neurological defects, compared with an incidence of 12 percent in those without neurological defect. The incidence of major and minor neurological deficits in the VLBW population ranges from 4 to 15 percent, depending on whether the babies were born in a hospital other than the one in which the intensive care nursery was contained and on the availability of fetal monitoring and neonatologists (Fitzhardinge, 1980; Fitzhardinge, Kalman, and Ashley, 1978.) The incidence of hearing loss among VLBW infants is 14 times greater than that expected in the general population (Downs, 1982). Punch (1983) indicated that the incidence of hearing loss in the general population of children less than 5 years of age was 0.63 percent.

Mencher (1975) has stated that the greatest numbers of hearing impaired children fit into one of five categories, one of which is infants who weigh less that 1,500 g at birth. The Joint Committee on Newborn Hearing issued a position statement in 1981 that lists birth weight of less than 1,500 g as a category of infants with an appreciably greater risk of displaying a hearing deficit (Gerkin, 1984). Hearing loss is usually most marked in the high frequency range. Complete deafness is rarely present; most affected infants hear low and middle frequency tones. These infants consequently will startle at noise, locate towards a sound of mixed frequency, and do not appear to be hearing impaired on casual observation.

Vision

Visual disturbances may be present in as many as 44 percent of VLBW survivors (Pape et al., 1978). Infants weighing less that 1,000 g are particularly susceptible to retrolental fibroplasia. Strabismus is the next most common eye disorder seen in the VLBW population. The majority of infants who display strabismus do so as a result of an imbalance in visual acuity; however, others display this condition as a result of ocular muscle imbalance. A full ophthalmological evaluation is warranted any time after 40 weeks postconception if persistent nystagmus, failure to fixate, or persistent squint are noted. Visual adequacy is crucial to the early development of infants. Thus, the presence of a visual disturbance must be detected as early as possible and necessary intervention provided thereafter.

Speech Development

VLBW infants have been observed to develop nonvocal communication early; they fixate and brighten before term and smile socially at or slightly after term. However, expressive speech development frequently lags behind. At 18 to 24 months postterm, when vocabulary size for the full-term healthy child is expanding, the VLBW child may display only a few recognizable words. The incidence of delayed speech and language development, in the absence of mental retardation or severe hearing loss, appears to be high. Incidence figures range from 15 to 35 percent of VLBW infants with delayed speech and language development at 2 years of age (Fitzhardinge and Ramsey, 1973). The National Health Interview Survey reported that the prevalence rate of speech and language impairments in children less than 5 years of age was 0.92 percent for children not identified as mentally retarded (Fein, 1983). The prevalence of language impairment has been reported to be 2 to 3 percent in normal healthy full-term infants at 3 years of age (Leske, 1981). The Collaborative Perinatal Project of the National Institute of Neurological and Communication Disorders and Stroke (Lassman, Fisch, Vetter, and La Benz, 1980) reported that premature children exhibited more difficulties in language comprehension and production at 8 years of age than their age-matched counterparts with normal gestational ages did. In addition, the children with birth weights of less than 1,500 g performed even more poorly than children with birth weights from 1,500 to 2,500 g. What emerges from a comparison of these studies is a rather paradoxical picture. Although more at-risk infants than ever before are surviving because of improved intensive care, a new population of children is emerging for whom prevention of speech and language disorders is a high priority (Cupples, 1985).

Hubatch, Johnson, Kistler, Bruns, and Moneka (1985) presented data on the language ability of VLBW infants at 18 to 20 months of age. The mean birth weight of the children studied was 1,197 g. Both language comprehension and expressive language skills were measured. Results indicated that at the time of single word usage the adjusted ages of the VLBW infants exceeded the ages of the control group by 4 months. Despite their younger ages, the receptive vocabulary and expressive verbosity of the control group were significantly better than those of the VLBW group. The control group children were more successful in pointing to body parts, in pointing to actions in pictures, and in demonstrating knowledge of spatial concepts. The significance of these differences in receptive measures alone demands attention because of the relationship between receptive language delays and related problems. Research of this nature is quite valuable. Hubatch and her colleagues have presented it in a manner that allows for additional investigations relevant to language functioning in VLBW infants.

Intellectual Status

The majority of data available on the intellectual status of VLBW children during the preschool years was obtained through the administration of standardized psychometric tests. Although such tests give an objective measure of intelligence, they must be interpreted cautiously. Variations in the intellectual performance of VLBW infants are present and are due to factors such as intrauterine growth retardation, extreme prematurity, and neonatal asphyxia. Other factors include the type of obstetric care, whether neonatal transport was needed and the quality of the transport, the quality of the neonatal care received, and the socioeconomic level and parenting ability of the family. The detection of cognitive deficiency in the preschool years may be more readily determined by observing variations in verbal performance, visuomotor coordination, and other behavioral characteristics. Because of factors specified previously, as well as others, the reliability of objective measures of intellectual status must be kept in mind, particularly for younger survivors of VLBW. When skill acquisition is viewed as the mastery of specific behavioral competencies and the absence of these competencies as a reflection of cognitive delay, then perhaps a more reliable picture of cognitive performance apart from that revealed through a global IQ score may be attained. A more complete coverage of assessment strategies is presented in later chapters.

A review of the literature on the intellectual performance of VLBW children makes it readily apparent that results must be interpreted in light of the population sample as well as the assessment strategies. In general, however, reports have indicated that VLBW children score approximately 10 points below the mean for the general population, with the overall distribution of scores skewed toward the lower scores. Siegel (1982) used several infant development scales to assess the performance of VLBW infants between 4 and 24 months of age. The results of this series of test administrations was shown to be helpful in determining which children would display later cognitive delay. Each of the children in the Siegal study was administered the Bayley Scale (both motor and cognitive index), a modified version of the Uzgiris-Hunt Scale, and the McCarthy Scales of Children's Abilities. The preterm group (less than 1,500 g at birth) differed significantly from the full-term group on quantitative, memory, perceptual performance, motor, and general cognitive index subscales on the McCarthy. A closer review of the results revealed that the preterm group displayed significantly poorer performance at 5 years of age on specific skill categories that were part of the broader categories. These included memory for numbers, sorting and counting, tapping sequencing, block building, design drawing, arm coordination, and imitative action. Ross, Schenchener, Frayer, and Auld (1982) used the Bayley Scale to assess the performance of a population of VLBW infants. Children in the study had an average Bayley score of 92.2 on the Mental Scale and 87.8 on the Motor Scale. The results further revealed that 30 percent of the children had mental scores and 37 percent had motor skills on the Bayley that were less than 85.

Other researchers have followed the cognitive development of VLBW infants. In almost every instance the overall performance of the experimental group differed from that of the control group. These differences were seen for specific tests as well as for overall behavioral observations (Cohen, Sigman, Parmelee, and Beckwith, 1982; Hines, Minde, Marton, and Trehub, 1980; Lasky et al., 1983; Rawlings, Reynolds, Stewart, and Strang, 1971; Smith, Sommer, and von Tetzchner, 1982; Vohr, Oh, Rosenfield, Coviett, and Bernstein, 1979). A guarded picture of the developmental performance of the VLBW infant was provided by Jones, Cummins, and Davis (1979). Data from Hammersmith Hospital in England on 357 VLBW infants revealed that 58 percent of the infants died. Of those that survived only 27.8 percent were totally normal. Jones and colleagues also suggested that there was no significant improvement in the proportion of handicapped infants in the VLBW category went on to state that "neither we, over a 15 year period, nor others, over a 10 year period, were able to show that the proportion of handicapped babies among those born <1500 grams had dropped significantly. Thus it becomes difficult to judge the true achievements of the increasingly expensive technology involved in the care of the VLBW infant" (p. 1335).

In summary, Kitchen and colleagues (1982) commented on both the survival prospects and developmental sequelae for infants with birth weights of less than 1,500 g: "The survival prospects for infants or birth weights less that 1500 grams born in recent years have improved. Evidence for a corresponding decrease in long-term morbidity of survivors is conflicting but recent reports from some centers indicate that high morbidity rates are occurring" (p. 386). Clearly, the VLBW preschool child is one who must be followed closely in terms of the presence of any form of developmental delay.

SCHOOL-AGE PERFORMANCE

The intellectual outcome of small, preterm, or sick infants whose survival has required neonatal intensive care is of great concern. As pointed out previously overall developmental problems occur with greater than normal frequency in the high-risk population. The incidence of developmental problems has been shown to be related to the age of assessment, the level of neonatal care provided at birth, specific medical conditions, and birth weight and gestational age.

Silver (1983) pointed out that as long as there have been schools, there have been children who have had difficulty learning. He further noted that over time these children were differentiated into groups based on known or presumed causal factors. Advances in neonatal intensive care have resulted in the survival of an increasing number of individuals at biological risk for intellectual delay and school deficits. It is clear that a new category of children is advancing through the schools.

What level of school performance is present in the high-risk population? Do high-risk infants, once they reach school age, display an increased incidence of academic difficulties? The present section is designed to answer these questions. The information that follows is divided into two main sections. The first one deals with general intellectual functioning of school-age survivors of neonatal intensive care (NICU); the second deals with specific skill areas and school performance in general.

Intellectual Functioning of School-Age Survivors of NICU

Data available on the intellectual functioning at school age for NICU survivors reflect the results of a variety of research methodologies. Investigators use multiple strategies to assess the high-risk population as a whole as well as specific subcategories determined by a number of variables. What has emerged is a fairly consistent picture of the intellectual functioning of school-age high-risk infants.

Francis-Williams and Davies (1974) reported on the results of intelligence testing of a group of infants born in Hammersmith Hospital, London who weighed less than 1,500 g at birth. The purpose of the follow-up was not only to report on the intellectual status of the infants but also to correlate that status with other variables present in the follow-up group. The differences in the distribution of IQ scores between the SGA group and the AGA group were significant. Although most of the children scored fairly evenly on both verbal and performance scales, some showed quite significant differences between the two. Twenty-two percent showed a difference of 15 points or more between verbal and performance scores on the Weschler Intelligence Scale for Children—Revised and have consequent learning difficulties as shown by school performance. Steiner, Sanders, Phillips, and Maddock (1980) similarly found a significant difference between verbal and performance IQ scores for a population of SGA and AGA infants. No significant correlations between birth weight, gestational age, or neonatal illness and IQ performance were detected by Francis-Williams and Davies (1974). Social class differences in IQ were also noted.

Data provided by Stewart and Reynolds (1974) described the intellectual performance of a population of infants who weighed less than 1,500 g at birth. They used the WISC-R to measure the IQ of the children when they ranged from 3 to 6 years of age and found that 92 percent of the children followed had an IQ of 80 or higher. These children were not followed relative to the presence of specific school problems; thus, the score of 80 or higher on intelligence testing may be an underestimation of the number of children who would display later cognitive and school problems.

Taub, Goldstein, and Caputie (1977) followed a group of preterm infants and administered the WISC-R when the children were between 7 and 9 years of age. Results indicated that verbal IQ scores for the premature infants were not significantly different from those of the nonpremature group. In contrast, however, performance IQs were significantly lower for the premature group; subtests requiring visually mediated behavior were particularly affected. Thus, the supposition that premature infants show deficits in perceptual organization and visually mediated activities was supported. Additional testing, by means of Visual Motor Gestalt Test, revealed that the premature group had significantly poorer scores. It should be pointed out that the population studied by Taub and colleagues had a mean birth weight of 2,153 g and a mean gestational age of 240 days (266 days = 38 weeks). Thus, the true risk status of the preterm infants is questioned.

A 1980 study by Drillen, Thomson, and Burgoyne provided helpful data on the intellectual status of LBW children at early school age. (A variety of other factors were studied also, and the results of these are presented in subsequent sections.) The WISC-R was used to assess general intellectual function in a population of infants who weighed less than 1,500 g at birth and an additional sample of LBW children who weighed between 1,500 and 2,000 g at birth. A further breakdown of the LBW children included those who were judged to be neurologically normal in the first year.

In the Drillen et al. study the LBW children presented an interesting picture of intellectual performance at 6 to 7 years of age. What emerged was the significance of neurological status prior to 12 months of age and its relationship to the later intellectual status of the population followed. The study suggested that transient abnormal neurological signs in the first year of life, present in more than 40 percent of infants with birth weights less than 2,000 g, were predictive of later intellectual and scholastic impairments.

Further detailed study of the intellectual performance of a population of VLBW (less than 1,500 g) infants was done by Kitchen and colleagues (1980) who administered a battery of psychometric tests when the children were 8 years of age. The VLBW infants had a significantly lower performance on all scales of the WISC-R than the normal birth weight children did. This discrepancy was even more pronounced when results from the 10 children with birth weights less than 1,000 g were examined separately: 40.5 percent of the children had a mean full scale IQ score below 84. The authors considered the results to accurately reflect the intellectual status of the LBW population they evaluated.

The intellectual outcome of 102 children with birth weights less that 1,500 g was determined for two separate time periods (1965 to 1969 and 1970 to 1975) by Hunt, Tooley, and Harvin (1982). The data is summarized in Table 3–2 and is discussed here as the averages for the two time periods. The total with IQs in the retarded range was approximately 8 percent and comparable to data from other studies of VLBW populations. Another 17 percent of the children had definite intellectual problems, with scores in the borderline range of intelligence (IQ 68 to 83). A substantial group of the children (20.6 percent) had scores in the normal range but had intellectual disabilities that were expected to interfere with normal school progress and achievement (problems with language comprehension or visual motor integration or both). Another subgroup (22.5 percent) was rated as suspect by the examiners. Although survival rates across the two periods of time increased, a corresponding increase in the number of handicapped children was not observed.

Further comparisons for the same population of subjects included viewing intellectual status at later ages. Fifty-three children (born 1965 to 1973) were tested at two separate ages. Data are summarized in Table 3–3. Of most concern for this comparison was a shift to less satisfactory intellectual status for 16 of the 20 children who had been considered normal at the time they entered school. In this group the shift in status was accompanied by a decrease in average IQ. The authors concluded by stressing the importance of monitoring high-risk infants well into childhood. Currently, the true incidence of handicaps cannot be detected in any other way. Also, parents and children may need professional support and intervention for the first time at much older ages than was previously supposed.

One final relevant investigation is that of Noble-Jamieson, Lukeman, Silverman, and Davies (1982) who made comparisons between a group of survivors of neonatal intensive care and matched controls. The results of the WISC-R subtest scores from this study are presented in Table 3–4. The children were 9 years of age at the time of testing and had been patients in the Hammersmith Hospital, London, England. The preterm children scored significantly lower in 4 out of 5 WISC-R subtests. The high mean IQ score for the control group is partially a reflection of the social class distribution of the population tested. These

Table 3-2. Outcome by IQ Categories For 102 Children 4 Years Or Older, Born 1965 to 1975 With Birth Weights Less Than 1500 Grams

IQ	Category	1965–69 (%)	1970–75 (%)
<68	Retarded	15.8	3.1
68–83	Borderline	15.8	17.2
>84	Handicaps	21.1	20.3
Total	Handicap	52.6	40.6
>84	Suspect	18.4	25.0
>84	Normal	28.9	34.4
Total	No Handicap	47.4	59.4

results are in full agreement with other follow-up studies. The authors' conclusions included the concept that children who may be designated as normal or healthy in the short term deserve truly long-term surveillance. These follow-up efforts should certainly extend into the school years and be directed toward all functional areas that have an impact on overall academic and intellectual performance.

School Performance and Specific Skill Areas

Data in the previous section were presented in chronological order to enhance the practitioner's understanding of what is currently known about the intellectual status of high-risk infants at school age. The material presented in this section also is presented in chronological order.

In a paper presented at the American Orthopsychiatric Association Convention in New York, De Hirsh, Jansky, and Langford (1965) reported on extensive comparisons made between prematurely born and maturely born children at three age levels (kindergarten, first, and second grades). The children had weighed less than 2,500 g at birth and had been less than 37 weeks gestational age. Comparisons were made on specific skill areas, both within the preterm group and between the preterm and term groups. An interesting finding for the preterm group was that preterm girls performed better than boys in reading, writing, and spelling at the end of both grades 1 and 2. Also, within the preterm group those children who weighed less that 1,500 g at birth scored lower on four of five scholastic tests, thus supporting the increased vulnerability of the VLBW infant. Comparisons between the term and preterm children on kindergarten tests were striking and showed that the term group scored better in most skill areas. These included concomitant movements, fine motor patterning, figure-ground organization,

Table 3–3. Comparisons at 4 to 6 Years and 8 Years for 53 High-Risk Infants

IQ	Category	Binet IQ (4–6 yr)	Wisc-R IQ (8 hr)
<68	Retarded	57.5	46.0
68–83	Borderline	75.9	77.0
>84	Handicaps	99.1	93.4
>84	Suspect	100.5	105.5
>84	Normal	112.4	105.1

auditory perceptual patterning, word recognition, language comprehension, word finding, story organization, category skills, name writing, copying of letters, letter naming, word matching, word rhyming, and word recognition. Each of these differences were at the 0.05 level of significance or better. Subsequent evaluation of reading, writing, and spelling skills in grades 1 and 2 revealed significant differences between the preterm and term groups. The results of this study suggested that prematurely born infants whose IQ fell within the average range of intelligence did less well than maturely born peers on a large battery of tests. Significant lags persisted well into the second grade. These children therefore must be regarded as an academic high-risk group. It must be recalled, when considering the results of this study, that the children used as subjects represented a time period when neonatal intensive care was a relatively new medical subspeciality.

Francis-Williams and Davies (1974) reviewed the school performance and academic skills (reading and visuomotor skills) in two cohorts of high-risk infants born during two different time periods. More than 50 percent of the children 5 years and older scored 1.0 and 2.0 standard deviations below normal for their age and IQ on the Bender Gestalt Test. The children showed greater difficulty in separating two superimposed patterns. These results appeared to be common perceptuomotor deficits in preterm infants with normal IQ and were related to later specific learning disabilities. Further evaluation of the reading ability of the follow-up group revealed that as many as 30 percent of the children were displaying problems in learning to read.

A corollary investigation conducted on Swedish children who were identified as at-risk at birth was conducted by Bjerre and Hansen in Malmo, Sweden (1976). The focus of this investigation was to assess both the psychomotor and school adjustment of 7-year-old children with low birth weight. Data collection was through the use of a specially constructed questionnaire that covered the child's attitude toward school as well as toward schoolmates and adults. Parental responses indicated that they feared problems at school more than the

Table 3-4. Results of Intelligence Testing (Mean & Ranges)

Test	High Risk n=23	Controls n=23	p
Similarities	9.8 (2-17)	11.6 (7-17)	n.s.
Vocabulary	10.2 (3-15)	12.2 (8-16)	<0.02
Arithmetic	9.6 (5-16)	11.6 (7-18)	<0.02
Block Design	10.4 (6-16)	12.4 (8-19)	<0.02
Object Assembly	9.1 (5-17)	11.4 (5-16)	<0.01
Verbal I.Q.	98.4 (83-123)	106.8 (90-126)	<0.02
Performance I.Q.	98.5 (83-119)	106.6 (84-128)	<0.005
Full Scale I.Q.	98.0 (81-129)	109.0 (88-129)	<0.003

Note: From "Low Birth Weight Children at School Age: Neurological, Psychological, and Pulmonary Function" by C. Noble-Jamieson, D. Lukeman, M. Silverman, and P. Davies, 1982, Seminars in Perinatology, 6, p. 268. Copyright by Grune & Stratton, Inc. Reprinted by permission.

the parents of healthy infants. The children with birth weights less than 2,000 g were more often regarded as being dependent on adults, lacking self-confidence, and having a defiant attitude toward parents. In comparision to general population a higher percentage of LBW children were found to be attending different forms of special classes or special preparatory schools before starting the ordinary school. More than 25 percent of the LBW children displayed school performance that was judged as below average. Vocabulary skills for the LBW group were inferior to those of the control group. Other areas in which the LBW group differed from controls included gross motor function, fine motor coordination, and intellectual status. Within the LBW group differences were present between those who weighed less than 2,000 g at birth and those who weighed 2,000 to 2,500 g. In addition, gestational age was related to skill areas and performance; those children whose gestational age was more than 35 weeks performed better than those whose age was less than 35 weeks. Evaluation of other behaviors revealed that the LBW children were regarded as being less active and more compliant than the control group. Teachers were more inclined to regard the LBW group as shy and having poorer contact with their schoolmates, more dependent on contact with adults, and less active and very compliant. Parents of the LBW group also displayed an overprotective attitude to a significantly greater degree than the parents of the control children. The results of this investigation point to several important characteristics that differentiate the LBW group from controls.

The performance of VLBW infants at 8 years of age was assessed by Kitchen and colleagues (1980). Overall intellectual status, which was reported on in the previous section, as well as school achievement were evaluated. Ninety-two percent of the children were attending normal schools. The results did not adequately address the level of performance of these children. The fact that they were attending normal schools does not indicate that they were performing adequately within grade levels. Fifteen percent of the children were reported to be reading 18 months or more behind age level. It seems reasonable to assume that a higher percentage of children were reading 6 to 18 months behind age expectations. Thus, a significant percentage of children in the follow-up group can be assumed to have academic difficulties. The authors concluded by stating that only 43 percent of the group followed could be said to have no degree of measurable deficit at school age.

In a similar study Drillen and colleagues (1980) examined the performance of a group of children at 6 to 7 years of age who had weighed less than 1,500 g at birth. Infants who had weighed 1,500 to 2,000 g were an additional group in the study. Both of these groups were compared to a control group. Specific differences between the LBW and control groups were seen for reading ability, social adjustment, tests of motor impairment, visuomotor ability, and speech and language skills. These differences were likewise related to the neurological status of the LBW children during the first year of life. An overall impairment score was derived based on performance on each of the subtests included in the total examination. The LBW group differed significantly from the controls on the overall impairment score. The authors further reviewed the relationship between social status and problems in school. In both the LBW and control groups tests of intelligence and educational achievement showed a marked decline in score and grading between the best homes and the worst. In the control group social differences were not significant for perceptural skills, speech and language performance, or general behavior. In the LBW group, however, major differences were found between the higher and lower social classes in performance in many of the skill areas tested. Thus, an additional variable, namely social class, appears important relative to school performance of LBW infants.

Steiner and colleagues (1980) reported on the learning problems present in a group of 122 VLBW infants who had received only minimal neonatal intensive care intervention. Follow-up at school age revealed that poor reading performance was characteristic of the group as a whole. The reading performance of more than 50 percent of the children was 2 or more years below average. Ten of the children were not reading at all. Further analysis of teachers' ratings of behavior revealed that the preterm group displayed poorer concentration and overall attention span than the full-term control group. The long-term effect of these deficits on school achievement led the authors to conlude that children of VLBW are nine times more likely to display problems of this nature as either an isolated disability or part of a larger handicap.

School achievement and the behavior of children who were small for their gestational age was the focus of a follow-up investigation by Parkinson, Wallis, and Harvey (1981). Forty-five infants whose birth weight was below the 10th percentile for gestational age were included in the study. School performance and ability were scored in each of 10 different areas. These included reading, writing, arithmetic, drawing, music, games, creative activities, activities requiring reasoning ability, activities requiring independence, and activities requiring imagination. Separate scores were obtained for each of these areas as well as an overall achievement score. Results were compared to the scores obtained for a group of AGA birth weight infants. All children were from 5 to 9 years of age when tested. What was particularly interesting about this study was that head growth had been monitored prenatally to see if there were relationships between length and onset of growth retardation and particular school deficits later on. Similar research was conducted by Harvey, Prince, Bunton, and Campbell (1976) with results identical to those reported by Parkinson and colleagues.

Findings indicated that the children with the longest period of intrauterine growth retardation (IUGR starting before 34 weeks) had lower scores than those children whose IUGR started later in pregnancy or who displayed no IUGR. The SGA infants had significantly lower scores in reading, writing, drawing, creative activities, imaginative activities, and reasoning abilities. The greatest difference was in writing ability. In addition, significantly poorer handwriting was noted in the SGA group. Boys who had experienced longer periods of IUGR were also characterized by more atypical behavior. They were more clumsy, more worried, fidgety, unhappy, and upset by new situations. Teacher reports mentioned additional problems in the SGA group. These included more frequent absences from school, overprotective parents, problems in communicating with teachers and other children, problems related to being small for their age, and specific problems with school work. They were also reported to be less able to concentrate than AGA controls. These findings point to increased school and behavior problems for SGA infants. The severity of these problems is determined in part by the sex of the child, social class, and the stage in pregnancy when IUGR begins. These results are consistent with those of Noble-Jamieson and colleagues (1982) who found marked reading ability differences between AGA and SGA infants.

The presence of specific learning disability in high-risk infants has been discussed by Hunt and colleagues (1982). Children who function in the borderline range of intelligence, or who have scores in the normal range but have evidence for specific learning disability, constitute the majority of intellectual problems identified in the LBW population at school age. The incidence rate for learning disability for VLBW survivors has been reported to be as high as 37 percent, or roughly twice that of the general population. Data from the Collaborative Perinatal Project revealed that the risk of learning disability was higher for low birth weight children, although other factors such as socioeconomic status and demographic variables were also important (Nichols and Chen, 1981).

A population of NICU survivors in Quebec, Canada was followed up to their school years with subsequent evaluation of their school performance by Gunn, Lepore, and Outerbridge (1983). All children were between 5 and 12 years of age when assessed. School performance and behavior questionnaires were sent to teachers. Areas of concern most frequently reported by teachers were students anxiety about school achievement (31 percent), poor motor or handwriting coordination (30 percent), excessive attention seeking or continual talking in class (25 percent), overactivity (23 percent), excessive shyness or timidity (22 percent), short attention span or daydreaming (18 percent), and fighting with other children (16 percent). These findings are in agreement with previous reports of overall school behavior.

The information presented in this section is quite consistent. It describes the high-risk infant as one who displays increased school, adjustment, relational, and behavioral problems. This view is shared by teachers, parents, and researchers. It is apparent that schools are dealing with a new category of "special students" who can attribute their special needs to insults suffered in the neonatal period. This category of students may grow in number as NICU expertise increases and smaller and younger children survive neonatal intensive care.

FACTORS PREDICTIVE OF SCHOOL AND DEVELOPMENTAL PERFORMANCE

The ability to correlate specific neonatal conditions with later developmental performance would be of great help to the practitioner, as parents and others desire to know what to expect from a sick baby later in life. Certain medical and neonatal complications are known to have an impact on later development, and several of these have been discussed previously in this chapter. What needs to be kept in mind, however, is that human development is a highly complex process and the result of interaction between influences from within (the organism itself) and without (the environment). The purpose of this present section is to review data that can help the practitioner in assessing risk potential based on prenatal and neonatal factors. The use of powerful statistical techniques has afforded the researcher the opportunity to more stringently measure the impact of various neonatal factors on later development. Previous data reviewed have clearly shown that the high-risk population as a whole is more vulnerable to developmental delay. What specific factors surrounding the neonatal period have been found to correlate with later developmental performance?

Method of delivery and developmental outcome at 5 years of age were the focus of a study conducted by McBride and colleagues (1979). Several modes of delivery were examined relative to their relationship to later performance. Physical development, motor skills, and intellectual functioning were the areas evaluated. The only method of delivery that appeared to be related to motor skills was breech delivery. Breech children tended to score less well on tasks of motor function. Caesarean section deliveries were not significantly related to later intellectual or motor deficits. The authors concluded by stating that delivery complications in and of themselves constitute just one part in a continuum of risk factors. In the absence of other complicating events delivery methods are early risk factors that the growing child is readily able to overcome in the presence of adequate environmental support.

Wallace, Cecelia, McCarton-Daum, and Vaughan (1982) were interested in determining whether neurobehavioral performance in the neonatal period would be predictive of congnitive outcome at 6 years of age. The authors were also interested in detecting what effects socioeconomic status would have on the intellectual ability of LBW infants when the infants were 6 years old. Results indicated that the relationship between neonatal behavioral factors (audition, visual motility) and cognitive functioning at 6 years of age was significant. A strong relationship between neonatal neurobehavioral performance and intellectual levels at 6 years of age was present and was made even stronger by the addition of socioeconomic status as a variable. These results support previous data that have linked neurological functioning present at less than 1 year of age with later intellectual ability.

The relationship between perinatal risk factors and performance at 1 year of age on the Bayley Scale of Infant Development was the focus of an investigation by Rossetti (1984). Birth weight, gestational age, Apgar scores, and length of stay in the NICU were used to predict performance at 1 year of age. In addition, all combinations of variables were assessed. Significant relationships were found between birth weight and length of stay in the NICU, Apgar scores and length of stay, birth weight and Bayley scores, and gestational age and Bayley scores.

Hartlage, Nooman, Catterson, and Telgrow (1983) conducted an extensive investigation to determine if a relationship exists between birth conditions and mental status at 6 years of age. The relationship between specific neonatal variables and subsequent mental development was assessed. Forty-one survivors of NICU were followed over a 6-year period. For each child 58 measures of neonatal condition were made and correlated with intellectual performance at 6 years of age. Variables that correlated significantly with Stanford-Binet scores obtained at 6 years of age included duration of labor, trauma, respiratory distress, and length of stay in the NICU. Additional variables were found to be significantly correlated with levels obtained on the Weschler Preschool and Primary Scale of Intelligence (WPPSI). These included respiratory distress, temperature control, maternal eclampsia, and cardiac disease. These data suggest that specific neonatal conditions may affect specific aspects of mental function (specific neonatal problems correlate with specific deficit areas reflected on measured abilities as was presented in the section on school performance), rather than with more global aspects of mental status at age 6.

SUMMARY

One clear and significant statement can be made on the basis of the previous discussion of the developmental performance of high-risk infants: The term high-risk encompasses a hetergeneous group of infants placed in the category by one or several prenatal, neonatal, or postnatal factors. Thus, any discussion of the high-risk population can be confusing because of the overlapping nature of the factors that place an infant at risk.

In sharp contrast to the heterogeneity of the population of high-risk infants is the homogeneity of results revealed on both short- and long-term follow-up studies. Numerous investigators have evaluated the physical, neurological, intellectual, behavioral, and school performance of very young, preschool, and school-age survivors of neonatal intensive care. Although not all survivors of neonatal intensive care display developmental deviations throughout the preschool and elementary years, what emerges is a clear and concise description of neurodevelopmental performance that differentiates many high-risk infants from the healthy full-term infant. These differences extend into school age and can be expected to account for a growing number of children with school problems as the number of infants surviving at younger gestational ages and lighter birth weights increases.

A summary of the previous review of the developmental status of high-risk infants includes the following (Rosen, 1982):

1. The incidence of low birth weight is about 8 percent. It has changed only slightly in the past 25 years.
2. Approximately 1.5 percent of LBW infants weigh less than 1,500 g at birth. About 25 percent of these infants will die and 50 percent will display some form of neurodevelopmental delay ranging from mild to severe.
3. Both the physical growth and the neurological development of the high-risk infant differ from that of the full term healthy infant. Growth rates vary according to the degree of intrauterine growth retardation present in the SGA infant. Catch up growth is observed, but varies. Aberrant neurological development under one year of age is related to both preschool and school age intellectual and school performance. Growth differences can be observed into teen years.
4. Behavioral observations of the high-risk infant reveal consistent differences in overall performance during the neonatal period. Even at postconceptual ages of 40 weeks or greater the high-risk infant differs from the full-term infant.
5. Specific medical conditions such as hemorrhage and respiratory disease, are known to contribute to preschool developmental delay.
6. Very low birth weight infants are at greater biological risk relative to survival as well as the presence of long and short term developmental delays which are reflected in intellectual and school performance. VLBW infants differ from other LBW children. Likewise, all small for gestational age infants present greater risk for neurodevelopmental sequelae.
7. Low birth weight infants consistently display a greater incidence of school problems than do healthy infants. These differences are reflected in deficits in specific academic areas as well as in intellectual functioning. Even for those high-risk infants that fall within the normal range of IQ, a greater incidence of school interpersonal, adjustment, and learning problems are observed.
8. Certain neonatal factors have been found to be predictive of later developmental performance. These include birth weight, gestational age, length of labor, method of delivery, neurological status under one year, and specific medical conditions.
9. Adequate diagnosis of neurodevelopmental performance based on single test administration is not possible in the early days of life. Until such tests are available, long term follow-up is needed to accurately identify those infants who will be in need of intervention to eliminate or reduce neurodevelopmental delay.

REFERENCES

Abramowich, S., Gregory, S., Slemuk, M., and Stewart, A. (1979). Hearing loss in VLBW infants treated with neonatal intensive care. *Archives of Disease in Childhood, 54,* 421.

Babson, S. (1970). Growth of low birthweight infants. *Journal of Pediatrics, 77,* 11.

Babson, S., and Kangas, J. (1973). Preschool intelligence of undersized term infants. *American Journal of Diseases of Children, 117,* 352.

Bjerre, I., and Hansen, E. (1976). Psychomotor development and school adjustment of 7 year old children with low birth weight. *Acta Paediatrica Scandinavica, 65,* 88.

Brandt, I. (1978). Growth dynamics of low birth weight infants with emphasis on the perinatal period. In F. Falkner and J. Taune (Eds.), *Human Growth* (Vol. 2). New York: Plenum Press.

Brazelton, T. (1973). *Neonatal behavioral assessment scale.* Philadelphia: J. B. Lippincott.

Cohen, S., Sigman, M., Parmelee, A., and Beckwith, L. (1982). Perinatal risk and developmental outcome in preterm infants. *Seminars in Perinatology, 6,* 334.

Cruise, M. (1973). A longitudinal study of growth of low birth weight infants: 1. Velocity and distance growth, birth to three years. *Pediatrics, 51,* 620.

Cupples, W. (1985, October). *Child language disorders.* Proceedings of a Conference on Prevention of Speech, Language and Hearing Disorders. Paper presented at the Annual Convention of the American Speech-Language-Hearing Association, Washington, D.C.

Davies, P. (1976). *Recent advances in pediatrics.* Edinburgh: Churchill-Livingstone.

Davis, P., and Tizard, J. (1975). Very low birth weight and subsequent neurological defect. *Developmental Medicine and Child Neurology, 17,* 3.

De Hirsch, K., Jansky, J., and Langford, W. (1965). *Comparisons between prematurely and maturely born children at three age levels.* Paper presented at the annual meeting of the American Orthopsychiatric Association, New York.

De Souza, S., and Richards, B. (1978). Neurological sequelae in newborn babies after perinatal asphyxia. *Archives of Disease in Childhood, 53,* 564.

Di Vitto, B., and Goldberg, S. (1979). The effects of newborn medical status on early parent-infant interaction. In T. Field, A. Sostek, S. Goldberg, and H. Shuman (Eds.), *Infants born at risk.* New York: Spectrum Publications.

Downs, M. (1982). Early identification of hearing loss. In M. Lass, L. McReynolds, J. Northern, and D. Yoder (Eds.), *Speech, language and hearing: Vol. III. Hearing disorders.* Philadelphia: W. B. Saunders.

Drillen, C. (1964). *The growth and development of the prematurely born infant.* Edinburgh: Churchill-Livingstone.

Drillen, C. (1967). The incidence of mental and physical handicaps in school age children of very low birth weight. *Pediatrics, 39,* 238.

Drillen, C., Thomson, A., and Burgoyne, K. (1980). Low birth weight children at early school age: A longitudinal study. *Developmental Medicine and Child Neurology*, *22*, 26.

Ellison, P. (1984). Neurologic development of the high-risk infant. *Clinics in Perinatology*, *11*, 1

Ellison, P., Browning, C., and Trostmiller, T. (1982). Evaluation of neurologic status in infancy: Physical therapist versus pediatric neurologist. *Journal of the California Perinatal Association*, *2*, 63.

Ellison, P., Horn, J., and Browning, C. (1983). A large sample many variable study of motor dysfunction in infancy. *Journal of Pediatric Psychiatry*, *8*, 345.

Fein, D. (1983). The prevalence of speech and hearing impairments. *ASHA*, *25*, 37.

Ferrari, F., Grosoli, M., Fontance, G., and Cauazzuti, G. (1983). Neurobehavioral comparison of low risk preterm and full term infants at term conceptual age. *Developmental Medicine and Child Neurology*, *25*, 4.

Fitzhardinge, P. (1980). Current outcome of NICU population. In A. Brann and J. Volpe (Eds.), *Neonatal neurological assessment and outcome: Report of the 77th Ross Conference on Pediatric Research*. Columbus, OH: Ross Laboratories.

Fitzhardinge, P., Kalman, E., Ashley, S. (1978). Present status of the infant of very low birth weight treated in a referral neonatal intensive care unit in 1974. *Ciba Foundation Symposium*, *59*, 139.

Fitzhardinge, P., and Pape, K. (1981). Follow-up studies of the high risk newborn. In G. Avery (Ed.), *Neonatology, pathophysiology and management of the newborn*. Philadelphia: J. B. Lippincott.

Fitzhardinge, P., Pape, K., Arstikaitis, M., Boyle, M., Ashley, S., Rowley, A., Netley, C., and Sawyer, P. (1976). Mechanical ventilation of infants of less than 1500 grams birth weight: Health, growth and neurological sequelae. *Journal of Pediatrics*, *88*, 531.

Fitzhardinge, P., and Ramsey, M. (1973). The improving outlook for the small prematurely born infant. *Developmental Medicine and Child Neurology*, *15*, 447.

Fitzhardinge, M., and Stevens, E. (1972). The small for date infant: 1. Later growth patterns. *Pediatrics*, *49*, 671.

Francis-Williams, J., and Davies, P. (1974). Very low birth weight and later intelligence. *Developmental Medicine and Child Neurology*, *16*, 709.

Gerkin, K. (1984). The high risk register for deafness. *ASHA*, *26*, 4.

Gunn, T., Lepore, F., and Outerbridge, E. (1983). Outcome at school age after mechanical ventilation. *Developmental Medicine and Child Neurology*, *25*, 305.

Hartlage, L., Nooman, M., Catterton, Z., and Telgrow, C. (1983). *Birth conditions associated with mental status at age six*. Paper presented at the Southwestern Psychological Association, San Antonio.

Harvey, P., Prince, J., Bunton, W., Campbell, S. (1976). Abilities of children who were small for dates at birth and whose growth in utero was measured by ultrasonic cephalometry. *Pediatric Research*, *10*, 891.

Hatcher, R. (1977). The neuropsychological examination of the preterm infant. *Acta Medica Aurologica*, *9*, 95.

Hines, R., Minde, K., Marton, P., and Trehub, S. (1980). Behavioral development of preterm infants: An ethological approach. *Developmental Medicine and Child Neurology*, *22*, 623.

Howard, J., Parmelee, A., Koop, C., and Littman, B. (1976). A neurological comparison of preterm and full term infants at term conceptual age. *Journal of Pediatrics, 88,* 995.

Hubatch, L., Johnson, C., Kistler, D., Bruns, W., and Moneka, W. (1985). Early language abilities of high risk infants. *Journal of Speech and Hearing Disorders, 5,* 195.

Hunt, J., Tooley, W., and Harvin, D. (1982). Learning disabilities in children with birth weight less than 1500 grams. *Seminars in Perinatology, 6,* 280.

Jones, R., Cummins, M., Davis, P. (1979). Infants of very low birthweight. *Lancet, 6,* 1332.

Kimble, K., Ariagno, R., Stevenson, D. (1982). Growth to age three years among very low birth weight sequelae—free survivors of modern neonatal intensive care. *Journal of Pediatrics, 100,* 622.

Kitchen, W., Ryan, M., Rubaids, A., Astbury, J., Ford, G., Lissenden, J., Kieth, C., and Keir, E. (1982). Changing outcome over 13 years of very low birth weight infants. *Seminars in Perinatology, 6,* 373.

Kitchen, W., Ryan, M., Rubaids, A., McDougal, A., Billson, F., Keir, E., and Naylor, F. (1980). A longitudinal study of very low birth weight infants: 4. An overview of performance at eight years of age. *Developmental Medicine and Child Neurology, 22,* 172.

Knobloch, H., Malone, A., Ellison, P., Stevens, F., and Zdeb, M. (1982). Considerations in evaluating changes in outcome for infants weighing less than 1501 grams *Pediatrics, 69,* 285.

Kramer, L., and Pierpoint, M. (1976). Rocking waterbeds and auditory stimuli to enhance growth of preterm infants. *Journal of Pediatrics, 88,* 297.

Kurtzberg, D., Vaughan, H., Daum, C., Grellong, B., Albin, S., and Rotkin, L. (1979). Neurobehavioral performance of low birth weight infants at 40 weeks conceptual age: Comparison with normal full term infants. *Developmental Medicine and Child Neurology, 21,* 590.

Lasky, R., Tyson, J., Rosenfeld, C., Priest, M., Krasinski, D., Heartwell, S., and Gant, N. (1983). Differences on Bayley's Infant Behavior Record for sample of high risk infants and their controls. *Child Development, 54,* 1211.

Lassman, F., Fisch, R., Vetter, D., LaBenz, E. (1980). *Early correlates of speech, language and hearing: The Collaborative Perinatal Project of the National Institute of Neurologic and Communicative Disorders and Stroke.* Littleton, ME: PSG Publishing.

Leske, C. (1981). Prevalence estimates of communication disorders in the U.S. *ASHA, 21,* 229.

Lester, B., and Zeskind, P. (1979). The organization and assessment of crying in the infant at risk. In T. Field, A. Sostek, S. Goldberg, and H. Shrunar (Eds.), *Infants born at risk.* New York: Spectrum Publications.

Lubchenco, L. (1976). *The high risk infant.* Philadelphia: W.B. Saunders.

Manser, J. (1984). Growth in the high-risk infant. *Clinics in Perinatology, 11,* 19.

Maisels, J., and Marks, K. (1981). Growth chart for sick premature infants. *Journal of Pediatrics, 98,* 66.

McBride, W., Black, B., Brown, C., Dolly, R., Murray, A., and Thomas, D. (1979). Method of delivery and developmental outcome at five years of age. *The Medical Journal of Australia, 1,* 301.

Mencher, G. (1975). *Early identification of hearing loss.* Basel: Karger.

Michaelsson, K., Ylinder, A., and Donner, M. (1981). Neurodevelopmental screening at five years of children who were at risk neonatally. *Developmental Medicine and Child Neurology, 2,* 427.

Nichols, P., and Chen, T. (1981). *Minimal brain dysfunction: A prospective study.* Hillsdale, NJ: Earlbaum.

Noble-Jamieson, C., Lukeman, D., Silverman, M., and Davies, P. (1982). Low birth weight children at school age: Neurological, psychological, and pulmonary function. *Seminars in Perinatology, 6,* 4, 266.

Pape, K., Buncie, R., and Ashley, S. (1978). The status of two years of low birth weight infants born in 1974 with birth weights of less than 1001 grams. *Journal of Pediatrics, 92,* 253.

Parkinson, C., Wallis, S., and Harvey, D. (1981). School age achievement and behavior of children who were small for dates at birth. *Developmental Medicine and Child Neurology, 23,* 41.

Paz, M., Ruiz, J., LeFeuer, A., Hakanson, D., Clark, D., and Williams, M. (1981). Early development of infants of birth weight less than 1000 grams with reference to mechanical ventilation in newborn period. *Pediatrics, 68,* 330.

Punch, J. The prevalence of hearing impairment (1983). *ASHA, 25,* 27.

Rawlings, G., Reynolds, E., Stewart, A., and Strang, L. (1971). Changing prognosis for infants of very low birthweight. *Lancet, 1,* 516.

Rosen, M. (1982). The biological vulnerability of a low birth weight infant. In D. Parron and L. Eisenberg (Eds.), *Infants At Risk For Developmental Dysfunction* (Health and Behavior: A Research Agenda: Interim Rep. No. 4). Washington, DC: National Academy Press.

Ross, G., Schenchener, S., Frayer, W., and Auld, P. (1982). Perinatal and neurobehavioral predictors of one-year outcome in infants less than 1500 grams. *Seminars in Perinatology, 6,* 317.

Rossetti, L. (1984). *A longitudinal study of the developmental status of high risk infants.* Paper presented at the annual convention of the American Speech-Language-Hearing Association, San Francisco.

Rothberg, A., Mansils, J., Baguato, S., Murphy, J., Gifford, K., and McKinley, K. (1983). Infants weighing 1000 grams or less at birth: Developmental outcome for ventilated and nonventilated infants. *Pediatrics, 71,* 599.

Rubin, R., Rosenblatt, C., and Balow, B. (1973). Psychological and educational sequelae of prematurity. *Pediatrics, 52,* 352.

Scarr, S., and Williams, M. (1971). *The assessment of neonatal and later status in low birth weight infants.* Paper presented at the annual meeting of the Society For Research In Child Development, Minneapolis.

Siegel, L. (1982). Reproductive, perinatal, and environmental variables as predictors of development of pre-term (<1500 grams) and full term children at five years. *Seminars in Perinatology, 6,* 274.

Silver, L. (1983). Introduction. In C. Braun (Ed.), *Childhood learning disabilities and prenatal risks.* Johnson & Johnson Baby Products.

Smith, L., Sommer, F., and von Tetzchner, S. (1982). A longitudinal study of low birth weight children: Reproductive, perinatal, and environmental pressures of developmental status at three years of age. *Seminars in Perinatology, 6,* 294.

Steiner, F., Sanders, E., Phillips, E., and Maddock, C. (1980). Very low birth weight children at school age: Comparison of neonatal management methods. *British Medical Journal, 281,* 1237.

Stewart, A., and Reynolds, E., (1974). Improved prognosis for infants of very low birth weight. *Pediatrics, 54,* 724.

Taub, H., Goldstein, K., and Caputie, D. (1977). Indices of neonatal prematurity as discriminators of development in early childhood. *Child Development, 48,* 797.

Vohr, B., Oh, W., Rosenfield, A., Coviett, R., and Bernstein, J. (1979). The preterm small-for-gestational age infant: A two year follow-up study. *American Journal of Obstetrics and Gynecology, 133,* 425.

Wallace, I., Cecelia, S., McCarton-Daum, C., and Vaughan, H. (1982). Neonatal precursors of cognitive development in low birth weight children. *Seminars in Perinatology, 6,* 327.

Westwood, M., Kramer, M., Munz, D., Lovett, J., and Watters, G. (1983). Growth and development of full term nonasphyxiated small for gestational age newborns: Follow-up through adolescence. *Pediatrics, 71,* 376.

Wright, F., Blough, R., Chamberlin, H., Halstead, W., Meier, P., Moore, R., Naunton, R., and Newell, F. (1972). A controlled follow-up study of small prematures born from 1952–1956. *American Journal of Diseases of Children, 124,* 506.

Chapter 4

Parental Concerns for High-Risk Infants

During the past two decades neonatal intensive care has developed into a highly specialized and effective system of treating newborn infants who have life-threatening disease. Because of their apparent success in reducing neonatal mortality, there has been a nationwide proliferation of neonatal intensive care units.

Even under the best of circumstances the birth of an infant, especially a firstborn infant, is a time of enormous change on the part of the parents—and much more so in the case of a high-risk infant. Of necessity, the bulk of concern in the NICU is directed toward infants who are literally fighting for their lives to overcome a vast array of medical complications associated with prematurity or other potentially fatal conditions to which newborns are susceptible. Clinical observations reporting an increased incidence of divorce, child abuse, failure to thrive, abandonment, and other family problems in the high-risk population have been available for years. Only recently, however, have controlled studies been undertaken in an effort to understand the unusual and confusing environment that the parents of premature infants encounter as they try to meet the needs of their fragile offspring, and as they attempt to deal with their own feelings toward their infants, their spouses, and their other children. In the years since parental visiting has been permitted in the NICU numerous studies have revealed that most parents continue to suffer severe emotional stress and that this stress occurred even when parents had frequent contact with their infants.

It is the purpose of the present chapter to alert the practitioner to the unusual set of circumstances faced by the parents of a very sick neonate, as well as the potential effects of this set of circumstances on later family well-being. In addition, a discussion of family intervention strategies is presented.

FOUNDATIONS OF NORMAL ATTACHMENT

A variety of researchers over several decades have elaborated on the process by which the human infant becomes attached to its mother (See Chapter 2 also). What has emerged is a description of the critical importance to the survival and development of the infant of early attachment to a primary caregiver.

Attachment can be defined as a unique relationship between two people that lasts over time (Klaus and Kennell, 1976). Although quantifying attachment during the early periods of the infant's life can be difficult, behaviors such as fondling, prolonged gazing, and physical touch are barometers that have been used in an effort to describe and measure attachment behavior. These activities involve both opportunity and ability on the part of the mother and infant.

Early theories of infant development viewed the child as not fully able to benefit from sensory stimuli. However, intensive study of the sensory ability of newborn infants from birth has revealed that the infant does possess a remarkably sophisticated ability to benefit from early environmental exposure (see Chapter 2). These sensory capabilities, in the presence of normal environmental opportunity generally afforded the healthy newborn, are the foundations upon which attachment behavior is initiated.

Attachment works in both directions, mother toward infant and infant toward mother. Table 4–1 presents a view of the steps involved in forming normal attachment between mother and infant. Pregnancy for a woman has been viewed as a period of maturation, involving a series of adaptive tasks, each dependent on the successful completion of the preceding one. A wide range of stressful factors may take place during the pregnancy and neonatal period that have the potential to profoundly influence a woman's subsequent mothering behavior and, ultimately, the developmental outcome of her child (Caplan, 1960).

During the first 60 to 90 minutes after birth the infant is alert, responsive, and especially appealing. In short, the infant is ideally equipped to meet the parents for the first time. Klaus and Kennell (1976) suggested that "there is a sensitive period in the first few minutes and hours of life during which it is necessary that the mother and father have close contact with their neonate" (p. 149). A strong

Table 4–1. Steps in Attachment

1. Planning the Pregnancy
2. Confirming the Pregnancy
3. Accepting the Pregnancy
4. Fetal Movement
5. Accepting the Fetus as an Individual
6. Birth
7. Hearing and Seeing the Baby
8. Touching and Holding the Baby
9. Caretaking

Note: From Care of the High-Risk Neonate (p. 149) by M. Klaus and S. Fanaroff (Eds.), 1979, Philadelphia: W.B. Saunders Co. Copyright 1982 by W.B. Saunders Co. Reprinted by permission.

interest in eye-to-eye contact is expressed by mothers of both full-term and premature infants. Statements such as "let me see your eyes" or "open your eyes" are common during the first few minutes of mother-infant contact. Eye-to-eye contact appears to elicit maternal caregiving responses (Robinson, 1967). Mothers make conscious attempts to elicit eye contact (en face) with their infants. The infant's sensory and motor abilities evoke responses from the mother and begin the communication that is especially helpful for attachment to begin. Stern (1971) has observed that patterns of interaction between a mother and her child have a characteristic rhythm. Intricate interchanges take place within a few minutes. If these interactions are interrupted for any reason, or not allowed to form, many aspects of the relationship between the two individuals are disturbed. This interdependency of rhythms seems to be at the root of their attachment as well as their communication (Brazelton, Koslowski, and Main, 1974). Thus, it seems important that the family have privacy in the first hours of life in which all family members have the opportunity to become attuned to each other.

Although the concept of a sensitive period during the early hours of life has received considerable attention, some researchers have reported that full attachment to the baby may also take place other a period of time. McFarlane (1978) reported that a group of English women became attached or felt that their baby was theirs according to the following schedule: 41 percent during pregnancy, 24 percent at birth, 27 percent during the first week, and 8 percent after the first week. Clearly, the importance of the early minutes and days of life for the formation of proper attachment is well established.

Klaus and Kennell (1976) summarized quite clearly what they see as several principles that are thought to be crucial components in the process of attachment:

1. There is a sensitive period in the first minutes and hours of life during which it is necessary that the mother and father have close contact with their neonate for later development to be optimal.
2. There appears to be specific responses to the infant in the human mother and father that are exhibited when they are first given their baby.
3. The process of attachment is structured so that the father and mother will become attached optimally to only one infant at a time.
4. During the process of the mother's attachment to her infant it is necessary that the infant respond to the mother by some signal such as body or eye movements.
5. People who witness the birth process become strongly attached to the infant.
6. Some early events have long-lasting effects. Anxieties about the well-being of the baby with a temporary disorder in the first day may result in long-lasting concerns that may cast long shadows and adversely shape the development of the child.

CHANGING ATTITUDES TOWARD MOTHER-INFANT SEPARATION

Increasingly, neonatologists and other health care professionals working with the parents of high-risk infants have become concerned with the effects of separating mother and child in the newborn period. These concerns have been made especially salient by observations that have concluded that early maternal-infant separation leads to deviant caretaking behavior that may develop into patterns of abuse and neglect later in infancy (Jeffcoate, Humphreys, and Lloyd, 1979; Klaus and Kennell, 1976). The issue of mother-infant attachment comes to the center of attention when care of the premature infant is studied. When the mother of the premature infant who is placed in the NICU is finally permitted to take her child home, she often reports her experiences as one of receiving a stranger. Her feelings about her baby appear to be quite different from those of the mother of the healthy full-term baby. Various attempts have been made to assess the consequences of separation on the behaviors of mothers who are kept from their infants placed in the NICU.

The feelings of physicians concerned with the care of the high-risk infant relative to the role of the parent have changed remarkably in the past 40 years. A 1942 report by Gleich listed the following "don'ts" concerning premature infants.

1. Don't handle the infant unnecessarily.
2. Don't allow anyone except the nurse and the physician into the premature infant's room. Friends and relatives should be kept out.
3. Don't feed the average premature infant oftener than every three hours.
4. Don't allow premature infants to sleep in a room with other children. Premature infants contract disease easily.

It is clear from statements such as these that the premature infant was relatively isolated from regular and intentional exposure to caretakers with a view toward establishing attachment. How times have changed. Increasingly, NICU policy today permits unlimited parental visiting as well as handling when possible. A practice that is gaining increased acceptance is the provision of a 24-hour toll-free number for parents to call. Parents are free to call and inquire about the status of their child at any time of day or night. They are permitted to speak to the pediatric nurse caring for their baby at that time, or the neonatologist if so desired. However, a certain degree of mother-infant separation is unavoidable. This is particularily true in the case of the mother who must leave her infant in the NICU for an extended period of time and who lives any distance from the hospital. Maternal-infant separation does take its toll and the information that follows is designed to alert practitioners to the potential effects of mother-infant separation in the newborn period.

EFFECTS OF EARLY MOTHER-INFANT SEPARATION

Barnett, Leiderman, Grolistern, and Klaus (1970) indicated that initially the primary focus of those interested in mother-infant separation was on the infant. This type of research has not fully addressed the importance of early contact relative to the stimulation of maternal behavior so necessary for a normal caretaking routine to be established. Barnett and his colleagues interviewed mothers while their infants were still in the nursery as well as after the infants were discharged. Their results indicated that the mothers who were separated from their infants displayed differences in three areas: commitment to the infant, self-confidence in the ability to mother the infant, and other nurturing behaviors such as stimulating the infant and skill in caring for the baby.

Leiderman (1980) conducted a detailed and controlled study designed to measure the effects of early separation on mother-infant behaviors. Three groups of mothers were included: two groups with premature infants and one group with full-term infants. The premature infants of both groups were separated from their mothers after birth and placed in an NICU for 3 to 12 weeks until they weighed 2,100 g. One group of mothers were allowed visual contact only with their infants. These mothers did not participate in caretaking activities while the babies were in the NICU. The other group of mothers were allowed to be in contact with their babies in the NICU. They handled their infants and participated as much as possible in the normal caretaking. When both groups of premature infants weighed 2,000 g they were placed in a discharge nursery until they weighed 2,500 g. During their stay in the discharge nursery (7 to 10 days) both groups of mothers were allowed to be with their infants as much as they desired.

The mother-infant interactions of the three groups were observed at three points: the first just before leaving the hospital, the second 1 week after discharge, and the third 1 month after discharge. During these observations it was seen that the full-term mothers smiled at their infants more and held them close to their bodies more than both groups of the mothers of the premature infants. Further differences were detected in the mothers' attitudes of self-confidence and in the marital situations. Only 1 of 22 of the mothers who were allowed close contact with their premature infants subsequently became divorced. In the group allowed no contact 5 of the mothers became divorced and two infants within the no-contact group were given up for adoption. Although follow-up when the children were 8 years of age revealed no differences between those who had had contact and those who had been separated, the impact of early separation is clearly observed.

Additional studies have examined the interaction of mothers and their premature infants during the first year of life. What has emerged is a consistent finding that whereas the total amount of interaction may be similar to that for full-term infants, the quality of the interaction differs. Minde (1982) devised an objective scale to rate medical complications suffered by infants while they were in the NICU. One group of infants, who suffered no medical complications during their stay in the NICU as identified by the scale, was matched with a group of infants who were seriously ill (severe medical complications) while in the nursery. The 10 well and 10 ill infants were matched individually, based on birth weight and gestational age. Both infant and parental behavior was observed at three points in time. Observation 1 took place while the infant was seriously ill; observation 2, 1 week after the ill infant had recovered; and observation 3, approximately 3 weeks after observation 2. Observations on well infants took place according to the same schedule. The infants were observed one final time during a home visit, matched within 1 week of birth for both groups of infants. The results obtained were as follows:

1. The 10 ill infants showed signifinantly fewer arm, leg, and head movements and eye openings during observation 1 than did the matched well infants, but no differences were found during observations 2 and 3 at home.
2. Mothers of ill infants touched and smiled at their infants significantly less during all three nursery observations, but at home they not only touched and smiled less but also looked at their at their infants and vocalized to them less than did the mothers of the well infants.
3. When the total group of ill infants was divided into those who were seriously ill for more than 30 days (long group) versus less than 17 days (short group), it became clear that the mothers of the short group showed an initial decrease in smiling and touching but increased their level of touch and smiling during observations 2 and 3 to the level of the well parents. The parents of the long group showed a consistant lag in their caretaking behavior toward their infants.
4. The psychological background factors between the mothers of the long and short group were not different; hence the differences in caretaking behavior between the groups more than likely reflected the length of illness of individual infants.
5. Mothers' actual behavior with their infants on a particular day were correlated more with their perceptions of how ill their infant was rather than the infant's actual degree of illness.

These results demonstrate that the quality of interactional patterns may differ during the early stages of caregiving, but that as time progresses, the amount of interactional time cannot always be used to describe differences between preterm and full-term infants. The quality of interaction through the first year of life has been observed to differ between full-term and preterm infants (Brown and Bakerman, 1979; Field, 1980). Observations of human mothers separated from their infants consistently show that attachment, bonding, and interactional patterns do differ between the mothers of healthy and high-risk newborns.

Abuse and Neglect

The previous section suggested that early and prolonged hospitalization may set the stage for patterns of deviant parenting during the first weeks and months of life. Could it be that interference in the early formation of attachment results in even greater distortions in parenting at a later date? Perhaps one of the best barometers of the effect of mother-infant separation on later parenting patterns is an examination of the relationship between high-risk status and child abuse. Literature available on child abuse has suggested that abnormality in the child predisposes the child to abuse and neglect. Because of the rapid growth of NICUs and the survival of larger numbers of infants with a difficult neonatal history, the systematic study of the relationship between child abuse and prematurity has been possible.

Klein and Stern (1971) examined the relationship between low birth weight and later patterns of abuse and neglect. Their study, conducted at Montreal Children's Hospital, involved the systematic review of all hospital records of children who had been classified as abused during a 9 year period. A total of 51 cases of abuse met the pre-set criteria established by the investigators. Seventy-six percent (39) of the abused children were full-term infants and 24 percent (12) were low birth weight infants. Of the 39 children who were not premature (although abused) 15 had had significant medical illness while quite young. The analysis of the records of the low birth weight infants revealed that in 9 of the 12 cases major neonatal problems were present that resulted in an average length of stay in the NICU of 41 days. Further review of the histories of the low birth weight infants revealed that 10 of the 12 battered infants came from deprived home environments in which the mothers themselves usually had suffered maternal and environmental deprivation during childhood. These data suggest that multiple factors have an influence on child abuse, one of which is the neonatal history of the child.

Other investigators have addressed the relationship between low birth weight and the potential for later abuse and neglect. Smith and Hanson (1974) in Birmingham, England noted that 25 percent of a group of 134 abused children they followed were low birth weight babies. Prematurity or serious illness in the newborn period was noted in 23 to 31 percent of abused children in studies conducted by Elmer and Gregg (1967), Klaus and Kennell (1970), and Weston (1968). Lynch (1975) examined the factors present in historical data for a population of 25 abused children and determined that six factors emerged as significantly overrepresented when compared to comparable non-abused children. These were abnormal pregnancy, abnormal labor and delivery, neonatal separation, other separation in the first 6 months of life, illness in the first year of life, and illness in the mother in the first year of the infant's life. Fomufod, Sinkford, and Lovy (1975) presented data from a retrospective study of child abuse cases over a 12 month period, with special emphasis on birth weight, gestational age, neonatal problems, and duration of the hospital stay. In addition a series of studies on child abuse and high-risk history were reviewed. Results indicated that low birth weight and mother-infant separation appear to be significant factors in the etiology of child abuse. Although many high-risk infants do not suffer abuse and neglect later in childhood, separation in early infancy can serve as one of several predisposing factors relative to the possibility of deviant parenting behaviors. Factors such as socioeconomic status, educational levels of the parents, whether the parents were themselves abused or neglected, and marital stability can contribute to increased incidences of abuse and neglect.

The role of the clinician-educator may vary, depending on the particular setting in which services to the high-risk infant and family are provided. At the very least, however, the practitioner needs to be familiar with the potential for parenting behaviors, predisposed by factors in the newborn period, that may lead to later patterns of deviant parenting.

SOURCES OF PARENTAL STRESS

The normal set of circumstances surrounding birth and the neonatal period are of necessity interrupted when an infant is ill and unable to receive the amount and type of early maternal exposure afforded the healthy newborn. Parents lose much when their infant is born prematurely. The psychological preparation that takes place during the later weeks of pregnancy is lost. Thus, the earlier the delivery the greater the frustration on the part of the parents. Failure to produce a full-term baby contributes to the grief and depression usually experienced after the birth of a premature infant. Taylor and Hall (1979) pointed out that in addition to fearing that the infant will die or survive but be severely handicapped, parents feel guity, angry, depressed, and preoccupied with the infant. They further pointed out that when an infant is delivered prematurely, unexpected realities replace expectations, and each of these represents a further loss.

In discussing the unexpected realities that replace expectations on the part of the parents Taylor and Hall concluded by stating that:

1. A scrawny, underweight, high-risk infant, who is either seriously ill or likely to become so, replaces the expected healthy full-term infant.
2. An unreactive or underactive infant replaces the responsive and reactive infant with whom the parents had expected to actively interact.
3. Separation of the premature infant from the parents replaces the anticipated frequent close contact between them.
4. An incubator in a sophisticated NICU replaces the expected bassinet beside the mother's bed in the rooming-in unit.

5. Nurses and doctors, strangers but awesomely knowledgeable and competent, replace the parents as the primary caregivers.
6. The mother especially has failed to produce the expected baby; hence the parents' perception of failure and its accompanying loss of self-esteem replace the expected success and increase in self-esteem. (p. 75)

These are certainly potent and serious barriers to the formation of attachment. Each of these must be overcome by the parents if they are to begin to ultimately accept and become attached to their child. Table 4–2 represents the parents' usual emotional reactions to both a full-term and a premature birth.

In addition to the harsh aforementioned realities, a host of other adjustments are forced upon the parents of high-risk infants. The first of these is the abrupt disruption of normal family routine. If the mother is hospitalized for any period of time before delivery, or if she chooses to remain close to her baby after delivery, her absence in the home poses a difficult problem for the rest of the family. The single parent or unmarried mother who gives birth to a high-risk infant faces an even more serious disruption in family routine. Transportation to and from the NICU may become a concern, especially if the baby is transferred to a NICU many miles from home. Child care for siblings becomes quite difficult. Parents are devoting increased time to and concern toward their sick baby, often at the expense of other children in the family. Parents may feel quite torn between their newborn and other children and family responsibilities. If the mother works outside the home, another source of stress may be added, namely, her desire to be close to her baby, perhaps for an extended period of time, and her possible need to return to work. These stresses may be compounded by the individual characteristics of each family relative to other children, employment, finances, family routine, proximity to support groups (extended family), proximity to the NICU, and parental resources for coping with an unusually stressful time. These forces cannot be ignored.

Parental Reports

Ellen Galinsky (1976), in an attempt to describe her experiences as the mother of a premature baby, presented in great detail her personal observations. Her first opportunity to view her premature son (32 weeks gestation, 1,330 g) resulted in the following:

> Probably the most startling thing about a premature nursery is the appearance of the babies themselves. They look more like little old people curled up—worn out by life—rather than like new babies. Their rib cages protrude, their bellies, probably the only round part on their bodies, heave in and out, seeming to strain with each breath. Their skin hangs on

Table 4–2. Parents Usual Emotional Reactions to Full-Term and Premature Births

	Full-Term	Premature
Perception of Events	Gain, success	Loss, failure
Reactions to Birth	Joy, relief	Grief, concern
Emotional Preparation	Complete	Incomplete
Expectations Confirmed	"Wished for baby"	Feared baby
Self-esteem	Increased	Decreased
Baby's Primary Caregivers	Mother or father	Nurse or doctor
Parents and Infants	Together	Separated
Baby's Social Responsiveness	Well developed	Decreased or absent
Mother Goes Home With	Baby	Empty arms
Psychological Tasks Remaining	Reconciling real baby and fantasized baby	Grieving for expected baby, accepting baby

their bony arms and legs in folds, not the soft clear skin of a newborn, but coarser more saggy skin. Their noses, because they do not have have fat cheeks, spread almost from ear to ear. Their eyes are still closed. And some are covered with downy fetal hair. They bear little resemblance to the children and adults they will become. (p. 51)

It is no wonder that the mother of the high-risk infant faces an unusual emotional trauma at the birth of her child.

Further comparison of the experiences of the mothers of full-term and premature infants amplifies the plight of the mother of a high-risk infant. In contrast to the normal pregnancy there are distinct differences in the experiences of the mothers of high-risk infants. The average pregnant woman, apart from past history or previous medical indications, does not appear to be overly concerned about premature delivery. As a result premature labor comes as a shock and the woman, even though intellectually aware of the possibility, is emotionally unprepared when it happens to her. The actual atmosphere of the hopsital is more characteristic of an emergency situation than of a normal labor. The rush of activity, the added concern on the part of the professional staff, paternal apprehension, and preparation for the needs of the preterm infant all serve to heighten maternal anxiety. All of these confirm the woman's feelings that she is involved in, and powerless to alter, a dangerous situation for her baby. A tremendously heightened concern for the welfare of the baby is experienced by the mother. She wonders if the baby is alive, and if it will survive. Later she wonders if it will be normal. If she is afforded the opportunity to see her baby, she may be quite dismayed at its size, overall appearance, and unusual color.

In many instances the mother returns to her room with a complete feeling of loneliness and inability to do anything of significance for her baby. Her initial discussions with hospital staff about the condition of her baby may answer immediate questions for her, but a rising feeling of failure on her part and worry for her baby result. Her inability to be close to her baby is quite frustrating for her. If the mother is required to leave the baby in the NICU and return home, her feelings of failure are enhanced. She may be reluctant to visit the baby and take part in its care. Once the baby arrives home, a tremendous amount of anxiety may accompany the event. The mother may feel quite inadequate to meet the needs of her baby. In reflecting back on the early caregiving opportunities afforded her, Galinsky (1976) stated: "Not being able to take care of Phillip in the hospital, I guess, made me wonder if I am capable of doing so" (p. 72). Laney and Sandler (1982) in an attempt to identify relationships between maternal stress and preterm delivery discovered that mothers of preterm infants had larger numbers of stressful events present in their lives than did mothers of full-term infants. The impact of these events, and the patterns of response they may have engendered, appeared to contribute to the manner in which the mother adjusted and reacted to her preterm infant. Faulty and inadequate patterns of handling previously experienced stressful events may in part have established less than desirable strategies for handling the current set of circumstances, namely the birth of a premature and ill infant. The authors concluded their investigation by stating that maternal stress is clearly implicated as a contributive factor to preterm delivery as well as later developing patterns of inadequate parenting. Although it is a fact that only some infants sent to the NICU sustain significant damage, the very need to be on such a unit is ample threat to a parent that his or her child may be damaged.

Father's Role

Sherman (1980) pointed out that fathers have a unique role in an NICU. Because their wives and infants are often simultaneously hospitalized in separate facilities, they assume a central role in maintaining family stability during the crisis. They may be first to visit the infant on a regular basis and to commuicate with staff about the infant's condition. They play a key role in reporting progress of the infant back to the mother. Because of the early disruptive separation of the mother from her sick infant, the father plays a more crucial role in stabilizing the family in this setting than he does following the birth of a healthy baby. Many mothers feel reassured based on the husbands' detailed reports of how the baby is doing. It is the reality of having to deal with the ambiguity of uncertain outcomes for their babies that is perhaps the single most anxiety-producing element facing the parents of the high-risk infant.

PARENTAL PATTERNS OF ADJUSTMENT

Kaplan and Mason (1960) described the birth of a premature infant as an acute crisis. They delineated four normal psychological tasks that the mother of a sick newborn must complete if she is going to establish a healthy relationship with her child.

The first task confronts the mother at the time of delivery. It is the preparation for the loss of the baby whose life is in danger. This anticipatory grief involves withdrawal from the relationship already being established during pregnancy with the expected child. The mother hopes the baby survives, but simultaneously she prepares for its death.

The second task faced by the mother involves her identifying and facing her feelings of failure because she has not delivered a normal full-term baby. The mother struggles with both of these tasks until the baby's chances for survival seem secure. Based on the child's weight and physical condition, the baby may continue to remain in the hospital for a further 2 to 10 weeks, and during this period the next two tasks must be performed.

The third task is the resumption of the process of relating to the baby that previously had been interrupted. The mother has lost the usual opportunity provided by delivery of a full-term healthy infant for the development of readiness for the mothering role. Characteristically, there is a point at which the mother really begins to believe that the baby will survive. The event that stimulates activity on this task may be the baby's gain in weight, a change in feeding patterns, a change in its activity or appearance, or a change in the staff's manner.

The final task is that the mother gain an understanding of how her premature baby differs from a healthy full-term baby in terms of its special needs and growth patterns. To provide the baby with the needed extra care and protection, the mother must begin to view the baby as having special needs and characteristics. But it is equally important for her to see that these special needs are temporary and will yield in time to more normal patterns. Her task is to take satisfactory precautions without depriving herself and the child of enjoyable interactions.

Parental Responses While the Baby Is in the NICU

Variability in actual parental behavior is quite likely while the infant is in the NICU. During crisis times parents may become alternately angry, demanding, and critical. They may withdraw and refuse to visit the child. As the child's condition varies, so will the parents' response and ability to relate to the child. If the child is unresponsive, sick, passive, and displays poor feeding, the parents are likely to derive little pleasure from being with the child. It is in just such circumstances, as the need for specialized nursing care is heightened, that mothers tend to lose confidence in their ability to care for their babies.

Sherman (1980) pointed out that the parents who appear to manage well are those who have stable marriages, receive support from family and friends, and are adept at actually seeking information from the staff. These are parents who more than likely have an additional healthy child at home. They often have strong religious beliefs and are able to understand the child's medical problems relatively easily. Parents who tend to respond in this manner are more likely to be spontaneously sought out by the staff to report on the infant's progress. The process of caring for the infant becomes the mutual responsibility of the staff and the parents, thus multiple contacts with supportive professionals is the result.

Other parents whose response is not characterized by these patterns may be identified by staff as "problem parents." Although these parents may be managing well, their behavior may cause discomfort to the staff. Some of the behaviors characteristic of this category of parents may include a reluctance to leave the NICU, repeatedly asking the same questions from many staff, and a desire to talk only to the physician or someone else "in charge." Depending on the seriousness of the infant's illness and the medical and long-range sequelae of the illness, problem parents may be quite vocal about their desire to discontinue life support measures. It is the problem parent who most likely evokes opposition from the staff. Communication between problem parents and staff is less pleasant and reciprocal thus spontaneous contact may be less frequent. Staff perceptions of parental behaviors, and the ability of staff to deal with less than desirable atmospheres for communication, may vary, however. It is possible that as coverage in the NICU changes around the clock parents may find one or more staff members better able to effectively communicate with as well as handle the types of behaviors that tend to alienate staff and parents.

Financial Concerns

One final area of parental stress that is worthy of discussion is financial concerns. Neonatal intensive care is very expensive care because it deals to a large extent with low birth weight infants who have a prolonged hospitalization and who require the same expensive life support methodology used in adult intensive care (Cullen, Fenara, and Briggs, 1976; Hawes, 1985). Newborn infants have been shown to be among those patients generating the highest hospital costs in recent years (Schroeder, Showstack, and Roberts, 1979). Additional data obtained on selected subgroups by Pomerance, Ubrainski, and Ubia (1978) and McCarthy, Koops, and Honeyfield (1979) indicated that very low birth weight infants and those born in hospitals other than the one in which the NICU is contained thus requiring transport to a regional NICU, showed high average costs. Phiblis, Williams, and Phibbs (1981) indicated that the average cost per admission to a NICU is approaching $10,000, with an average daily cost approaching $500. Phiblis further reported that the average cost for infants free from any significant risk factors was $2,000. In contrast, however, other infants (less than 25 percent of admissions and displaying significant risk factors) had an average cost of $19,800. Pomerance and colleagues (1978) reported on the costs of 75 infants who weighed less than 1,000 g at birth. Of the population studied, 45 infants did not survive (average cost per infant: $14,625; average length of survival: 17 days) Thirty infants survived with an average cost per infant of $40,286 (average length of stay in the NICU: 89 days). Although the initial concern of the parents of a high-risk infant is not directed toward financial costs, as the length of stay in the NICU increases parents are of necessity faced with the reality of paying for enormous medical bills. These are sobering realities for parents and constitute only part of parental adjustments necessitated by the birth of a high-risk infant.

PARENTAL INTERVENTION

Perhaps an area in which the practitioner can have the greatest impact on the long-term well-being of the high-risk infant and family is intervention, with the parents. This is designed to foster realistic and nurturing patterns of parental behavior, as well as to help the parents become aware of the special needs of their baby. The goal is to encourage the parents to create an atmosphere in the home that allows for the optimal development of their baby. In general intervention strategies designed to aid parents may occur prenatally, if the possibility of a premature birth is known; during the neonatal period, while the mother and baby remain in the hospital or after the mother goes home and the baby remains; or postnatally, during the early weeks and months when the establishment of a normal caregiving routine in the home is crucial. Both prenatal and neonatal intervention information are presented in the following section.

Prenatal Parental Intervention

There are definite advantages to advance indentification of mothers who are more likely to have special difficulties relating to their babies.

Mothers who have a high incidence of mothering disorders often have one of the following characteristics: the previous loss of a newborn infant, including miscarriage; a fertility problem with no living children; a previously seriously ill newborn infant; primiparity if younger than 17 or older than 38 years; a medical problem with which the infant may be affected; and the unmarried status of the mother (Klaus and Kennell, 1979).

Although it is a fact that only some infants sent to the NICU have significant delay or long-term serious deficits, the potential that a particular baby may need special care of this nature is quite threatening to the parents. No matter what the outcome, parents have significant adjustments to make, and the practitioner can be active prenatally to answer questions and provide support for these parents. In almost all high-risk situations, the odds are in favor of the birth of a live baby who can be expected to display reasonably normal developmental patterns in the long run. It is thus reasonable and comforting to stress to the parents a positive and relatively optimistic attitude toward the birth of their potentially high-risk baby. This is quite important for the mother's later relationship with her baby, which is in turn important for the development of normal parenting behaviors. In most instances the physician will be the primary provider of information and advice. However, as the number of neonatal follow-up clinics increases, nonmedical practitioners are increasingly involved in prenatal contact with parents. Although most high-risk births are not known beforehand, the potential exists that the practitioner will be able to provide valuable support for parents prenatally.

Intervention While the Child Remains in the Nursery

For the clinician-educator employed in a hospital setting, the input provided while the child is in the NICU can be a most valuable source of information for parents. Neonatologists are relying with increasing frequency on members of the neonatal follow-up team to enhance the parents' understanding of the special situation in which both the parents and infants find themselves after the birth of a high-risk infant. Specific intervention strategies with parents designed to foster attachment and enhance proper parenting behaviors have taken a variety of forms. Several of these are discussed in the following.

Proximity of Mother and Infant

In recent years there has been increased interest in how to help parents become attached to their high-risk babies. One strategy shown to be of help in reducing mothering disorders is to encourage parents to be close to and have regular contact with their infants. Terms, such as rooming-in and nesting, have been used to describe this intervention technique. In many instances after a premature delivery the infant must be transported immediately to a perinatal center that contains a NICU. The perinatal center may be many miles away from the hospital where the infant was delivered. This is a particularly stressful situation for the mother, as she immediately loses all contact with her infant. A practice that is gaining increased acceptance is transporting the mother, either before delivery if a high-risk situation is suspected or as soon after delivery as possible, to be near her infant. Several researchers have documented the effectiveness of close and regular contact between mother and infant relative to a reduction in both mortality and later parenting problems. One strategy, used in Baragwanath Hospital in South Africa, allowed the mothers of premature infants to live in a room adjoining the NICU. At feeding time the mothers entered the nursery to feed and handle their babies (Kahn, Wayburne, and Fouche, (1954). Tafair and Ross (1973) permitted mothers in Ethiopia to live in the NICU 24 hours a day. They found that the number of surviving infants increased 500 percent as more mothers chose to breast-feed. James and Wheeler (1969) described the successful introduction of a care-by-parent unit in the United States to provide a homelike caretaking experience for the mother. Nursing support was available for parents of premature infants if help was needed. Klaus and Kennell (1982) described a nesting program in which mothers were allowed to live in with their premature infants prior to discharge from the hospital. In their program once the babies reached 1,720 to 2,110 g, each mother was given a private room with her baby where she provided all the caregiving. Impressive changes in the mothers allowed to be a part of the program were reported. Even though the mothers had fed and cared for their infants in the intensive care nursery on many occasions before living in, eight of nine mothers observed were unable to sleep during the first 24 hours. During the second 24 hours, however, the mothers' confidence and caretaking skills improved greatly. Several mothers for the first time began discussing early discharge of their infants and even began making initial preparations for the infants' arrival home.

Another strategy involves transporting the healthy premature infant to the mother. Rather than bringing mothers into the NICU with its frightening sights and sounds, strange equipment, and unfamiliar faces, the baby is brought to the mother in her own room. In this way the mothers have an opportunity to become acquainted with their premature newborns under circumstances similar to those experienced by mothers of full-term infants. There are, however, medical limitations to this practice because of infants' ability to tolerate an environment other than the NICU, which has readily available any special medical equipment that may be needed at a moment's notice. This practice may not be the most appropriate if the infant is subject to respiratory problems or other problems such as cardiovascular disorders, seizures, feeding difficulties, and the need for additional special procedures.

Parent Groups

Communication of information to parents is complicated by the contact they have with a large number of professionals and thus may receive disparate and occasionally conflicting information. Parents are in communication with neonatologists, pediatricians, obstetricians, nurses neurologists, laboratory personnel, and several other professional staff members. In the early days following the birth of the baby the discussion centers naturally on the medical condition and survival prospects for the baby. However, as time passes, and as the parents work their way through the needed stages of adjustment, attention turns more and more toward the possibility of later problems, the parents' fears about the special needs of their baby and the parents' ability to meet special needs. One group that has been somewhat overlooked relative to providing help to the parents of high-risk infants is other parents of sick newborns. It is apparent that mothers and fathers who have been through similar experiences would have a wealth of information and insight to share. Some of the ways in which parent groups can be of immeasurable help to parents who have babies in the NICU relates to possible fears about taking the child home. The mother in particular may have been overwhelmed by the expertise and skill she observed in the NICU when others were providing the primary care for her baby. Now as it is nearing the time when she will have to assume that role she is naturally apprehensive about her competency. Mothers who have shared this experience can be a source of emotional support and practical advice about caretaking. It is also possible for experienced mothers to visit the home and make themselves available to families on a regular basis until fears about caretaking are eliminated.

The value of parent groups in the NICU cannot be underestimated. The practitioner may be in a position to introduce a group of this nature or to participate in a group already in existence. One major objective of any parent group is education. In addition, the provision of emotional support can be very helpful. The establishment of better lines of communication is often a by-product of groups of this nature. Staff-parent interaction is crucial for the overall adjustment needed on the part of the parents. One possible strategy is to encourage parents to have professionals from a variety of disciplines discuss topics of interest. Questions can be asked by the parents, and much valuable information can be provided. Parent groups are usually formed to meet the urgent need for information. The parent may, however, experience a degree of support and understanding from other parents often not possible from professionals, relatives, or friends. They also may obtain highly specific information about problems encountered. One important result of parent groups may be the fostering of more acceptable parenting behaviors.

A controlled evaluation designed to assess the impact of parent groups in the NICU was conducted by Minde and colleagues (1980). A group of parents of premature infants (birth weight less than 1,500 g) met once weekly for 90 to 120 minutes. In addition, the group was assigned a "veteran mother" who had had a similar baby in the NICU during the previous year. The initial objective of the group was to provide parents with a forum in which they could talk about and learn to cope with the stresses associated with having a very small, premature infant. An additional objective was to assist the parents in learning how to cope with the daily routines employed in the NICU. The parents talked initially about their intense feelings of depression, fear, and guilt about having given birth to a small, sick baby. Parenting styles and caregiving ability were assessed by means of later visits both in the nursery and in the home. The results of this investigation indicated that mothers of high-risk infants who had the opportunity to meet with each other for 7 to 12 weeks, with guidance from professional staff and a veteran mother, visited their infants more frequently and interacted more with them during visits in the nursery and at home. The mothers also felt more competent in their caregiving role than did mothers who did not attend such groups.

Early Discharge

Several researchers have discussed the parental benefit of allowing earlier discharge of premature infants. Obvious benefits are less separation of mother and infant, less stress for the mother when she is unable to visit the NICU as frequently as she would like, a reduction in fears (if the baby is able to go home, it must be doing reasonably well), and the quicker restoration of normal family routine (of great benefit when there are other children in the family). Of course deciding on a discharge date is dependent upon the medical condition of the infant as well as a judgment about the mother's ability to meet the special needs of her child. However, no negative effects as a result of early discharge were reported by Dillard and Korones (1973). It is entirely possible that when early discharge is allowed that experienced personnel can visit the home and assess caretaking routine. Additional studies of early discharge have not revealed any adverse effects on the physical health of the infants (Berg and Salisbury, 1971; Davies, Herhert, Haxley, and McNeish, 1979).

SUMMARY

The birth of an infant with perinatal complications is viewed as an emotional crisis that impinges on the well-being of the entire family. A variety of investigators have documented a higher incidence of financial stress, divorce, adjustment problems, and child abuse in families of high-risk infants. Clinician-educators are in a unique position to aid in the overall process of adjusting to the presence of and special needs created by the birth of a high-risk infant. The benefits to the parents and infant are enormous if a healthy relationship is established. As summarized by Klaus and Kennell (1976) seven tasks are needed in the practitioner's work with the parents of high-risk infants:

1. To help the mother adapt her previously conceptualized image of an ideal normal infant to the small infant she has produced.
2. To help relieve the mother's guilt about producing a small infant.
3. To help the mother begin building a close affectionate tie to her infant, developing a mutual interaction so that she will be attuned to her baby's special needs as the baby grows.
4. To permit the mother to learn how to care for her infant while he is in the hospital so that after her child's discharge, she will be competent and relaxed while caring for him.
5. To encourage the family to work together during the crisis of the premature birth, helping the father and mother discuss their difficulties with one another as they attempt to arrive at satisfactory solutions.
6. To help meet the special needs of individual families.
7. To assist the families in the transitional period that takes place after the infant is discharged from the NICU. (p. 122)

Although the bulk of these suggestions relate to the mother, the role of the father in increasing the probability of normal family adjustments in the presence of difficult circumstances cannot be ignored. As has been stated previously, the father is in a unique position to assume a central role in maintaining family stability during the crisis. Fathers play a more crucial role in stabilizing the family unit after the birth of a premature infant than they do after the birth of a healthy newborn.

Local support groups, home visits, putting parents in contact with other parents of high-risk infants, interventions in the nursery, early discharge, and increased contact in the NICU are considerable tasks involving the skills and expertise of a variety of professionals. The benefits of accomplishing these, however, are too far reaching to ignore.

REFERENCES

Barnett, C., Leiderman, H. Grolistern, R., and Klaus, M. (1970). Neonatal separation: The maternal side of the interactional deprivation. *Pediatrics, 45*, 2.

Berg, R., and Salisbury, A. (1971). Discharging infants of low birth weight: Reconsiderations of current practice. *American Journal of Diseases in Children, 122*, 414.

Brazelton, T., Koslowski, B., and Main, M. (1974). The origins of reciprocity: The early infant interaction. In M. Lewis and L. Rosenbaum (Eds.), *The effect of the infant on its caregiver* (Vol. 1). New York: John Wiley & Sons.

Brown, J., and Bakerman, R. (1979). Relationship of human mothers with their infants during the first year of life: Effects of prematurity. In R. Bell and C. Smotherman (Eds.), *Maternal Influence and early behavior.* Holinwood, England: Spectrum.

Caplan, G. (1960). *Emotional implications of pregnancy and influences on family relationships in the healthy child.* Cambridge, MA: Howard University Press.

Cullen, D., Fenara, L., and Briggs, R. (1976). Survival, hospitalization charges and follow-up results in critically ill patients. *New England Journal of Medicine, 294*, 982.

Davies, D., Herhert, S., Haxley, V., and McNeish, A. (1979). When should preterm babies be sent home from neonatal units? *Lancet, 1*, 914.

Dillard, R., and Korones, R. (1973). Lower discharge weight and shortened nursery stay for low birth weight infants. *New England Journal of Medicine, 288*, 131.

Elmer, E., and Gregg, D. (1967). Developmental characteristics of abused children. *Pediatrics, 40*, 596.

Field, T. (1980). Interactions of high-risk infats: Quantitative and qualitative differences. In D. Sawin, R. Hawkins, L. Walker, and J. Penticuff (Eds.), *Exceptional infant: Vol. 4. Psychosocial risks in infant-environmental transactions.* New York: Brunner/Mazel.

Fromufod, A., Sinkford, S., and Lovy, V. (1975). Mother-child separation at birth: A contributing factor in child abuse. *Lancet, 2*, 549.

Galinsky, E. (1976). *Beginnings.* Boston: Houghton Mifflin.

Gleich, M. (1942). The premature infant: Part 3. *Archives of Pediatrics, 59*, 172.

Hawes, W. (1975). A survey of newborn intensive care centers in California. *Western Journal of Medicine, 123*, 81.

James, V., and Wheeler, W. (1969). The care-by-parent unit. *Pediatrics, 3,* 488.

Jeffcoate, J., Humphreys, M., and Lloyd, J., (1979). Disturbance in parent-child relationship following preterm delivery. *Developmental Medicine and Child Neurology, 21,* 344.

Kahn, E., Wayburne, S., and Fouche, M. (1954). The Baragwanath premature baby unit: An analysis of the case records of 1000 consecutive admissions. *South African Medical Journal, 28,* 453.

Kaplan, D., and Mason ,E. (1960). Maternal reactions to premature birth viewed as an acute emotional disorder. *American Journal of Orthopsychiatry, 39,* 539.

Klaus, M., and Kennell, J. (1970). Mothers separated from their newborn infants. *Pediatric Clinics of North America, 17.*

Klaus, M., and Kennell, J. (1976). *Maternal-infant bonding.* St. Louis: C. V. Mosby.

Klaus, M., and Kennell, J. (1979). Care of the parents. In M. Klaus and S. Fanaroff (Eds.), *Care of the high risk neonate.* Philadelphia: W. B. Saunders.

Klaus, M., and Kennell, J. (1982). Interventions in the premature nursery: Impact on development. *Pediatric Clinics of North America, 29,* 5.

Klein, M., and Stern, L. (1971). Low birth weight and the battered child syndrome. *American Journal of Diseases in Childhood, 122,* 15.

Laney, M., and Sandler, H. (1982). Relationships among maternal stress, infant status, and mother-infant interactions. In J. Lipsit and R. Field (Eds.), *Infant behavior and development: Perinatal risks and newborn behavior.* Norwood, NJ: Ablex Publishing.

Leiderman, P. (1980). Human mother to infant social bonding: Is there a critical phase? In G. Barlow, M. Maine, and L. Petrinovich (Eds.), *Behavioral development: An interdisciplinary approach.* Cambridge: Cambridge University Press.

Lynch, M. (1975). Ill health and child abuse. *Lancet, 8,* 317.

McFarlane, A. (1978). Maternal attachments. In S. Kitsinger and J. Davis (Eds.), *The place of birth.* New York: Oxford University Press.

McCarthy, J., Koops, B., and Honeyfield, B. (1979). Who pays the bills for neonatal intensive care. *Journal of Pediatrics, 95,* 755.

Minde, K. (1982). Low birth weight infants: A psychosocial persepctive. In D. Parron and L. Eisenberg (Eds.), *Infants at risk for developmental dysfunction* (Health and Behavior: a Research Agenda Interim Report. No. 4). Washington, DC: National Academy Press.

Minde, K., Shosenberg, B., Marton, P., Thompson, B., Ripley, J., and Bruns, S. (1980). Self-help groups in a premature nursery: A controlled evaluation. *Journal of Pediatrics, 96,* 933.

Phiblis, C., Williams, R., and Phibbs, R. (1981). Newborn risk factors and costs of neonatal intensive care. *Pediatrics, 68,* 3.

Pomerance, J., Ubrainski, C., and Ubia, T. (1978). Cost of living for infants weighing 1000 grams or less at birth. *Pediatrics, 61,* 908.

Robinson, K. (1967). The role of eye to eye contact in maternal-infant attachment. *Journal of Child Psychology and Psychiatry, 8,* 13.

Schroeder, S., Showstack, J., and Roberts, H. (1979). Frequency and clinical description of high cost patients in 17 acute care hospitals. *New England Journal of Medicine, 300,* 1706.

Sherman, M. (1980). Psychiatry in the neonatal intensive care unit. *Clinics in Perinatology, 7,* 33.

Smith, S., and Hanson, R. (1974). Battered children: A medical and psychological study. *British Medical Journal, 14,* 665.

Stern, D. (1971). A micro-analysis of mother-infant interaction. *Journal of the American Academy of Child Psychiatry, 10,* 510.

Tafair, N., and Ross, S. (1973). On the need for organized prenatal care. *Ethiopian Medical Journal, 11,* 93.

Taylor, P., and Hall, B. (1979). Parent-infant bonding and opportunities in a perinatal center. *Seminars in Perinatology, 3,* 73.

Weston, J. (1968). The pathology of child abuse. In R. Helfer and C. Kempe (Eds.), *The battered child.* Chicago: University of Chicago Press.

Chapter 5

Infant Assessment

Clinical activity for the practitioner involved in providing services for high-risk infants may take a variety of forms, including curriculum development, working with parents, and the actual provision of early intervention services. One activity that is of interest to most if not all practitioners, however, is the collection of accurate and reliable assessment data upon which a host of subsequent decisions hinge. Although the term assessment may have various meanings to practitioners, *infant assessment* as presented in this chapter is defined as any activity either formal (through the use of standardized norm referenced criteria) or informal (through the use of developmental profiles or checklists) that is designed to elicit accurate and reliable infant behaviors upon which inferences relative to developmental skill status may be made. The purpose of infant assessment may vary, depending on the setting in which assessment activity is conducted and the individuals involved. Infant assessment data are important to researchers who are interested in monitoring developmental progress as a means of describing the normal process of child development. Researchers also may be involved in assessment activity as a means of gauging the results of various medical and environmental factors on developmental performance. The clinician-educator is interested in accurate assessment data as a means of detecting developmental delay at an early age, providing appropriate intervention activity, and checking the developmental progress a child is making as a result of early intervention efforts. Assessment data also aid the clinician-educator in detecting specific skill areas that reflect developmental delay, thus allowing specific remedial effort to be directed toward that area. Assessment activity also aids the practitioner in determining which children are in need of closer monitoring relative to the potential for later developmental deviancy. Thus, the predictive purpose of assessment is fulfilled. Although no single assessment tool may be suitable for all the aforementioned purposes, the practitioner must be familiar with a variety of instruments as one or more of these tools may be used at different points in time. Data contained in Appendix D alerts the practitioner to a variety of assessment instruments as well as their purposes.

Professional concern with the detection of developmental delay in young children with a high-risk history spans several decades and involves a variety of professions. Neonatologists are concerned with the quality of life of the survivors of the NICU. The developmental pediatrician is directly concerned with the diagnosis and supervision of child development. Early childhood educators have demonstrated the increased efficacy of early intervention, and assessment is an important part of those efforts. Special education teachers as well as speech-language pathologists and developmental psychologists all have an interest in the accurate, reliable, and early detection of developmental delays.

Researchers in the United States and other countries have contributed to a virtual explosion of psychological research on the human neonate. A good portion of this research has been directed toward accurately determining developmental potential based on observations of infant and child performance.

Whereas in the first half of the twentieth century the infant was considered a helpless, passive receptor, shaped primarily by environmental forces, the current view affords the infant the ability to perform as a competent organism, skilled, selective, socially influential, and actively interacting with and making demands upon its environment. This view drastically changes the concept of child development and has salient implications for those interested in the assessment of developmental performance.

As pointed out previously, in any area of study description usually precedes explanation. This is particularly true in the area of infant development. It is precisely upon these early observations of normal infant performance that infant assessment is based. How can one know what is abnormal apart from a complete familiarity with normal and maturationally appropriate behaviors? The two are inextricably linked. The relationships between high-risk history and developmental delay as pointed out in Chapter 3 was based on close observation of populations of high-risk infants at various ages. What formed the basis of these observations? Clearly, a thorough knowledge of normal development was applied in these studies, and accurate assesment was performed to determine whether the developmental status of these populations was appropriate or not.

Chapter 5 is structured to alert professionals to a wide range of issues related to infant assessment. Both pretest and actual test administration are covered. A philosophy of test administration as well as interpretation and communication of results are presented. Practical issues such as how to recognize infants in need of assessment, when to initiate testing, and how frequently to test are addressed. Additional topics include possible settings in which assessment may take place, who should perform the assessment, the predictive ability of tests of infant development, correcting for prematurity, and the significance of catch-up growth. Material of this nature should prove useful to those practitioners currently involved in or anticipating involvement in assessment activity.

THE NEED FOR EARLY ASSSESSMENT

Perhaps the best manner in which to underscore the importance of infant asessment is to point out the wide applications of assessment data for an increasing array of professionals. Those who are concerned with early intervention and teaching of young handicapped children are bombarded by conflicting messages. The growing national emphasis on early identification, screening, diagnosis, and treatment emphasizes the need for more intense and specific diagnostic or assessment procedures at earlier and earlier ages. Investigators are trying to define the variables in each of the developmental areas that will reliably identify those children who need intervention in the early weeks and months of life. Comprehensive early screening systems and automated computer analysis are allowing for more systematic and accurate detection of developmental delay. The results of these assessment endeavors are of interest to researchers, who are striving to better understand the sequelae of various neonatal complications and aberrations in intrauterine development; to practitioners, who are interested in reliable and valid determination of developmental status for follow-up and early intervention; to physicians, who must make difficult decisions relative to patient care; and to state and federal legislators, who are charged with the responsibility of writing statutes to govern the provision of services to the handicapped population. When the issue of infant assessment is viewed along these lines its importance is clearly established.

For the clinician-educator perhaps the greatest need for reliable assessment lies in the necessary interactions with parents. In many instances the practitioner has the responsibility of communicating with parents about the developmental performance of their child. In that sense the practitioner serves as a liaison between the physician, who may not be intimately concerned with developmental skill acquisition but rather with physical health, and the parents who are quite concerned with the developmental progress their child is making. As indicated previously, parents face severe stress and anxiety at the birth of their sick baby. If the baby survives, their attention naturally turns toward how well the child is doing relative to children of similar age. Questions of this nature cannot be answered apart from an ability on the part of many professionals to reliably and accurately determine developmental status at any given point in time.

In the midst of this vigorous effort to refine and apply to a wide range of professionals diagnostic and assessment data in all developmental areas, there appears to be a large effort away from the use of norm referenced (standardized) measures of development and toward developmental checklists of observable behavior. An example of an instrument that combines a norm referenced standardized approach as well as an observational checklist format is the Bayley Scale of Infant Development. An increasing number of practitioners are advocating the use of functional analyses of young childrens' behavior as a more valid basis for intervention (instructional programming) than test data collected through the use of standardized assessment tools. As a result clinician-educators have available to them an increasing array of developmental scales covering all aspects of development. Those intimately involved in assessment find themselves looking for help in determining the best approach toward the whole issue.

An additional value of infant assessment lies in the availability of assessment results to those designing and implementing early intervention programs. There is a direct link between early identification and early intervention. In fact, in one sense early identification is a needless activity unless sufficient resources exist to implement strategies designed to remediate delays detected at an early age. The magnitude of developmental disorders in the United States alone is staggering. Six percent or more of all persons suffer from developmental disorders that are manifest at birth or in early life. These range from severe to mild, from curable through remediable, to untreatable or even lethal. This applies to 12 to 15 million persons. Although these figures represent a broader spectrum of etiological factors than high-risk history alone, they serve to amplify the importance of early detection (Dinno, 1977).

Other benefits of early diagnosis and detection of developmental delay for the high-risk population exist. It improves the outcome for children and families by preventing secondary understimulation or excessive pressure to perform, and it allows for the utilization of existing strengths in the child, the family, and the community. It also alerts a broad spectrum of professionals to the presence and unique needs of high-risk children. Most of all it affords the infant the opportunity to develop to its maximal potential.

A PHILOSOPHY OF INFANT ASSESSMENT

The concept of infant assessment is predicated on the notion that children develop more or less according to a relatively predictable pattern in a relatively set manner. That is not to say that variations in this pattern are not present. Rather, the underlying philosophy is that a series of skills must be mastered by a child before new and more difficult skills can be learned. Thus, a developmental sequence, leading toward skill mastery, is set in motion even before birth.

Tens of thousands of infants each year face life-threatening events during the first days and weeks of life. Although advances in medical care have enhanced survival rates for these children, there has been an accompanying increase in the numbers of surviving infants at risk for a host of sequelae. Even with the research advances of the past 10 to 20 years the ability to precisely determine which factors will predict developmental outcome for these infants does not exist. Although much is currently known about normal infant development, little is understood about the process of aberrant development other than the fact that it differs from the norm. Another factor that in part contributes to a limited understanding of abnormal development is the homogeneity of classification applied to developmental problems. The term most frequently applied to infants when a question arises relative to skill learning is *developmentally delayed.* The use of terms other than developmentally delayed may be more appropriate for certain categories of children.

Murphy, Nichter, and Liden (1982) have proposed three categories of aberrant development in infants. These categories may serve to influence the manner in which the practitioner interprets infant assessment results.

1. Aberrant rate of development: This may include a delayed rate of acquisition in a particular skill area such as cognitive or motor learning and functioning. For example, preterm infants may show a

delayed rate of acquisition for motor or cognitive skills. Skill acquisition is taking place in the expected sequence; however, the ages at which specific skills are learned is later than would normally be expected. The developmental delay may be global or may be related to specific skill areas. The child may also display different rates of development at different time spans. Thus, spurts of development are observed that may be followed by periods in which little additional progress is observed.

2. Developmental disorder: This term applies when a developing skill is currently operating inefficiently or maladaptively. A child who displays motor performance that is uncharacteristic for a particular age may have a motor development disorder. The same may hold true for an infant whose visual skills show less than appropriate development. This child may learn certain strategies to help compensate for the disorder.

3. Developmental deficit: This would include functions that are relatively static and upon which experience and maturation will have little impact (blindness and hearing loss are examples of developmental deficits).

The use of such categories makes it possible to view inter- and intra-individual differences in the quality of skill development rather than focusing solely on narrower parameters of performance such as mental age. These concepts have a direct bearing on infant assessment and play an important role in the manner in which the practitioner chooses to view the product of assessment.

The practitioner who is involved in infant assessment has important choices available about the way in which assessment results will be reviewed. Remember, physicians, other health professionals, and, more importantly, parents want to know about the developmental status of a particular child. Everyone wants answers, but answers are difficult to provide in an area in which so little is understood.

The best possible way in which the practitioner can view assessment results is as an indicator of the child's performance on the day the testing was performed, not as an indicator of future potential for developmental skill acquisition. Oftentimes the word diagnosis is applied to infant assessment. The use of this word is best left in the medical model because a medical diagnosis leads to definitive statements about etiology, clinical symptomatology, treatment, and prognosis. Educational or psychological testing provides little or no information about etiology, some but not much about clinical symptomatology, and absolutely none about prognosis. A single testing can be viewed as only a glimpse into child behavior on a particular day and under a particular set of circumstances. A single testing permits some decisions about the presence or absence of some clinical conditions, but the younger the child the less reliable even these observations are. As a means of amplifying this point a review of data on the predictive ability of tests of infant development should serve to alert the practitioner to the limitations inherent in placing too much emphasis on a single test administration.

THE PREDICTIVE ABILITY OF TESTS OF INFANT DEVELOPMENT

Knowledge of infant development and existing technology for studying infant behavior have matured to the point where a fresh look can be taken at past and present procedures for assessing infant performance. Taking a fresh look is by no means an easy task. The usefulness of infant tests as predictors of subsequent development has been the subject of vigorous debate, ranging from assertions of the tests' uselessness to cautious optimism concerning their value. Thus, there is still disagreement as to whether developmental tests in infancy have predictive value.

A review of existing literature on the predictive ability of tests of infant development for healthy infants reveals that available tests have not fared well. The expectation that infant tests would be predictive of subsequent behavior stems from the hypothesis that there are continuities in mental development. The expectation that there are relationships between cognitive abilities allows for the supposition that measuring cognitive functions at one point in time should be closely related to measuring similar functions at other points in time. Although present knowledge of normal infant development does support the presence of a developmental sequence that leads to increased skill mastery, knowledge of the relationship between certain aspects of skill learning and other developmental performance areas is still limited. Thus, it is possible that a child at a young age will display a delay in a particular area that may have only minimal impact on other parameters of development. Delays noted in specific areas are generally detected through the child's failure to perform adequately on test items assumed to be reliable measures of skill performance for that particular area. Zelazo, Zelazo, and Kolb (1972) have pointed out that there are at least three major considerations that are important for the practitioner to keep in mind relative to specific skill areas on assessment tools. First, it appears that brain damage can be extensive and severe without necessarily impairing cognitive ability. Second, environmental factors are often more destructive of intellectual development than are neurological insults per se. And third, a complete understanding of the significance of specific test items is not available. Thus, the items the examiners have placed so much emphasis on relative to determining developmental adequacy in a particular developmental domain may not fully reflect actual skill mastery. A review of specific items on currently available infant assessment tests reflects basically three main categories: measures of gross and fine motor performance, usually measures of imitative behavior that necessitates an intact fine and gross motor capacity, and meaures of both receptive and expressive language ability.

To fully appreciate the problems inherent in attempting to predict later IQ on the basis of tests given during infancy, a discussion of predictive correlations arrived at by various investigators is helpful. Predictions from infancy to later IQ tests are not high. McCall, Hogarty, and Hurlburt (1972) presented data that reveal a linear effect between later IQ and the age at which the infant test was administered. The later in infancy the test was given, the higher the prediction to childhood IQ. Thus, the shorter the developmental period spanned, the higher the correlation. Data of this nature were derived from populations of normal healthy infants.

Siegel (1981) undertook a study to determine if infant test scores were predictive of subsequent cognitive and language development, to determine if infant tests could be used to detect infants at risk for subsequent developmental problems, and to assess the effects of the quality of the environment in which the infant was developing on subsequent developmental performance. The results indicated that although correlations between infant test scores and later development were statistically significant, the infant tests accounted for only 50 percent of the variance at best. The infant tests used were the Bayley Scale of Infant Development and the Uzgiris-Hunt scale of infant performance. These tests were administered to 68 full-term and 80 preterm (birth weight less than 1,500 g) infants at 4, 8, 12, and 18 months of age. In addition the Caldwell Inventory of Home Stimulation (HOME) was used to measure the effect of home environment on later developmental performance. Siegal pointed out that other factors are obviously needed when attempting to predict developmental outcome. Infants who were performing in the risk range early in development but whose subsequent development at two years was normal came from more stimulating home environments as determined by the HOME scale. Thus, the quality of the home may have played a paramount role in overcoming poor performance early in infancy. In addition, infants who were not detected as being at risk early in development but who showed some developmental delay at 2 years of age tended to come from homes that provided less stimulation. It is apparent from these results that, when combined with careful measures of the environment, infant tests are somewhat better predictors of cognitive and language development. Predictive value would therefore appear to be strengthened by data on the type and degree of stimulation afforded a child in the home environment (Hunt, 1976; Hunt and Bayley, 1971).

Although the worth of infant assessment continues to be debated, traditional measures have been of some value. Clinical observations have indicated that appropriate performance in motor and language skills on traditional tests of infant development do indeed reflect, to various degrees, age-appropriate cognitive development. The problem, in part, is that inappropriate performance need not be indicative of delayed or impaired intelligence. The full nature of the relationship between delayed motor functioning and cognitive development is not as yet fully understood. What are the consequences of labeling a cognitively intact 20-month-old child as developmentally delayed or retarded simply because the child does not walk alone, lacks speech, fails to comply with the examiner's demands, or shows a combination of these? The evidence indicates that labels influence expectations, often with damaging results (Hobbs, 1975).

The previous discussion on the predictive ability of tests of infant development indicated that attempts to make predictive statements about developmental performance can be made only in the light of multiple assessment opportunities. The use of regular observations over time, regardless of the assessment tool used, has a number of distinct advantages, including the following (Murphy et al., 1982):

1. The ability to measure developmental patterns and rates of development
2. Aid in making decisions about intervention
3. Aid in monitoring the progress of interventions
4. The ability to recognize new problems as the child grows older

Regular reevaluation of developmental performance is of utmost importance to those involved in early intervention programming. Decisions about the need for early intervention and judgments concerning the effectiveness of intervention efforts for a particular child are in large measure dependent upon regular and reliable reevaluation of child performance.

As previously stated, an important concept is that changes in development occur with time. Thus, it is important to monitor the infant's development with serial observations. Determining if the infant is progressing steadily in all areas of functioning or if some areas are beginning to show delay or dysfunction can be accomplished only through repeated observations. For infants and the families of infants who are at mild risk good serial observations entail routine developmental evaluations. For infants at higher risk a more comprehensive schedule of evaluations may be indicated. A further discussion on the intervals between assessments is presented later in this chapter.

Perhaps Kagan (1971) has suggested the best possible way in which the results of infant assessment tests, either traditional or descriptive, should be viewed. He indicated that each of the infant's responses—smiling, vocalizing, looking time, heart rate increases and decreases, and any other behaviors called for in infant assessment tools—are analogous to windows on a house. Each window gives the viewer a different glimpse of the contents of the house. To provide a coherent and complete picture of the interior of the house, it is necessary to gain as many points of view as possible. In many ways past attempts at infant assessment have not recognized the need to repeatedly glimpse the interior of the child. McCarthy (1980) listed a series of considerations that should be kept in mind by any professional concerned with assessment and the predictive ability of tests administered in infancy. These are listed here in modified form:

1. In a testing situation the examiner is able to elicit a limited sample of the child's behavior at best. If the examiner cannot feel reasonably confident about the sample elicited, it should not be quantified or labeled but simply described. This is similar to a developmental checklist approach toward assessment.
2. The younger the child the less reliable predictions will be across the dimensions measured.
3. Traditional labels should be used with caution because a young child's IQ and response to stimuli are quite unstable. A term such as developmentally delayed, in a particular area, is preferable.
4. Time, spontaneous recovery of function, and maturation are on the side of the young child and may make liars out of the best of assessment tools.
5. Data from all sources relative to child behaviors should be treated with respect.

In summary, prediction of later developmental performance based on early assessment results is less than foolproof. A multitude of variables influence performance and these cannot possibly be taken into account by a single test instrument. Of necessity, the results of assessment tests must be viewed as only a small glimpse into the performance of the child. The ability to predict later developmental performance increases only in the presence of regular follow-up opportunities. Schedules for follow-up and strategies to employ are discussed later in this chapter.

GENERAL TEST CONSIDERATIONS

The practitioner must make a number of choices relative to various general and specific aspects of the actual process of infant assessment. Some of these decisions are dictated by the setting in which the assessment is conducted and how the results will be used. Other decisions are related to the particular set of circumstances surrounding each child to be assessed. Each of these areas is discussed in the material that follows.

Recipients of Infant Assessment

The basic rationale for identifying the infant who is at risk or handicapped is to make intervention programs available so that the child's condition does not interfere with normal developmental progress. Other reasons for identifying at-risk infants exist also. These include the need to gather research data, the need to measure developmental progress that takes place as a result of intervention efforts, and the need to determine the effectiveness of various approaches to stimulation efforts. Identification is, however, most useful when it results in intervention programs designed to remediate impending developmental delay. One of the major goals of identification of delayed infants is to direct them to needed early intervention services. With this in mind it becomes imperative that the practitioner be aware of those infants in need of assessment, the purpose of assessment, and potential sources for referral for assessment efforts.

Scott and Hogan (1982) indicated that the identification of handicapped infants may be thought of as presenting three main classes of problems: identifying clear disabilities; identifying hidden handicaps; and identifying high-risk situations. Each of these categories gives some clue as to which infants the practitioner should be concerned with relative to the need for early and systematic assessment.

Infants with gross perceptual or physical disorders are easily identified by any competent physician or practitioner. A large portion of these children will in all probability be identified by the neonatologist in the first few days of life. An infant not identified prior to hospital discharge will be identified by parents and other persons interacting with the infant, usually before the child is 1 year of age.

The other category of infants who should be recipients of regular and systematic follow-up assessment are those who are suspected of manifesting delayed or aberrant development due to a host of prenatal, neonatal, or postnatal factors. These children encompass the category of high-risk infants described in Chapter 1.

Risk factors and percentage of risk for infants at specific birth weight categories when accompanied by several possible neonatal complications are presented in Table 5–1. As may be observed, from 10 to 75 percent of all high-risk infants may be suspect for displaying neurological or cognitive sequelae or both. The sequelae that may be present in later childhood include specific cognitive deficits, specific academic difficulties, behavioral problems, and speech and language deficits. Chapter 3 presents a complete coverage of the deficits possible in cohorts of high-risk infants. The percentages listed by Fitzhardinge (1982) may not reflect all of the children who will display more subtle deficits traceable to factors in the neonatal period. The underlying concept behind the need for early assessment is that certain characteristics and events, such as those surrounding the neonatal period, are precursors of subsequent problems, not in all but in many cases. This concept is substantiated by the results of follow-up studies that have shown both long- and short-term sequelae related to high-risk status. The ideal situation, therefore, is one in which all high-risk infants are recipients of regular follow-up geared toward early identification and intervention if so indicated.

Potential Sources of Referral

The practitioner's sources of referral of infants for assessment will vary, depending upon the setting in which the practitioner is employed. In most instances setting dictates to a large degree referral avenues. However, several broad categories can be described that may account for most, if not all, of the practitioner's assessment efforts.

Primary health care referrals are made up of those that result from the direct input of health care professionals. This mode of referral has traditionally been the major method of identifying high-risk infants. Primary health care professionals may be neonatologists, pediatricians, or general medical practitioners. Because of recent advances in state and federal legislations relative to the provision of special services for young children (less than 3 years of age), many medical practitioners are not aware of the availability of such services. The clinician-educator therefore can be a valuable resource for informing health care professionals of the availability of evaluative and intervention services for high-risk infants. The practitioner employed in a medical setting may have ready access to the NICU for assessment activity. If this is not the case, it is possible to cultivate professional relationships with health care professionals that are geared toward initiating more systematic follow-up of the survivors of the NICU. Chapter 7 presents information on helpful strategies for expanding the referral base and for informing primary health care professionals about service delivery systems for high-risk infants.

Table 5-1.   Risk Factors for Major Neurological and/or Cognitive Sequelae

Birth Weight	Category	% Risk Factor
>2500 g	All admissions	<5
	RDS	5
	Post-asphyxia seizure	30-50
	Meningitis	30-50
1501-2500 g	All admissions	10
	SGA	<10
	RDS	<10
	BPD	20-30
	Post asphyxia seizure	30-50
	Meningitis	30-50
<1500 g	All admissions	10-30
	AGA, nonventilated	10-15
	AGA, ventilated	30-40
	SGA	30-50
	Seizures, decerbrate posture	75-80

RDS—respiratory distress syndrome
BPD—bronchopulminary dysplasia
AGA—appropriate weight for gestational age
SGA—small for gestational age
Note: From *Neonatology, Pathophysiology and Management of the Newborn* (p. 353) by G. Avery (Ed.), 1981. Philadelphia: J. B. Lippincott. Reprinted by permission.

A second source of referrals for the practitioner may be those originating from social service programs. Most communities provide several social service avenues of support for families with special needs. These agencies may be in contact with high-risk mothers prior to delivery. They may be aware of historical information on childbirth or parenting skills that result in an environment that will not afford maximal development opportunity to a particular child. In many instances social service agencies are able to make home visits and determine firsthand if a child is in need of evaluative or remedial intervention. These community service personnel are a significant resource for identifying infants who may be developmentally delayed or in an environment that places them at high social risk of neglect or outright abuse.

By far the most effective method of identifying young children at risk for delay and in need of assessment is through community referral. Referrals of this nature are greatly enhanced through efforts directed toward public education via the media, advertising, direct mail, and so forth. This method of referral produces contacts with the parents of the children at risk.

Although the sources of referrals mentioned are not exhaustive, they do constitute the major avenues by which the practitioner will gain initial contact with the families of high-risk infants and, for that matter, infants for whom developmental adequacy is in question. As the practitioner becomes more adept and skilled in infant assessment, the benefit and availability of such services will become known by a broad spectrum of persons who are in a position to refer a particular child for needed services.

Initiation of Assessment Efforts

Once the practitioner has determined those infants who are in need of systematic follow-up and referral avenues are established, the question arises as to when to initiate serial observations and what schedule to follow for subsequent evaluations. There is no clear-cut formula for when to initiate assessment and how often a child should be seen for reassessment. The employment setting the practitioner is functioning in, the source of the initial referral, parental willingness and resources to participate in follow-up, the individual characteristics of the child in relationship to present performance and medical history, the test instruments to be used, the need for support personnel, and other factors will, in part, be the determinants of when to start testing and how often to test. As has been indicated, the decision of when initial testing should be performed will depend in large measure upon employment setting. The practitioner employed in a hospital setting may have the opportunity to evaluate and talk to the parents of the high-risk infant prior to hospital discharge. This is an ideal situation. Although formal evaluation may be more difficult and possibly less reliable while the baby is in NICU, observations of this nature can prove quite valuable as subsequent evaluations are undertaken. The unique value of assessment while the baby is in the NICU, as well as potential problems, are discussed later in this chapter.

If the source of the referral for infant assessment is outside the hospital setting, the actual date on which initial assessment is performed may be delayed until a deficit is suspected by parents and others who interact with the baby. The probability of routine assessment for all high-risk infants is diminished if support for it does not originate with the neonatologist and family pediatrician. There are distinct benefits to early detection and intervention. These include an earlier start for following developmental skill mastery, earlier opportunity to provide parents with helpful data on activities to be performed in the home, and an earlier start for the actual provision of intervention services. Thus, testing, or at least intensive observation, should begin in the nursery or shortly after hospital discharge.

Parental willingness to participate in systematic follow-up evaluations must of necessity be considered when determining when to initiate and how frequently to perform serial observations of infant developmental status. Parents are usually most receptive to follow-up efforts if they are informed of the value of these efforts from a preventative standpoint. Parental concerns such as time involvement, cost, and other adjustments are more easily dealt with if the parents understand the need and value of assessment and follow-up. It is relatively simple to explain to parents that their baby has had a precarious neonatal period. They are quite aware of this. It is also relatively simple to further explain that experience has indicated that infants who have had neonatal histories similar to their baby tend to display a greater frequency of developmental delays. If the parents understand that the practitioner is interested in insuring optimal development for their child, and that early and regular assessment is an integral part of the process, they will more than likely be quite supportive of regular evaluation appointments.

Individual child characteristics will also play an important role in determining when to initiate follow-up. For the child who has been through a particularly difficult neonatal course, the need for initiating follow-up as soon as possible is much stronger. Table 5–1 can be used as a general guide in determining the importance of early assessment based on particular childhood characteristics. If the practitioner is aware that a child is being discharged to a home environment that is less than optimal, even in the absence of severe neonatal complications, early assessment may be desirable. It is quite important that the practitioner be appraised of the neonatal history, as well as potential sequelae based on known risk factors, in order to make accurate decisions on initiating assessment activity.

The need for support personnel as well as the actual content of follow-up visits will also play a part in determining when to initiate serial observations. If the practitioner wishes to perform a complete evaluative work-up of a child, and if the evaluation is part of a comprehensive neonatal follow-up program that involves a variety of other professionals, the start of formal assessment procedures may be delayed until the infant has been in the home setting for 1 to 3 months. This allows the parents the opportunity to familiarize themselves with their baby and to make observations on infant behaviors that will be an important part of later assessment data. This is not to say that there is no contact with professional staff before this time. The baby will have been seen by the pediatrician at least once prior to a follow-up visit, and the pediatrician is in a good position to determine the overall status and to initiate an earlier referral to the assessment process if needed. Other referral sources will, in large measure, determine when assessment efforts will begin.

In all probability community and social service referrals will be made as the child gets older and the potential for developmental delay is suspected. The overriding concern is that the assessment process begin at as early an age as possible, taking into consideration all the individual variables that will be present in each child, each referral source, each follow-up strategy, and each employment or assessment setting.

Assessment Intervals

The question of how often a particular child should be seen for developmental follow-up is not an easy one to answer. No set formula for frequency of visits exists. However, a number of variables such as those mentioned in the previous section are important to consider. Several additional variables are discussed in the following.

The age of initial referral in combination with the child's performance on assessment tests is one useful way in which to determine the frequency of follow-up visits. It must be kept in mind that the younger the child the greater the potential for change from evaluation to evaluation. Thus, if a child is evaluated before dismissal from the hospital and, based on behavioral observations is felt to be at risk for developmental delay, the frequency of visits may be increased to perhaps every 3 months. If the child at the initial observation is felt to display age-appropriate behavior, contact with the parents may be maintained, but formal reevaluation may be delayed until the infant is 6 months of age. If at any time the practitioner detects behavior that suggests delayed development, assessment every 3 months is a schedule to work toward. Three-month intervals for those infants for whom a delay is suspected appears to be optimal. This allows the parents ample time to implement home stimulation activities as suggested by the practitioner and allows the infant sufficient time to benefit from these activities.

The infant's neonatal history may also dictate the frequency of follow-up evaluations. For those infants who have serious neonatal complications with known relationships to later neurological and cognitive sequelae, more frequent evaluations are recommended. A schedule of reassessment every 3 months for the first year of life would appear to be most appropriate in these instances. Based on the child's status throughout the first year, the schedule can be readily altered. For family situations in which the availability of environmental stimulation is less than optimal, more frequent evaluations (every 30 days) may be needed. This serves to accurately monitor the infant's developmental progress and provides an opportunity for parents to receive valuable instruction on caring for their baby.

After the child is 1 year of age, the schedule of visits may be altered. For the child who appears to be displaying appropriate developmental progress evaluations may take place every 6 to 12 months, depending on the individual needs and growth of the child. For those children enrolled in an early intervention program, benefit is derived from reassessing developmental status every 6 months, up to 3 years of age. If accurate descriptions of developmental status and potential are to be made for the high-risk infant, regular, systematic, and detailed observations of child performance starting at an early age are essential. In the absence of systematic assessment of this nature, developmental delay cannot be detected, early intervention cannot be initiated, and optimal skill acquisition may not be achieved by infants who have survived a difficult neonatal period.

Personnel Involved in Assessment

There are many similarities in skills and interests among professionals with expertise in child development. The question then arises as to which professionals should be contacted to perform infant assessment. For example, if a child appears to be displaying delayed development in motor skills, should the child be seen immediately by the pediatrician, the developmental psychologist, the physical or developmental therapist, or the early childhood educator? How do we decide which professionals should be consulted? The scope of most developmental disabilities goes beyond the expertise of any one profession. The professional who works alone is at a disadvantage because of what may be called tunnel vision, that is, the child may be viewed from a narrow professional framework that reflects the academic background of the person involved in assessment.

The ideal situation is one in which the practitioner is part of a comprehensive team effort that includes input from a variety of professions. Of course the availability of input from various disciplines depends on the setting in which the child is seen. In a hospital or public education setting the probability is high that a team concept of assessment is in operation. The exact composition of the team in a specific setting may vary considerably. A comprehensive child development-assessment team may include developmental pediatricians, pediatric neurologists, developmental psychologists, child psychiatrists, social workers, physical therapists, occupational therapists, speech-language pathologists, special educators, and child development specialists. Any effort to assess both physical or organic and environmental or functional aspects of child development and developmental deviations will require at one time or another the expertise of those professionals. Holm

(1978) indicated that the strength of assessment teams lies in their broad coverage and comprehensiveness. The professionals involved have the unique opportunity to associate with persons with similar interests but with different tools of the trade. This model allows for exchange of ideas and a chance to sharpen professional skills. Although the potential for role conflict is enhanced when a variety of professions are involved, the benefits of a team approach to assessment are more than enough to compensate.

The professionals on the team can turn the apparent overlap of skills and expertise into an advantage by sharing professional responsibilities in one of two ways: either a multidisciplinary or an interdisciplinary mode of service delivery. In the multidisciplinary mode the team members work side by side. Each profession is concerned with its own area of expertise. Once assessment is completed a systematic review of all results is made and combined into a single format for reporting purposes. If the need arises, additional professionals may become part of the assessment process. On the other hand, the interdisciplinary team shares expertise. On teams of this nature the role definition (who does what) is decided on the basis of each child and family. Such teamwork requires mutual trust and respect for professional competency: Those involved trust that persons in other disciplines are not just knowledgeable in their own fields, but that they are also aware of their limitations. They rely upon each other to build on and compliment the skills and expertise of the entire team.

In a study designed to examine the correlation between neonatal factors and later developmental performance, Rossetti (1984) found it helpful to have at least two members on the assessment team: a neonatologist and a speech-language pathologist. The neonatologist performed a general physcial and neurological evaluation, and the speech-language pathologist administered the Bayley Scale of Infant Development. Both were involved in gathering information from the parents and in providing home intervention guidelines. In addition to the physical and neurological screening the neonatologist also administered the Knobloch Developmental Scale. One way in which to determine the reliability of a team made up of two members would be to examine the correlation between the developmental scores obtained by each professional. In the Rossetti study the correlation between the Knobloch and Bayley scores was .87. This indicates the degree to which team members were in agreement about the infant behavior they were evaluating and observing.

The answer to the question of who should gather infant assessment data is simple. Any one of a number of professionals with expertise in child development and behavior are capable. The exact professionals involved depend on the setting, the model, the child, and the test instruments used.

Possible Settings for Assessment Activity

In considering where actual infant assessment procedures should be conducted the choice is relatively limited. There are basically three choices available (with minor variations), and each has its strengths and weaknesses.

In the Hospital Prior to Discharge

As mentioned previously there is great value in affording the assessment team the opportunity to observe and evaluate a particular infant prior to hospital discharge. Even though the results of an assessment at this early date provide only a single glance into the child's behavioral competence, the data obtained can provide valuable baseline descriptors that can be compared with later performance. Inpatient evaluations or observations can be performed just prior to discharge, or observations can be made over time while the baby is in NICU. The administration of formal test measures in the NICU is, in most instances, not possible because of the nature of the environment. As the condition of the baby improves, however, and it demonstrates greater awareness of its surroundings, in particular when it begins to respond to others in its environment, the time may be ripe for detailed observations of behavioral competence. The parents can and should be a part of any evaluations or observations conducted while the child is in the NICU. Assessment and monitoring of the infant's state is a very important part of the total evaluation process. In fact, all observations or judgments on infant behaviors must be made in light of the state an infant is in at any particular time. A more complete discussion and description of the importantce of infant states is presented later in this chapter.

Any efforts to observe behavior and evaluate performance while the baby is in the NICU must be made in light of what is known about the impact of that environment on the baby. The amount of visual, auditory, and tactile stimulation to which the infant is exposed while in the NICU is at a high level. Healthy full-term as well as preterm infants have been shown to display neurological habituation when bombarded with sensory stimulation. For example, when a bright light is flashed into a neonate's eyes, constriction of the pupils is not the only result. In addition, the neonate blinks, contracts the eyelids and whole face, and withdraws the head by arching the whole body, often setting off a complete startle as withdrawal occurs. Repeated stimulation of this nature induces diminished responses because of the infant's capacity to shut down these responses. Brazelton (1962) subjected a group of infants to 20 bright light stimuli at 1 minute intervals. By the tenth stimulus, the subjects had decreased not only their observable motor responses but also their cardiac and respiratory responses. By the fifteenth stimulus electroencephalographic results reflected the induction of a quiet, unresponsive behavioral state. Thus, the infant's capacity to shut out disturbing visual stimuli provides protection from having to respond to visual stimulation and at the same time frees energy to meet physiological demands. This capacity of the neonate has been considered a kind of neurological habituation and is present in neonates with intact central nervous systems. This capacity is present, although somewhat decreased, in premature infants.

Another important factor to consider, if observations are conducted in the NICU, has to do with the impact of normal nursery routine. Porter and Marshall (1985) have examined the physiological results of certain hospital procedures on newborn infants both in the NICU and the normal nursery. In 1984 they began investigating the physiological results of certain bedside procedures on infants in the NICU. They discovered that babies have between 50 and 130 daily bedside intrusions. Although some are quite painless (like changing a diaper or taking a temperature) others are not. Blood transfusions, spinal taps, and even the insertion of a chest tube are all bedside procedures that many of the babies must endure, often without anesthetic. The researchers monitored the babies' heart rates, respiration rates, blood pressures, and levels of oxygen and carbon dioxide in the blood. All of the monitoring procedures were noninvasive, with readings taken from the skin's surface. A summary of the results revealed that none of the monitored physiological characteristics returned to base line within 10 to 20 minutes of the procedures. Thus, babies in the NICU appear to be significantly disturbed by these bedside procedures; and their performance on neurobehavioral assessment measures is affected negatively.

In a practical way, it is important for the practitioner to realize that any newborn baby in a brightly lighted, noisy nursery who is subjected to multiple bedside procedures, some quite invasive in nature, is not likely to display behavior that appropriately reflects behavioral competence. If assessments are to be reliable, inpatient evaluations must be conducted in an environment that is more conducive to obtaining valid indices of behavioral competence. It may be possible for the mother to care for the infant for a day or two in a regular hospital room before discharge, thus reducing the effects of the excessive stimulation present in the NICU. At the very least the infant can be moved to a vacant hospital room for several hours prior to testing.

Outpatient Settings

There are several possible choices for the setting for follow-up assessments based on an outpatient model. Follow-up efforts may be conducted in the hospital as part of a regular follow-up program; in a physician's office as part of normal routine well-baby appointments; in a child center designed for both assessment and intervention; in a university setting, possibly as part of ongoing research efforts; through public school programs in those states mandating the provision of services to children from birth; or in any other setting in which the practitioner is employed. The previous discussion on the value of a team approach is important as outpatient avenues of assessment are considered. The goal in follow-up efforts of this nature is to have the opportunity to observe, over time, the behavioral competence of high-risk infants. If the child is already involved in intervention efforts, either center- or home-based, all persons interacting with the family may provide valuable insight on developmental status and progress. The composition of the assessment team in an outpatient model is quite variable from setting to setting and may vary because of the child's age, suspected areas of deficit, and additional concerns relative to family and medical status. It is most helpful if at least one member of the team is either the neonatologist (especially helpful during early assessment, birth to 6 months) or a pediatrician familiar with normal early developmental skill acquisition and its relationship to later skill mastery and school performance. Over time the practitioner, regardless of specific primary discipline, will develop a more global understanding of all aspects of child development and be able, in conjunction with the physician, to provide reliable and accurate serial observations and assessments of skill status. No definitive statements can be made about the best setting for outpatient follow-up efforts. The practitioner, based on employment setting and team composition, is in the best position to decide the best avenue of outpatient follow-up.

In-Home Testing

A substantial number of practitioners may have the opportunity to make home visits in an effort to monitor developmental performance. There are both benefits and liabilities to home visits. One major benefit lies in the fact that the practitioner is able to observe the child in its natural setting. A more realistic setting is thus presented in which to view infant behaviors. Evaluations in the home setting also may be more relaxing for the parents, thus allowing them to be more accurate and detailed in providing data and in asking pertinent questions. A more realistic pattern of mother-infant interactions is present for observation as well. The home setting may also be the best one in which to provide instruction about parent-conducted infant stimulation efforts. Specific intervention strategies as well as a demonstration of these techniques may be more plausible and of greater benefit if conducted in the home. A major benefit that can be attributed to home visits for follow-up purposes is the opportunity it affords the pracititioner for observation of the home environment. As may be recalled, follow-up studies of high-risk infants have revealed that the quality of the home and the potential for environmental stimulation are as important in many instances as the high-risk history in relationship to developmental progress. Valuable insight can be gained by the practitioner who has the opportunity to observe in the home the degree to which the child's needs for stimulation are being met. Throughout normal caretaking routine the child is processing auditory, visual, and tactile stimuli—not to mention other sources of stimulation. These are valuable sources of stimulation for the baby, and testing in the home affords the practitioner the opportunity to observe these events in a natural setting. The home setting, therefore, provides a valuable opportunity for the practitioner to view firsthand the quality of the environment available to the high-risk infant.

A liability inherent in the home setting is the limited number of professionals able to make home visits. The probability of a follow-up program in which several team members visit the home for evaluation purposes is small. In situations such as this it is imperative that the individual conducting the visit have a broad understanding of normal child development as well as specific expertise with high-risk infants so that proper referrals to other professionals can be made when indicated. A key concept for the home visitor who works alone is to be aware of one's limitations and be ready to make appropriate referrals to other professionals. Failure to do so may increase the probability of missing a subtle delay in developmental performance, thus inhibiting long-term developmental skill acquisition.

Variations of the three basic settings for follow-up evaluations are possible. In some instances a child may have be seen as part of a team evaluation in addition to being seen in the home setting by a person specifically trained for home visits and parental interviewing.

Considering Data From Other Sources

Regardless of who conducts follow-up evaluations or the setting in which the evaluations are performed, all practitioners involved in follow-up activity must be alert and receptive to information about a child's performance that may emanate from a variety of sources. As the infant gets older, and if infant stimulation is being offered, the professional involved in providing the stimulation can be a valuable source of data when judgments are being made about developmental status. Although data from this source are helpful, by far the most important source is that provided by the parents.

Traditionally, data from all sources are important to the clinician involved in the process of assessment and management. This is true regardless of whether the concern relates to physical ailments or developmental progress. For the practitioner involved in systematic follow-up of high-risk infants parental data are indispensable. Some criticism, however, has been directed toward using data obtained from parents. These assertions have maintained that parents are quite unreliable in their descriptions of their children's development and behavior and that they are more likely to report their fantasies or distortions than realities (Vaughn, Deinard, and Egeland, 1980). The question arises then that if the parents are unable to judge their child's developmental status, who is?

A large body of literature on correlations between subjective judgments of IQ and various groups of professionals does not exist. There are, however, data available on the ability of pediatricians to judge cognitive performance. In several studies designed to compare physicians' subjective estimate of IQ with actual scores, the correlations ranged from .32 to .65. The tendency was to lump all patients into the middle of the distribution curve, cutting off both the upper and lower ends (Coplan, 1982). Despite these kinds of data, only about 25 percent of pediatricians reported that they used any type of formal developmental assessment tool (Shonkoff, Dworkin, and Leviton, 1979). Most pediatricians rely solely on their subjective clinical judgment to determine the preschool child's status, despite evidence that such judgment is frequently in error.

Are parents able to do a better job of estimating the developmental status of their children? The question is broader in nature and in application than might be initially assumed. If it cannot be demonstrated that parents are able to reliably estimate performance and describe behavior, then all data provided to professionals attempting to monitor skill acquisition are called into question. In an attempt to clarify the reliability of data provided by parents, McCormick, Shapiro, and Starfield (1982) examined factors associated with maternal opinions of infant development. Parent interviews and child observations were performed on 4,783 1-year-old children. The majority of infants in the study (87 percent) were considered to be developing normally for age by their mothers. Of those considered to be slow by their mothers, however, nearly 70 percent were found to be within a normal range, based on direct observation of child performance. Thus, although those in the appropriate group considered slow are a small percentage of this group (4.9 percent), they represent the majority of those whose rate of development was thought to be slow by their mothers. (See Table 5–2 for further data on this study.) Maternal opinions of slow development reflected infant health status (birth weight), hospitalization, congenital anomalies, and use of physician services. Social factors found to influence maternal opinions of development included low maternal education and sex of the child. Thus, factors other than actual performance on developmental tasks may heavily influence maternal opinions of developmental adequacy.

An additional study conducted by Coplan (1982) attempted to examine parental estimates of the developmental performance in a high-risk population. In this investigation 46 children (mean age 2 years, 8 months) were referred for developmental assessment. Each child underwent formal testing of language and intellectual development. Each child's mother was then asked to provide a subjective estimate of her child's level of function. The correlation coefficient between maternal estimate and formal test results was found to be .85 (p<.001). This investigation established an important point. For high-risk infants, parental estimates of their child's developmental level can be accurate. This is particularly important because this is the group of children for whom pediatricians' own developmental estimates appear to be the weakest. As a corollary to the study, Coplan reported that parents' descriptions of their children's behavior were usually accurate, even though their interpretations frequently were not. Parents often preferred to perceive their children as stubborn, lazy, or spoiled rather than cognitively delayed.

Studies of this nature reveal that there is some assurance that properly derived parent ratings of development and behavior can be counted on to give a fairly accurate picture of the child. If parental data are detailed and precise, and the parents are of average intelligence, their comments should at the very least be moderately valid in light of the studies cited. Such data should, of course, be supplemented by further interviewing and observations to gain a more complete picture of the child and the setting and interactions. Parental perceptions of development and behavior should not be discarded as worthless; they should be viewed as quite valuable if the parents are asked the right questions.

The practitioner involved in follow-up efforts with high-risk infants must always bear in mind that the results of formal testing are just a glimpse into overall performance. A major avenue of expanding that glimpse into a detailed and prolonged view of skill learning is to pay close attention to data from all sources and, in particular, to data obtained from parents. Later in this chapter the value of a developmental

Table 5-2. Maternal Opinion of Development of Infants by Observed Level of Gross Motor Performance

	Gross Motor Classification*	
	Appropriate	Inappropriate
Total Number of Infants	4,417	366
Infants Considered Normal	3,993	201
Infants Considered Slow	424	165

*Appropriate, observed gross motor activities correspond to a developmental quotient (DQ) of 80 or greater. Inappropriate, observed gross motor activities correspond to a DQ less than 80 on the Bayley Scale of Infant Development.

log is discussed. In conjunction with formal assessment results it can be a highly reliable source of data upon which judgments of developmental adequacy may be based.

SPECIFIC TEST CONSIDERATIONS

Once basic pretest considerations have been evaluated and thought through by the practitioner, a variety of additional concerns surface about actual test administration procedures. These concerns are related to issues such as determination of infant state at the time of testing and its effect on test interpretation, the need to correct for prematurity when reviewing assessment results, the significance and concept of catch-up growth, the need for the evaluator to be an astute observer of behavior, the use of a developmental log to supplement assessment results, and general categories of tests available for follow-up efforts. Each of these issues is discussed in the material that follows.

Determination of Infant State

The practitioner who has any degree of experience in the assessment and measuring of developmental competence for very young children, high-risk or otherwise, can readily attest to the fact that the particular level of consciousness or state an infant is in at any given point has an impact on response patterns during test administration. *Infant state* can be defined as the level of consciousness or alertness and environmental interaction patterns present in an infant at a given point in time. Brazelton (1973) was one of the first to discuss the importance of infant states for the normal healthy newborn. The infant's reactions to stimuli presented during an evaluation therefore must be interpreted within the context of the initial state of consciousness, as reactions may vary markedly as the infant passes from one state to another. State depends on physiological variables such as hunger, nutrition, degree of hydration, and the time within the wake-sleep cycle of the infant. The pattern of states and the movement from one state to another appear to be important characteristics of infants in the neonatal period, and this kind of evaluation may be predictive of the infant's receptivity and ability to respond to stimuli in a cognitive sense (Brazelton, 1973).

In a discussion of infant states presented in The Neonatal Behavioral Assessment Scale (NABS), Brazelton (1973) provided a description of states as they apply to the healthy newborn. Although the infant states presented are specifically important if the NABS is being used for assessment purposes, knowledge of these states is imperative regardless of the test instrument used. The infant's responses to test items may vary, depending on the particular state an infant is in at the time of assessment. The particular characteristics of each state are summarized in Table 5-3.

In a more recent discussion Brazelton (1981) elaborated on the usefulness of state assessments. He indicated that neonatal state observations are used not only to help interpret infant response to test stimuli, but also as an aid to parents. After state observations are made, the parents can be informed of the manner in which their baby responds to external stimuli and can be provided with specific suggestions on caregiving for a fussy or unresponsive baby. For example, in the case of an overresponsive, rapidly upset, intensely motor-reactive neonate, the parents can be informed that the baby may cry for unpredictable reasons and not be consoled as easily as they might like. They may then be provided with suggestions for handling behavior of this nature. Brazelton (1981) went on to state that "in the neonatal period, state behavior can be assessed and used to predict normalcy or developmental delay, and may even predict other difficulties such as apnea and problems in organization that could lead to failure in the parent-child interaction" (p. 336).

The application of the concept of infant state to the high-risk neonate is a more recent development and would appear to have an impact on the early assessment of high-risk infants. Gorski, Davison, and Brazelton (1979) presented an insightful description of the stages of behavioral organization (state) in the high-risk neonate from both a theoretical and clinical standpoint. Basically three stages of behavioral organization were described that will mold the practitioner's view of the infant's interaction with its environment:

1. In Turning or Physiologic Stage: During the usual course of events for the stressed premature infant, normal reciprocal interaction

Table 5-3. Infant States

State	Characteristics
Sleep State	
Deep sleep	Deep sleep with regular breathing no activity, no eye movement
Light sleep	Rapid eye movements, random startle movements, sucking movements off and on
Awake State	
Drowsy, Semidozing	Eyes opened or closed, eyelids fluttering, movements usually smooth, mild startles noted
Alert	Bright looks, focuses attention on objects, motor activity at a minimum
Eyes open	Considerable motor activity, increase in startles, high activity level
Crying	Intense crying, difficult to break through even with novel stimulation

with caregivers, which leads to the establishment of a bond resulting in mutually satisfying interaction is not possible. The high-risk infant must first develop sufficient physical integrity and internal stability before the infant is able to use caregiver support and input needed to make continuing developmental gains. Simply stated, the stressed premature infant is not able to benefit fully from interactions with caregivers during the early period following birth because the infant's energy is directed toward survival and maintaining physiological stability. The practitioner who is afforded the opportunity to visit and observe an infant's performance in the NICU must be aware of both past and present medical status and be willing to interpret behavioral observations in light of the infant's physiological status. The infant during this period is quite sick and cannot pay attention to, much less respond in an appropriate manner to, the type of stimuli to which it is likely to be exposed during the course of the standard developmental assessment. Even the process of observing performance must be undertaken with the implicit understanding that the bulk of the infant's energy is directed inward.

2. Coming Out: The baby has now mastered a minimum capacity to control and maintain physiological systems. The baby must now begin to build upon these basic organizational patterns. This stage represents the first active response to the environment and implies a more active response to outside stimuli, both nutritional and social. This is the period when changes in the caregiver environment have an important impact on the physical well-being and growth of the

high-risk infant. It is at this time that initial attachment to a primary caregiver is established and strengthened. This is a period where the mother's presence can be helpful to both baby and mother as the infant is showing some awareness of the world and those in it. This second level of developmental awareness (stage of organization) is usually experienced while the infant is yet a patient in the NICU. Although this stage represents progress, there is also an inherent special vulnerability related to infant-caregiver interaction. This period spans the time from when the baby is no longer acutely ill and is able to breathe effectively and to absorb enough calories to gain weight, to the time when the baby can be discharged. The parents should be encouraged during this time to assume increasing responsibility for the care of the baby. This is a time when behavioral observations can point to caregiver interventions that can foster the infant's physical as well as social-interactive development. It is at this point that the practitioner with access to the NICU can play a valuable role in instructing parents on the basis of behavioral observations. Any observations of behavioral performance should be made with the knowledge that this is the first time the infant is displaying a greater awareness of its environment and is initially attempting to interact with it.

3.   Reciprocity: This is the ultimate state of environmental opportunity. At this point the infant is strong enough to breathe, feed, and respond to caregiver behaviors in specific and predictable ways. This stage may begin sometime before discharge and continue after the infant is in the home setting. The infant, however, must still face the task of overcoming the remaining handicaps inherent in experiencing a difficult start in life. The developing relationships between parents and infant play a key role in this final phase of early development. If practitioners have an opportunity to assess behavioral competence during this final stage, they must be aware that the infant's ability or inability to interact in a reciprocal manner with its environment may be an important precursor to developmental adequacy at a later date. The infant who is unable to demonstrate initial interest in the environment may be displaying behaviors that are precursors of impending developmental deficits.

In summary, it is apparent that any attempts to evaluate developmental adequacy in the early days or weeks of life for the high-risk infant must be undertaken with a full awareness of the particular state the infant is in at any given point. Initially the high-risk infant will direct all its energy inward in an attempt to regulate physiological status. Following this the infant will begin to show initial awareness of its environment and caregivers. The final stage includes the infant's interaction with caregivers in a reciprocal manner. Infant states as described by Brazelton (1973) may not be fully applicable to the high-risk infant until the infant begins to display interest in and interaction with its environment in a reciprocal manner. If developmental follow-up is performed at a later age, infant states as described earlier in this section are important to keep in mind when attempting to interpret behaviors elicited or observed during follow-up efforts.

Correction for Prematurity

One of the most basic premises upon which child assessment is founded is that an individual child's performance is considered to be appropriate or not in comparison to the expected performance of children of similar age. Thus, developmental adequacy is appropriate, whatever the area being evaluated or the test instrument being used, if a child's performance is consistent with age expectations. However, the survival of increasing numbers of premature and very low birth weight infants has raised salient questions about what constitutes the measuring stick to which these infants are to be compared. The survivial of increasing numbers of VLBW infants, including some born as early as 12 to 16 weeks prematurely, raises serious questions about developmental assessment. The issue of whether to calculate the age of the high-risk infant based on the date of its birth (chronological age) or whether to correct the chronological age for the degree of prematurity (corrected age) is an important one for the practitioner assessing developmental adequacy of high-risk infants. For example, a child who is born 2 months early (32 weeks gestational age instead of the normal 40 weeks) can be considered a 4-month-old or a 2-month-old when the child is assessed 4 months after the date of birth. This is an important consideration because the determination of normality or deviance of the child's performance on a particular test will depend on which age is used. Typically it has been the practice to correct for degree of prematurity in at least the first 2 years of life (Hunt, 1981). This practice is based in part on the acknowledgment of the significant degree of physical and neurological growth and maturation that is known to take place during the last trimester of in-utero development. Premature infants are deprived of these important weeks, and to compare their developmental performance to that of full-term infants has been suggested to be an inappropriate comparison.

Siegel (1983) studied the consequences of correcting developmental test scores for the degree of prematurity in matched groups of full-term and preterm children. The children were administered a series of developmental tests at various ages (4, 8, 12, 18, 24 months). At each point (age of test administration) the uncorrected scores of the preterm children were significantly lower than those of full-term children. Corrected scores for the preterm children during the first year of life were more highly correlated with test scores at 3 and 5 years. Thus, adding the degree of prematurity (weeks) to the score obtained for infants less than 1 year of age appeared to be a more accurate predictor and better reflected later developmental performance. From 12 months on the uncorrected scores were more highly correlated with test performance at 3 and 5 years. In other words, correcting for prematurity, and using the corrected score in judgments about developmental adequacy, appeared to be a more appropriate manner in which to view infant test results, in particular for children less than 12 months of age. The author concluded by stating that, "the use of a correction for degree of prematurity may be appropriate in the early months, but in most cases at one year of age and after, there were no significant differences between the predictive ability of the corrected and uncorrected scores" (p. 1187).

The decision about the most appropriate score is a complicated one. In the case of more subtle developmental delay the use of a corrected score may remove the apparent deviance for age norms. The practitioner must keep these considerations in mind as assessment is undertaken. The examiner must of necessity be aware of the degree of prematurity when examining a child. If the child is being seen for serial observations of performance, the lessening need to correct for prematurity because of the child's accelerated rate of developmental skill mastery, thus reducing the gap between expected age and actual age that is due to prematurity alone, may be an important indication of developmental expectations. Hence, catch-up growth, when observed, is important to note and monitor. A more complete discussion of catch-up growth is presented later in this chapter.

Test Selection

Once basic pretest considerations have been dealt with and the practitioner is in a position to initiate assessment efforts, the question soon arises about which tests to use. There is no shortage of tests available for use with infants and young children. The question is, which test or tests should a practitioner use? The answer to that question lies, in part, with the academic discipline the practitioner was trained in as well as the particular setting in which an infant is evaluated. The practitioner may be in a setting in which the practitioner is responsible for the bulk of the developmental assessment. In a setting such as this it is mandatory that the examiner become familiar and comfortable with several tests that measure global developmental adequacy as well as with instruments that assess specific skill areas. In settings that use a team approach with infants the practitioner may function more as a specialist representing a particular discipline.

The practitioner must address also the general type of assessment procedures to be followed. There are advantages as well as disadvantages to using test instruments that yield a global score resulting in a developmental quotient. The advantages of tests of this nature are that they are usually comprehensive and possess good reliability and validity. The global score achieved is designed to be a summary statement reflective of developmental performance across modalities. For research purposes and for charting general developmental progress there are advantages to measures of this type. The basic premise, however, of tests of this nature is that skill performance in all areas is equally reflective of general developmental mastery. Each skill area is weighted equally, and areas assessed can all contribute negatively to the overall score achieved on the instrument. The exact relationship between mastery or lack of mastery and subsequent cognitive development in each of several skill areas is simply not known. Thus, although motor performance may be low, this may not be reflective of cognitive impairment as well. For tests of this nature these factors must be kept in mind when interpreting and communicating assessment results to other professionals and parents.

The use of developmental profiles or checklists has gained increased acceptance and application in recent years. Instruments of this nature may or may not yield a score reflective of global performance. Instead, the checklist is generally divided into specific skill areas for which age-related behaviors are assessed for a particular child. The examiner is required, either through direct observation or parental report, to determine whether a specific behavior is present or absent. If present, more difficult behaviors are evaluated to determine their presence or absence. A general age level in each skill area or a more global age level of performance may be arrived at. Various test instruments, those that yield a global score (developmental quotient) and those that function as a checklist or profile of developmental adequacy are presented in Appendix D.

Regardless of the assessment instrument used, the practitioner must be a careful observer of behavior. The actual test administration should begin the moment the examiner sets eyes on the infant. Often spontaneous responses to environmental stimuli are more indicative of developmental adequacy than the infant's response to a particular test item. For example, an infant may spontaneously transfer an object from hand to hand while basic data is being taken from the mother, but does not transfer an object during test administration. Behavior such as this should be carefully noted and explained when reporting assessment results.

Test selection by the practitioner must be performed with several important considerations in mind. These include the following:

1. The general type of test selected, one yielding either a global score or a checklist of skills, must be taken into consideration.
2. The effects of strange surroundings, maternal apprehension, and the strangeness of the examiner may restrict the infant's responses during formal test administration.
3. Infant states as previously described are an important consideration as the infant's patterns of response and interaction with the environment are to large measure influenced by the state the infant is in at given points in time.
4. Data obtained from a developmental log kept by parents are a helpful source of information.
5. The examiner must also be aware, if at all possible, of the child's medical history. Data on degree of prematurity, specific medical conditions, the length of stay in the NICU, and the presence of subsequent medical problems aid in formulating opinions on developmental adequacy and intervention efforts.

One additional comment about the assessment of high-risk infants is needed. The point has been made previously that parents are a primary source of valuable data concerning the developmental progress of an infant. Data kept by parents over a period of time, which describes in chronological order the development of new skills, can be a rich source of supplemental information. The use of a developmental log is thus encouraged. There need be no set structure or format to the log, although the practitioner may find it quite helpful to structure the parents' entries. Parents have demonstrated that they are good describers of behavior, although their judgments of the adequacy of behaviors described is much less reliable. It seems a waste of insightful and firsthand input not to consider, and in some cases weigh equally, descriptive data provided by parents in forming judgments regarding developmental progress. As a result of the limitations inherent in any of the tests previously described, the practitioner's ability to detect and quantify developmental delay based on a single test administration is restricted. The practitioner is therefore providing developmental assessments on a serial basis over a period of time. As the practitioner gathers specific test data in a serial manner, detailed descriptions of developmental skill mastery by the parents can aid in formulating opinions about the rate of skill learning as well as about the new skills learned. The parents can be asked to simply chart new skills as their infants learn them. A notebook can easily be kept by parents that lists dates and skills learned. As follow-up continues over a period of months, and as specific test data are compiled, the two sources of information can be combined to provide a clear and indispensible resource. The practitioner is therefore encouraged to use the developmental log when long-term follow-up is indicated.

Interpretation of Results

Once the practitioner has gathered assessment data, either from a single test administration or from serial test results, a decision must be made about the performance of a particular infant. In the case of the infant who has serious neurological or cognitive problems, the determination of developmental status is relatively straightforward. The practitioner must keep in mind, however, the limitations inherent in attempting to determine developmental adequacy and potential on the basis of a limited sample of behavior.

The use of assessment data is of crucial importance as parents and other professionals desire some direction based on test performance. A host of decisions on intervention hinge on proper judgments based on assessment results. These include basic decisions about the need for additional medical intervention and evaluation; the need for early programming, either center- or home-based; the effectiveness of current intervention efforts; later school placement as the child approaches school age; and strengths and weaknesses in specific areas of development.

Test results can be viewed as either prognostic or prescriptive. A combination of the two is also possible. A prognostic interpretation of assessment results is in almost all instances a tenuous one. Previous discussions have centered on the lack of predictive ability of infant tests. The younger the child and the fewer the observational opportunities the less correlation there is between the test results and later performance in the absence of severe neurological damage or known mental retardation syndromes. As the child's age increases, and as additional assessments are performed over time, the prognostic benefit of assessment increases somewhat but is by no means foolproof. The clinician-educator is cautioned therefore about making medium or long-term judgements about a child's developmental potential on the basis of results obtained early in the child's life or on the basis of a limited sample of behaviors.

A second and more helpful way in which to view assessment results is in a prescriptive manner. This is simply to answer the question, What is the next step of action based on what has been obtained? A prescriptive approach toward viewing assessment data can result in a variety of outcomes. For the infant seen at an early age who performs below age expectations the decision may simply be to ask the parents to keep a developmental log and to schedule the baby for reassessment in 90 days. If a persistent pattern of developmental delay is present over a period of time (6 to 9 months), the decision may be to provide the parents with instruction and home stimulation materials to initiate intervention in the home setting. As the infant grows older the decision may be to refer the parents and child to an infant stimulation program or later a preschool program. If the child is already involved in intervention efforts, a prescriptive interpretation of assessment results may focus on specific areas of developmental delay for the purpose of directing intervention efforts more intensely in these areas. The effectiveness of the intervention being provided can also be gauged in this manner. The results of assessment efforts can also be the basis upon which additional referrals are made, either for medical evaluations or for detailed assessment in a specific skill area or developmental domains such as language or motor skills. In short, a prescriptive use of assessment results requires that the practitioner be thinking ahead to the next step of action for a particular infant. The choices range from no action to intense intervention and further assessment.

Catch-Up Growth

One final comment about test interpretation is related to the significance of catch-up growth observed in an infant. The degree of developmental delay that is detected after initial assessment is of particular importance as serial observations are scheduled. Initial test data can serve as a base line upon which comparisons of future results can be made. The practitioner initially is correcting for the degree of prematurity in interpreting test results. As the child matures and displays behaviors that are more age appropriate, the need to correct for prematurity lessens. Previous discussions have alluded to the importance of correcting for prematurity up to at least 1 year of age. Catch-up growth, therefore, may be said to occur when the child is less than 1 year of age, and the need to correct for prematurity is decreased due to the child's display of more age-appropriate behaviors. Thus, the presence and rate of catch-up growth displayed by an infant can be used in forming preliminary judgments about developmental expectations. The rate of catch-up growth displayed by high-risk infants is an area that has received little systematic study. However, it seems reasonable to assume that an infant who maintains a developmental delay over time, or for whom the gap between present performance and age-appropriate performance widens, would carry a less favorable prognosis. On the other hand, if an infant displays a developmental delay on early test administrations but subsequently displays rapid catch-up growth with no delay present by 12 to 15 months of age (no need to correct for prematurity), a more favorable prognosis is possible. The experienced practitioner is able to apply catch-up growth in forming judgments about developmental expectations. Judgments of this nature can be made only on the basis of multiple test administrations. Monitoring of catch-up growth may be one of the most valuable tools available to the practitioner in light of the limitations inherent in forming prognostic opinions on developmental potential.

Communication of Results

Ultimately, infant assessment results must be communicated to the parents and others concerned with the infant's developmental status. If the practitioner remembers the audience being addressed, confusion and lack of effectiveness in communicating results can be avoided.

Data transmitted to parents must be precise and clear and must be presented in a manner that allows the parents to fully understand assessment results. In many instances the child's performance is close to age expectations, and parents can be informed that although their baby is not doing all that can be expected, it is performing close to age norms and that future testing is recommended to monitor skill development. In the case of the infant whose performance reflects a moderate-to-severe delay, and who has been seen over time by the evaluator, the parents in most instances are aware that their baby is not doing well. Parents in this category have suspected for some time that their infant is not developing in a normal fashion and are usually most open and receptive to comments and suggestions for action. The emotional adjustments that are necessitated as parents become increasingly aware that their child is not developing normally and may be in need of special services for an undetermined period of time cannot be minimized. Discussions with parents at this time can center on the subsequent courses of action, with the parents fully involved in the decision-making process.

Communication with other professionals should also be with the intended audience in mind. Clear descriptions of the tests used, the child's performance, and test interpretation should be provided. Not all practitioners are familiar with the variety of assessment tools available for use. If the practitioner is assessing a specific skill area, other persons may not be familiar with the specific test used. Communication can be enhanced if a brief description of the test is provided. The developmental performance of the child should be transmitted clearly and in a manner that is easy to comprehend. This will of course depend in part on the instrument used and its scoring and reporting format.

If test results are to be communicated to early childhood educators or those involved in intervention efforts, the practitioner may need to make specific reference to skill areas and the progress or lack of progress in that area. Clear descriptions and reporting of results will serve to enhance services provided to an infant as well as allow persons from a variety of disciplines to feel a part of the total effort directed toward the high-risk child.

SUMMARY

A need clearly exists to provide accurate and reliable assessment data for infants who fall into the high-risk category. The following chapter discusses the effectiveness of early intervention efforts with young developmentally delayed children; however, the identification of those children hinges on early assessment and detection of delay. The practitioner has a host of factors to keep in mind as assessment efforts are initiated. Many of these depend heavily on the setting in which the practitioner is employed. Regardless of the setting, however, the evaluator must be aware of the strengths and weaknesses inherent in the assessment process. Of primary importance is the practitioner's skill at being an accurate and objective observer of behavior. Careful descriptions of infant behavior obtained through direct observation or parental report, and conducted over time, can provide accurate and reliable data on developmental progress. Data of this nature are indispensible as follow-up efforts are undertaken. Each child has the right to achieve its optimal developmental potential regardless of medical history or other high-risk factors. The monitoring of developmental progress for the high-risk infant is a crucial factor in ensuring that right.

REFERENCES

Brazelton, T. (1962). Observations of the neonate. *Journal of the American Academy of Child Psychiatry, 1*, 38.

Brazelton, T. (1973). *Neonatal behavioral assessment scale.* Philadelphia: J. B. Lippincott.

Brazelton, T. (1981). Behavioral competence of the newborn infant. In G. Avery (Ed.), *Neonatology, pathophysiology and management of the newborn.* Philadelphia: J. B. Lippincott.

Coplan, J. (1982). Parental estimate of child's developmental level in a high risk population. *American Journal of Disorders in Childhood, 136,* 101.

Dinno, N. (1977). Early recognition of infants at risk for developmental retardation. *Pediatric Clinics of North America, 24,* 633.

Fitzhardinge, P. (1982). current outcome of NICU population. In A. Brann and J. Volpe (Eds.), *Neonatal neurological assessment and outcome: Report of the severity* (Seventh Ross Conference on Pediatric Research). Columbus: Ross Laboratories.

Gorski, P., Davison, M., and Brazelton, B. (1979). Stages of behavioral organization in the high risk neonate: Theoretical and clinical considerations. *Seminars in Perinatology, 3,* 61.

Hobbs, N. (1975). *The futures of children.* Washington, DC: Jossey-Bass.

Holm, V. (1978). The rationale for child development teams: The limited scope of expertise. In E. Allen, V. Holm, and R. Schiefelbusch (Eds.), *Early intervention—A team approach.* Baltimore: University Park Press.

Hunt, J. (1976). Environmental risk in fetal and neonatal life and measured infant intelligence. In M. Lewis (Ed.), *Origins of intelligence.* New York: Plenum Press.

Hunt, J. (1981). Predicting intelligence disorders in childhood for preterm infants with birth weights below 1501 grams. In S. Friedman and M. Sigman (Eds.), *Preterm birth and psychological development.* New York: Academic Press.

Hunt, J., and Bayley, N. (1971). Explorations into patterns of mental development and prediciton from Bayley scale of infant development. *Minnesota Symposia on Child Psychology, 5,* 52.

Kagan, J. (1971). *Change and continuity in infancy.* New York: John Wiley & Sons.

McCall, R., Hogarty, P., and Hurlburt, N. (1972). Transitions in infancy sensory motor development and the prediction of childhood I.Q. *American Psychologist, 27,* 728.

McCarthy, J. (1980). Assessment of young children with learning problems: Beyond the paralysis of analysis. In E. Sell (Ed.), *Followup of the high risk newborn: A practical approach.* Springfield, MA: Charles C. Thomas.

McCormick, M., Shapiro, S., and Starfield, B. (1982). Factors associated with maternal opinion of infant development: Clues to the vulnerable child. *Pediatrics, 69,* 537.

Murphy, T., Nichter, C., and Liden, C. (1982). Developmental outcome of the high-risk infant: A review of methodological issues. *Seminars in Perinatology, 6,* 4.

Porter, F., and Marshall, R. (1985). Summary of a current research project. *The Micro Statistician, 1,* 3.

Rossetti, L. (1984). *A longitudinal study of the developmental status of high risk infants.* Paper presented at the annual convention of the American Speech—Language—Hearing Association, San Francisco.

Scott, K., and Hogan, A. (1982). Methods for the identification of high risk and handicapped infants. In C. Ramsey and P. Trohanis (Eds.), *Finding and educating high risk and handicapped infants.* Baltimore: University Park Press.

Shonkoff, J., Dworkin, P., and Leviton, A. (1979). Primary case approaches to developmental disabilities. *Pediatrics, 64,* 506.

Siegel, L. (1981). Infant tests as predictors of cognitive and language development at two years. *Child Development, 52,* 545.

Siegel, L. (1983). Connection for prematurity and its consequences for the assessment of the very low birth weight infant. *Child Development, 54,* 1176.

Vaughn, B., Deinard, A., and Egeland, B. (1980). Measuring temperament in pediatric practice. *Journal of Pediatrics, 56,* 510.

Zelazo, P., Zelazo, R., and Kolb, S. (1972). Walking in the newborn. *Science, 176,* 314.

Chapter 6

Early Intervention Programs: History, Effectiveness, and Implementation

The previous chapter alluded to the fact that one of the main goals of assessment is the early identification of children who need formal intervention designed to reduce the negative effects of a high-risk history. Early intervention programs are more readily available today than at any time in the past. Private and state agencies have become increasingly involved in the implementation of service delivery systems designed to remediate developmental delay in young children. This has not always been the case, however. A time did exist when the special needs of young children were not recognized, and services for children displaying delayed development were not available. Although the current status of early intervention services in the United States is much improved, refinement of service delivery models and intervention curriculum is constantly taking place.

The present chapter is designed to acquaint the practitioner with both broad and specific issues related to early intervention. A brief history of early intervention is presented. The effectiveness of early intervention and specific research data are included. Several model intervention programs, which have demonstrated the efficacy of early intervention, are described. An overall philosophy and various service delivery models are addressed also. Specific suggestions on the actual provision of services, as well as the critical components of programs, are included. Although the chapter is not designed specifically to be a how to chapter, the information contained should familiarize the interested practitioner with general and specific issues related to early intervention.

HISTORY OF EARLY INTERVENTION

A variety of influences have contributed over the years to the present status of early infant intervention programs. Several major forces, however, have influenced the growing interest in intervention programs for infants.

Early views of infant capabilities ascribed to the infant a limited sensory and motor capacity only. As a result institutions such as orphanages and homes for neglected or abandoned children provided mostly custodial care for younger residents. The child was by and large considered to be the responsibility of the parents and extended family. Thus, interest in providing an optimal experience for the child in homes of this nature during the early years was not present. As behavioral scientists began to realize the importance of early experience in the life of the child, and as an expanded view of infant capabilities emerged, interest was directed in a more energetic way toward establishing institutions that provided a higher quality of care to young children. Early research efforts indicated that the care received by a child early in life affected not only the health and biological development of the child but also the cognitive development of the child (Goldfarb, 1943; Spitz, 1945). Additional investigators demonstrated that individualized care of mentally disadvantaged children could prevent and reverse their course of development (Skeels and Dye, 1939). Thus, the realization that the early experiences of the child were linked to later cognitive performance, in combination with the awareness of the positive effect of extra stimulation for mentally delayed children, interacted in an efficacious manner and resulted in an increased interest in the early experience afforded children.

The results of research of this nature in the late 1940s had a profound effect on the state of child care in the United States. The philosophy of many institutions that were providing care to young children changed from that of purely custodial and impersonal to an emphasis on the child and a stability in the child-caregiver relationship. An additional area of research that added impetus to the concern for the early experiences of the child was that being conducted on the importance of the mother-infant bond during early infancy. Early nurturance and its impact on later personality and cognitive development were of great interest to researchers in the 1950s and 1960s. The results of these various avenues of research into the early months and years of the child's experiences paved the way for a more constructive and positive view of the early experiences of the child. Interest naturally turned to strategies that would provide for optimal early experiences resulting in optimal developmental performance later in the child's life.

Increased awareness of the importance of the early experience of the child in and of itself was not the sole motivator for current practice relative to early intervention, however. Social and political forces were important reasons why a national emphasis on early education, first for healthy normal infants and subsequently for infants with known handicapping conditions, exists today. Social influences emanated in part from the increased number of women in the work force and the resulting need for supplementary care for their children. Both group and family day care facilities for infants and young children have proliferated nationwide in an effort to meet the need for supplemental child care.

During the late 1960s another major impetus for the initiation of early intervention programs was realized. Known as the War on Poverty, an official policy of the U.S. government, its purpose was to alleviate poverty and improve the opportunities afforded children. It was widely known at that time that children from poor families were unable to fully benefit from the educational opportunities available to them once they entered school at 5 years of age. To alleviate this situation a massive federal effort was initiated to correct this deficit by offering preschool to children who were economically disadvantaged. This program was known as Head Start and is still in operation today. Early results of studies designed to evaluate the effectiveness of Head Start revealed promising results. Results showed that Head Start children showed larger gains in achievement than middle-class children not in Head Start (McCarthy, 1980). Follow-up evaluations conducted after a year or two in public schools, however, demonstrated a difference in IQ scores between the Head Start and middle-class children in favor of the non-Head Start group. These follow-up results were disappointing. Continued research into the effectiveness of the Head Start program has been more positive, however, and has highlighted the importance of the parents' role in preschool programs. Head Start has served to create a new interest in methods of teaching and preventing developmental delay in young children. It has also served to emphasize the fact that compensatory education must aim at changing attitudes and motivation as well as focusing on cognitive and linguistic skills.

At present Head Start programs funded under U.S. Public Law 92–424 are serving more than 32,000 handicapped preschool children nationally (McCarthy, 1980). Federal legislation requires that 10 percent of all children enrolled in Head Start programs be handicapped. This massive federal effort to provide a preschool experience for disadvantaged and handicapped children has served in large measure as the starting point for infant intervention programs in the United States. In 1968, the U.S. Congress was alerted to the fact that early intervention and programming for young handicapped children and their families could significantly reduce the number of children who would need intensive or long-term special education services. The result of this Congressional concern was the passage of U.S. Public Law 90–538, passed and signed into law in 1968. This act became known as the Federal Handicapped Children Early Education Assistance Act. It provided the following:

1. A program of model demonstration centers should be established to acquaint the community with the problems and potentials of handicapped children. The demonstration centers were to be established in settings that could be used for the training of teachers, speech pathologists and audiologists, clinicians, psychologists, physicians, paraprofessionals, aides, and others who may be required to alleviate the effects of early handicapping conditions.
2. These model programs were intended to stimulate all areas of development in the young child, including intellectual, physical, social and emotional. The bill urged that programs encompass not just children with disabilities but all age groups from birth to 6 years.
3. There was an emphasis on participation by parents to encourage their development of specific skills needed to respond effectively to the special needs of their handicapped child. The bill also enlisted the help of parents as allies of educators to provide a total program.

More than 224 model demonstration centers have been funded to public school districts, day care centers, nursery schools, and university-affiliated facilities since U.S. Public Law 90–538 was passed. The centers' programs differ widely in terms of ages and populations served. Some are designed primarily for infant stimulation, whereas others serve children with specific handicapping conditions. Some include only 3- and four-year-old children, whereas others focus on older age ranges. Regardless of the populations served all programs place a heavy emphasis on family involvement in the intervention process.

An additional major event that has had enormous impact on early intervention programs in the United States was the passage of U.S. Public Law 94–142, The Education of All Handicapped Children Act, in 1975. This law, which guarantees a free, appropriate public education for all handicapped children 3 to 21 years of age, has changed the public's perception of special services for handicapped children from that of a privilege for a few to the right of every child. U.S. Public Law 94–142 emphasizes educating handicapped children with nonhandicapped children as much as possible. It also mandates that school districts provide a continuum of alternative placements, including consultants, resource rooms, itinerant programs, self-contained classes, special schools, residential programs, and home and hospital services (McCarthy, 1980). The law is designed to match as closely as possible the child's specific educational needs with available resources. Each child is guaranteed due process, and decisions about the child's placement are made with the full involvement and participation of the parents.

One important component of U.S. Public Law 94–142 that has served in part to increase accountability of intervention strategies is the use of an individualized education plan (IEP) for each child. The IEP must be prepared for each child on a yearly basis and must include the following:

1. A description of the child's present level of performance
2. An outline of long-range goals in areas such as language, gross and fine motor functioning, cognitive development, preacademic skills, self-help skills, and social and emotional development
3. A statement of short-term instructional objectives
4. A description of the specific special education and related services to be provided, along with the projected dates for initiation of services and the anticipated duration of the services
5. A statement of appropriate objective criteria, evaluation procedures, and a schedule for determining if the instructional objectives are being achieved

In summary, a number of factors have interacted during the past 20 years and have resulted in the current effort to find and educate handicapped or at-risk children at younger and younger ages. Research data that ascribed to the infant a much greater sensory capacity, information on the detrimental effects of a disadvantaged or limited early environment, the increased number of working mothers in need of child care, a recognition of the importance of the child-caregiver relationship, and the growing realization that the effects of an early childhood handicapping condition can be reduced through early intervention have all given momentum to early intervention programs internationally. As the concept of early identification has changed, in part through the interest directed toward the developmental performance of children who would not have survived a precarious neonatal period, early identification and intervention have come to mean the provision of assessment and intervention services to children at ages undreamed of a decade ago. The results of this increased interest in the provision of special services for preschool handicapped children have been remarkable. In the United States all 50 states now have permissive or mandatory legislation to provide public school services for handicapped children, although the ages at which these services are available differ from state to state. Table 6–1 presents a state-by-state listing of mandatory ages relative to when special education services are available for handicapped children. These data were presented to the U.S. Congress in 1985 as part of the *Seventh Annual Report on the Implementation of the Education of the Handicapped Act* and was prepared by the U.S. Department of Education (Gary L. Jones, Acting Secretary). Not all handicapping conditions are covered by the legislation in each state at the ages indicated. Practitioners should be aware of the specifics of state mandates in their own states. Table 6–2 presents state mandates for the upper age limits for service eligibility.

A PHILOSOPHY OF EARLY INTERVENTION

As Soboloff (1979) has stated:

> It can no longer be accepted that treatment does not commence until the child is three years of age. The objectives of developmental enrichment programs are to help overcome blockages in the babies' developmental progress and to help parents understand the disabilities and their implications, to help them accept and be responsible for daily therapy, and to face the disability in a positive way. (p. 424)

With these goals in mind a variety of program models are available for the actual provision of services to the young developmentally delayed child. Each service delivery model shares a basic philosophy. In commenting on the overall importance of early intervention, Provence (1974) listed the following eight points as important elements in an early intervention program. These points can also serve as the outline for a general philosophy of early intervention.

1. The ability to establish a working partnership with parents and other caregivers on behalf of the child.
2. The ability to evaluate the parents' capacity for nurturing the child—their strengths and deficits and areas of conflict—and to find ways of helping them with their development as parents.
3. A commitment to assisting parents to develop personally in addition to developing as parents.
4. The ability to understand the meaning of development and behavior in the young child and to translate parental understanding into a prescriptive program.
5. The ability to recognize situations in the child's interpersonal, psychosocial or physical experience that are likely to enhance or threaten the child's development, that is, a supportive or impeding environment.

Table 6-1. Mandates for Serving Handicapped Children Aged 6 Years and Less, by State

Age Range (yr)					
0-5	2-5	3-5	4-5	5	6
IA	VA	AK	DE	AL	AR
MD		CA	MN	CO	AZ
MI		CT	OK	FL	IN
NE		DC	TN	GA	MS
NJ		HI	WA	ID	MT
SD		IL		KS	ND
		LA		KY	OR
		MA		ME	PA
		NH		MO	VT
		RI		NC	
		TX		NM	
		WI		NV	
				NY	
				OH	
				SC	
				UT	
				WV	
				WY	

6. The ability to mobilize the needed resources rapidly. This means not only creating resources but also, even more difficult, being able to use them properly. Time is often a crucial factor. Such mobilization means being able to respond to the unexpected in any given day: the sudden need for overnight care for a child; the need to take a child home from the center who has not been called for; the need to go into the home, help a sick mother get to the doctor, and to dress and feed and provide care for the child while getting the mother to the clinic.

7. Flexibility in attitude and practice. This flexibility means individualizing the program or intervention to meet the needs of a specific child; it also means adapting the program to fit the changing needs of children that characterize the process of normal development.

8. The establishment of a functioning group of colleagues with various skills who can provide expertise without fragmentation. Effective intervention in this definition implies continuity of interest and coordination of the efforts of those who provide service.

What these statements imply is that every child has a right to life with a caregiver who can facilitate the child's early development to the upper levels of the child's abilities. Inherent in the efforts to facilitate the child's maximal developmental skill mastery is the realization that

Table 6-2. State Mandates: Upper Age Limit for Service Eligibility

Age (yr)							
18	19	20	21		23	25	Other
GA	HI	AL	AK	OH	WV	MI	FL
IN		AR	AZ	PA			
MT		CO	CA	PI			
NC		DE	CT	RI			
NV		ID	DC	SC			
OK		IA	IL	SD			
		ME	KS	TN			
		MD	KY	TX			
		MN	LA	UT			
		MO	MA	VT			
		MS	NJ	VA			
		NE	NM	WA			
		NH	ND	WI			
		NY					
		OR					
		WY					

children are able to learn and benefit from stimulation provided at an early age. Efforts to meet the needs of young developmentally delayed children must take into account the importance of the parents as therapists for their baby. In essence, the younger the child the greater the role of the parents in providing actual intervention. This takes place, of course, under the supervision of early infant educators who are able to provide input to guide parental efforts. The actual number of professionals interacting with the parents may be limited to ensure optimal communication of intervention intent. With this in mind a transdisciplinary approach to remediation may be the most effective one for intervention. A more complete discussion of the transdisciplinary approach is presented later in this chapter. In an approach of this nature the practitioner providing input to the intervention efforts must be familiar with developmental norms and be prepared to provide intervention and programming advice in areas that do not constitute the practitioner's primary area of expertise. Practitioners must be aware, however, of their limitations and be willing to seek help and advice when appropriate.

One final consideration is the need for flexibility. The data provided by Provence (1974) made mention of this fact. The key concept relative to flexibility is the realization on the part of the practitioner that a variety of activities, which all make up the early intervention curriculum, can and should be used to enhance overall skill mastery for a particular child. The actual activities must be chosen with the specific child in mind and not the other way around. This mandates that the practitioner be familiar enough with each child and potential intervention activities to take full advantage of the particular learning style and specific needs presented by the child.

VARIOUS PROGRAM MODELS AND THEIR EFFECTIVENESS

An important consideration for legislators, educators, physicians, parents and other advocacy groups is the effectiveness of early intervention efforts. If, in fact, the time and resources expended in the identification and provision of services for young at-risk children is worth the effort, then aggressive attempts to provide intervention for all at-risk children should be made. Additional questions arise about the most effective model of program implementation. Both program setting and intervention audience become important considerations when determining the value of early intervention. Trohanis, Cox, and Meyer (1982) pointed out that 47 percent of early intervention programs are both home- and center-based; 25 percent are center-based only; 16 percent are home-based only; and the remaining programs are a combination of hospital or home-based and hospital. Home-based programs are those in which the intervention efforts take place in the child's natural home setting. Center-based programs are those in which intervention activity takes place after the child has been transported to a setting designed for this purpose.

The material that follows describes two basic program models and discusses the effectiveness of intervention efforts within these models. The intervention models are center-based and home-based service delivery systems. Regardless of the service delivery model used, early intervention efforts may be defined as any systematic activity designed to enhance the developmental performance of developmentally delayed or at-risk children. The purpose is to assist the child in compensating for the negative effects of a precarious neonatal period. This activity may take place primarily in the home or in a center designed for this purpose; the thrust of the effort is directed toward the child or the parents.

A recent project designed to provide home stimulation for a cross-section of children, not high risk and not solely from disadvantaged homes, conducted in the St. Louis, Missouri, school district had remarkable impact on the developmental status of 380 children (Mallory, 1985). In this project local school districts sent teachers into the homes on a regular basis, starting during the pregnancies of the mothers and continuing for 3 years. The teachers, who were experts in child development, met with each family twice a month, once in the home and once with a small group at a school, until the babies were 5 months of age. After that the teachers went into each home once a month, and parents met in groups every 6 weeks. Overall testing of the children revealed consistently higher scores on IQ tests for the children in the program. By age 3 the children in the program had mental and language growth exceeding that of other children of the same age. The children in the program also displayed significantly more aspects of positive development. These findings provide some of the most significant data to date on the efficacy of home stimulation and its impact on overall development skill acquisition.

When professional attention is turned toward populations of at-risk infants, accumulated information suggests that babies who are born with developmental disabilities or who are at high risk for acquiring them benefit from developmental enrichment programs begun early in life. Although programs of this nature may take a variety of forms, evidence has been available for a number of years that points out the various degrees of effectiveness of programs of early intervention.

Home-Based Programs

Home-based programs are those in which the intervention effort takes place in the home. The intervention efforts may be directed primarily toward the parent or toward the child. If directed toward the parent the goal is to better equip the parent to serve as the primary therapist for the child. Efforts of this nature include providing instruction for the parents, monitoring their acquisition of necessary skills, giving actual demonstrations of intervention techniques, observing the parents while they work with their infant, and assisting the parents in altering their home environment in ways that will serve to enhance the child's developmental performance.

Regardless of the actual setting in which intervention efforts are conducted, there are some general goals that are applicable to parental involvement in the intervention process. These are, however, particularly applicable when the primary setting for intervention is in the home and when the primary programmers are to be the parents. These include efforts to make the parents and family aware of the child's abilities and potential in all areas of development. Once this is accomplished, a program that is specifically designed to help each individual child reach the child's optimal level of functioning in all areas—motor skills, adaptive behavior, language, and social and emotional development—should be undertaken. The parents and family must realize that they are to be the primary programmers or educators of their child and must take pride in their role. In addition the family must begin to structure time, activities, equipment, and routine for maximal effectiveness in reaching the developmental goals set for their child in conjunction with the professional providing input.

A variety of strategies and intervention techniques have been used in home-based programs. Programs have been designed to enhance the intellectual and personality development of the child as well as to produce changes in the mother's self-esteem, to encourage an increase in the quality of verbal interaction in the home through a variety of stimuli, and to focus on equipping the parents to be the main agent of change as educational opportunities are offered (Gray, 1977; Levenstein, 1971). These intervention strategies have been examined for their long-term impact on later developmental performance. What has resulted is that prolonged and continuous intervention for 2 to 3 years during the first 3 years of life produces prolonged effects on intellectual and academic performance in school for 6 to 7 years after the termination of home-based intervention programs. Studies by Field (1980) and Ross (1984) investigated the efficacy of home-based intervention programs. In both studies significant gains in cognitive ability were observed when home-based programs were instituted. In the Ross study a team consisting of a nurse and pediatric occupational therapist visited the home of each family enrolled in the project twice a month for the first 3 months after the infant's discharge from the NICU and monthly thereafter until the children reached 12 months from term. The primary aim of the program was to maximize the mental and psychomotor development of the infants. At 1 year of age postterm children in the home visiting program showed significantly higher scores on the Mental Scale of the Bayley Scale of Infant Development than did children in a control group that received no home stimulation (experimental group mean = 99.2; control group mean = 89.4; $p < .001$) In addition, families that received home visits attained significantly higher ($p < .001$) measures of the home environment as measured by the Home Observation for Measurement of Environment Scale. An interesting corollary of these studies was the fact that measures on motor ability, taken at 8 months postterm, did not differentiate between those infants receiving home programming and those infants not receiving any home intervention. The mothers, however, who received home visits were found to show a higher degree of involvement and a greater emotional and verbal responsivity to their infants. They were also more likely to provide more appropriate play material and to organize more effectively the child's physical environment than mothers who did not receive home visits. What has emerged from studies of this nature is that the support, modeling, and information provided by the home visit professionals promoted maternal involvement and improvement in the child rearing environment, which facilitated the child's cognitive growth.

Williams and Scarr (1971) investigated the effects of short-term intervention on performance in a population of low birth weight and disadvantaged children. The effects of two programs of short-term educational intervention on intellectual performance were studied in a group of low birth weight children of poor socioeconomic background. Information on perinatal history, clinic history, and home environment was collected for each child. Performance on tests measuring motor function, social maturity, and intellectual abilities was determined before and after a 4-month period in which the infants were assigned to one of three groups: (1) tutoring plus the provision of educational materials, (2) provision of materials alone, and (3) no intervention. Four age ranges of children were included in the study: birth to 1 month, 1 to 2 years, 2 to 3 years, and 3 to 4 years. Both experimental groups, the group who received educational materials alone and the group who received educational materials plus home tutoring, demonstrated significantly better performance than the control group who received no intervention. For the experimental group gains were found to be largely dependent on the neurological status of the child. Those with known neurological impairment gained less than those who were neurologically intact, regardless of age group. The experimental program of tutoring and providing educational materials produced significant improvement in verbal performance in neurologically normal children and improvement in social maturity measures in the neurologically impaired children. The authors concluded by stating that the combination of physiologic and environmental handicaps present in many low birth weight children may severely limit both sensory input and the ability to process sensory input. For this group of children a special program of supplemental stimulation may be necessary.

Scarr-Salapatek and Williams (1973) conducted a follow-up evaluation designed to determine the effects of early stimulation on low birth weight infants. The infants chosen in this study weighed between 1,300 and 1,800 g at birth. A group of 30 infants were assigned to either a control or experimental group on an alternating basis. The infants came from a low socioeconomic group. A stimulation program designed to enhance sensorimotor development was provided for the experimental group throughout the first year of life. Home visits were made by a social worker for the purpose of instruction and demonstration for the mothers. At 1 year of age both the experimental and control groups were brought by their mothers for pediatric and behavioral observation. Significant performance differences were obtained in favor of the experimental group. These results indicated that early stimulation programs that provided for low birth weight, disadvantaged infants were effective in promoting behavioral development.

Schaefer and Aaronson (1972) described an additional early intervention program designed to be implemented in the home. The program, which involved high-risk infants, was designed to promote intellectual development through the provision of tutoring for infants in the acquisition of verbal skills and language development. Schaefer and Aaronson provided home tutoring for infants between 15 and 36 months of age for 1 hour per day, 5 days per week. At the end of the intervention period significant differences were found between the experimental group of infants who received home tutoring and the control group of infants who did not. An interesting finding of this study related to performance on IQ measures 36 months after the intervention ceased. Although differences 36 months postintervention were in favor of the experimental subjects, the differences appeared to be due more to a decline in performance on the part of the control infants than to an increase on the part of the experimental subjects. This trend continued until first grade. What emerged was a 5-point drop in IQ for the experimental children compared to a 12-point drop for the control group of children.

In summary, early intervention efforts conducted in the home have resulted in significant increases in developmental skill acquisition for high-risk, disadvantaged, and normal children and for children with already diagnosed handicapping conditions. These findings are important to the practitioner who is involved in early intervention efforts in the home setting.

Center-Based Programs

Center-based programs involve the provision of early intervention services in a child center or in the NICU. The efforts are directed toward either the child or the parents. In many instances programs of this nature are provided by local school districts, hospitals, and private agencies and may involve the child's participation and attendance on a varying schedule. Efforts certainly are made to involve the parents in the total educational program; however, in some instances the parents are either unwilling or unable to be fully involved in the intervention process.

Leib, Benfield, and Guidubaldi (1980) demonstrated the effectiveness of early intervention and stimulation for preterm infants while the infants were still in the NICU. A prescribed sensory enrichment program, within a regional NICU, was administered to 14 infants who weighed between 1,200 and 1,800 g at birth. An additional 14 infants with birth weights in the same range served as a control group. The stimulation program provided for the experimental group consisted of visual, tactile, kinesthetic, and auditory stimulation. The sensory enrichment program, administered by nurses during feeding times, was designed to provide an environment more like the one the infant would receive at home. The results indicated that the infants who received the early enrichment program had a significantly higher status than control infants, as measured by the Bayley Scales, at 6 months past the maternal expected date of confinement. Table 6–3 summarizes the findings obtained in this study. The implications of these results are that a program designed to provide the preterm infant with appropriate stimulation in the NICU may indeed enhance an infant's capability to respond behaviorally to the environment. If early intervention enhances the infant's responsiveness, this may in turn affect the infant's interaction with caregivers, thus creating an environment for reciprocal interaction that contributes to greater developmental performance.

Several investigators have followed the developmental progress of infants who have received center-based intervention. Palmer (1976), Caldwell and Richmond (1964), and Keister (1970) were early proponents of the center-based approach for infant intervention. Their results consistently revealed the effectiveness of center-based early intervention programs for at-risk children. One of the main obstacles to overcome for the center-based approach was the reluctance of some to allow a young child to spend time away from the mother and the home. As mentioned previously, the importance of a nurturing environment for infant development cannot be overstated. Thus, the danger exists, or was thought to exist, that placing a young child in a group setting for infant stimulation would negatively affect the child because of the lack of attachment to a primary caregiver. A basic objective of early providers of center-based group care for infants was that center-based care would not have damaging effects on the infants, especially when compared to infants who had been reared in the home setting. A second objective, which remains in effect today and is a basic premise for all center-based programs, is that intervention programs that are center-based will provide supplemental educational opportunties for the child, not substitute mothering, and will support and encourage the parent-child relationship in whatever way possible. An overview of center-based programs in terms of their impact on developmental progress and separation reaction reveals that significant skill acquisition takes place without differences between home-reared children and those receiving intervention outside the home. Of course, center-based programs need to realize the importance of the parent-child relationship, and the intervention provided must incorporate a variety of activities designed to strengthen and enhance that relationship.

Trohanis and colleagues (1982) presented summary information on several early intervention programs. The demonstration projects included programs that provided both center- and home-based inter-

Table 6-3. Group Comparison of Bayley Scales of Infant Development at 6 Month Follow-up

	Developmental Index Mean Score	
	Control Group	Treatment Group
Bayley Mental		
Uncorrected for gestational age	76.50	98.93*
Corrected for gestational age	105.21	125.36*
Bayley Motor		
Uncorrected for gestational age	78.86	97.86*
Corrected for gestational age	104.93	121.86*

*$p = <.001$

vention activities. A review of the effectiveness of these programs will serve to underscore the importance and effectiveness of early intervention efforts. Several of these programs are summarized in the following:

Peoria 0–3 Replication Project: The original Peoria 0–3 Replication Project in Illinois was funded in the summer of 1971 as a 3-year demonstration project by the U.S. government's Handicapped Children's Early Education Program. During the first few years the program provided center-based transdisciplinary diagnostic and evaluation services followed by home programming, which was often supplemented with outpatient occupational, physical, and speech or language therapy. The ages of the children served are birth to 3 years, and they are impaired or considered to be high-risk because of mental retardation, neuromotor handicaps, orthopedic handicaps, visual and hearing impairments, congenital anomalies, social or emotional disorders, psychomotor retardation, or developmental delay. On the basis of data from the third year of the demonstration services, a random sample of 99 children was selected. Statistically significant gains were found in the personal or social; cognitive or linguistic or verbal; and dressing and toileting areas. Additional data collected on the study group revealed that changes were effected on the part of the parents. Parent gains involved a greater acceptance of the child's handicap, greater attendance and participation in parent meetings and workshops, a greater frequency of parents individually working with their child on their own initiative, and a greater frequency of parent constructed adaptive equipment.

PEERS Project: The PEERS Project in Philadelphia was initiated in 1973. Two years later it was funded as a 3-year model demonstration project of the U.S. government's Handicapped Children's Early Education Program. The population served by the project includes children from birth to 4 years of age who have developmental delays that are the result of any type of handicapping condition. PEERS is a center-based program in which the parents work with parent educators one time per week. During this period of time the parents receive specific course instruction that includes information on child development, child assessment, and other related topics. At the same time that the parent is receiving instruction a trained volunteer is working with the infant. During the week the parents are expected to carry out the home instruction component of the program. Parents are encouraged to spend 30 minutes per day working with their infant. A home visit is made by a project staff member once each month. The general philosophy of the project is that the parents are the most effective teachers of their own children.

   An evaluation of the PEERS project indicated that significant changes in the children's developmental performance were observed in all developmental areas and that these changes were greater than would be expected through maturational effect alone. Parent involvement, commitment, and attendance at the weekly training sessions were all felt to be positive effects of the PEERS project.

Kindling Individual Development System (KIDS): The KIDS project was funded initially in 1975. The project is a home-to-school transition program for children from birth to 6 years of age who have developmental delays, mental retardation, serious emotional disturbances, learning disabilities, orthopedic impairments, and other health impairments. There are basically three avenues of service available for the child and family: home-based training for infants, center-based stimulation classes for toddlers, and early childhood school-based classrooms for preschool children. Consistent improvement in the children serviced through the KIDS project has been shown across several modalities; numerous replication projects have arrrived at essentially the same results relative to effectiveness.

An important component of each of these program models is the degree of parental involvement. No matter how skilled a professional staff may be in identifying a developmental delay and subsequently designing a program of individual stimulation, the effectiveness of the program hinges in large measure on the degree of parental cooperation and involvement in the actual provision of treatment. Less than optimal parent-infant bonding, which originates in many instances in the neonatal period, must be minimized. It is necessary that the practitioner realize that the early weeks of the child's life are important for both the child and the mother, and that these weeks may have a far-reaching impact on later intervention efforts. Intervention efforts are complicated by parents who do not become fully involved in the overall process of providing added stimulation for the child. On the other hand, when parents are receptive to professional advice, eager to learn from the practitioner, and willing to patiently implement an intervention program, the rewards are great for the practitioner, the family unit, the parents, and, most importantly, the child. Parents are able to incorporate suggestions provided by the practitioner in settings to which the practitioner has limited access. Follow-through of this nature is a great benefit to the intervention process.

In summary, a variety of researchers have examined the effect on overall developmental status of providing early stimulation opportunities to high-risk infants. Although these investigations have differed somewhat in the type of stimulation provided, the person providing the added stimulation, the setting in which the stimulation was provided, and the age at which the infants were tested, results consistently indicated that preterm infants do benefit from early intervention efforts (Beckwith, Cohen, Kopp, Parmalee, and Marcy 1976; Field, 1980; Powell, 1974; and Ross, 1984). For additional data on specific early intervention programs and the effectiveness of these programs see Trohanis and colleagues (1982) and Guralnick and Bennett (1986). The data presented in the preceding sections by no means represent an exhaustive review of all available information on the effectiveness of early intervention. Rather, it was designed to provide the practitioner with a data base upon which to make important decisions about the need and the effectiveness of early intervention efforts. What has emerged is a consistent description of the effectiveness of early intervention, whether home- or center-based.

CRITICAL COMPONENTS OF AN EXEMPLARY EARLY CHILDHOOD PROGRAM

When one considers the critical components of an early intervention program for handicapped children, at least six areas of concern emerge. These are setting, facilities and equipment, curriculum and instructional strategy, parental involvement, evaluation, and personnel.The importance of parental involvement has been stressed previously. The discussion that follows centers on personnel, curriculum and instructional strategy, and evaluation.

Personnel

All early intervention programs, to be effective, need qualified staff. Implicit in this statement is the need to hire appropriately trained staff and to provide systematic in-service training to upgrade skills. However, even after the appropriate staff are secured, careful thought must be given to the most efficacious use of the personnel. The effective use of staff as well as support staff is critical to the effective functioning of an exemplary program for young handicapped children.

As noted previously, there are basically three models available for staff utilization: multi-, inter-, and transdisciplinary. In the multidisciplinary model each profession interacts with the child in relative isolation, sharing information with other professionals most likely in the context of formal meetings. In the interdisciplinary model there is more sharing of information, but role definitions and areas of responsibility are strictly adhered to. In the transdisciplinary model there is both a sharing of information and, through reciprocal training, an actual sharing of roles. The transdisciplinary approach appears to be the most efficacious use of current staff as it allows for the training of staff by other professionals not available on a regular basis, thus increasing the data base and service provision skills of the entire early intervention team. Direct service staff may include teachers, parents, teachers' aides, teacher assistants, volunteers, student teachers, psychologists, speech pathologists, physical therapists, occupational therapists, nurses, physicians, social workers, parent involvement coordinators, audiologists, and other disciplines as needed.

In the transdisciplinary approach the parents and teacher are viewed as the primary direct service personnel, as they are likely to have more contact with the child than anyone else. Other professional staff members assist in meeting the needs of the child by playing three roles. The first is a consultative role. Specialists are brought in specifically because of their expertise and provide professional advice and counsel to the parents and teachers based on the unique needs of the child. Specialists then assume the second role of trainers. They must train the parents and teachers in those specialized skills and techniques that are required to effectively carry out the child's intervention program. The specialist not only is responsible for training the parents and teachers how to implement special techniques and intervention strategies but also should document the effectiveness of the training efforts through regular assessment of the child's progress toward specific training goals set by the personnel working with the child. Not only should effectiveness of the training be determined initially but also periodic checks should be made by the specialist to determine if the skills learned by the parents and teachers are being maintained as they interact directly with the child.

The third role of the specialist is the more traditional role of direct service provision to the child. This role is used when the service to be provided is so specialized that it must be provided by the professional. In many instances only appropriately licensed or certified specialists can legally provide direct service to the children (Cronin, 1979).

Curriculum and Instructional Strategy

Organizing an effective early intervention program requires insight into the variety of materials available for instructional purposes as well as familiarity with various instructional strategies. Although it is outside the scope of this chapter to provide a detailed discussion of available curricula, several general principles relative to the selection of materials are discussed. Appendix C provides a listing of available resources and materials that should be of help when curriculum decisions are made.

Curriculum Selection

An initial consideration in curriculum selection is the population of children being served. If the population to be served consists of infants who are at risk because of a difficult neonatal period, and for whom no specific developmental deficit has been detected as yet, then the materials used should reflect this fact. If, on the other hand, the population to be served is made up of children with known developmental deficits, the selection of materials should be viewed differently. Although many of the materials available for infant stimulation activity are well rounded and cover all developmental domains, some of the available materials are better suited to specific areas of developmental concern, such as motor development, social development, or self-help skill learning. If the population targeted for intervention is unique because of etiological considerations, such as children with known neurological deficits, materials designed for this population should be selected.

An additional factor is the age of the population being served. Any curriculum selected for program implementation should be broad enough in application to cover a significant age span (birth to 3 years, for example) or be sufficiently specific to provide detailed developmental data for a more narrow age range. Familiarity with age and infant population details as specified in the previous paragraph aid greatly in the selection of materials.

The setting of intervention activity must also be considered. If the activity is to be conducted in the home, materials better suited for this purpose should be used. There are a variety of infant stimulation curricula designed specifically to be used by either the parent or the practitioner in the home setting. The materials and equipment used in a center-based infant stimulation program may not be readily available or transported to the home. This factor must also be kept in mind when materials are selected. Appendix C presents several categories of materials, including reference materials, materials for parent curriculums, data on specific early intervention programs, and specific infant curricula.

The actual selection of materials to be used for intervention services must of necessity be made in light of the developmental domains targeted for stimulation and enhancement. Although not all children included in early intervention efforts will need developmental stimulation in all domains, the practitioner must be prepared to provide activities in one or all areas of development. Hence, the selection should be made with this consideration in mind. A listing of the developmental domains that may be included in an individual training program are provided by Bricker (1982):

1. Communication: This covers the sending and receiving of gestural, vocal, or gestural-vocal signals or symbols for the purposes of requesting, demanding, answering, greeting, or protesting.
2. Sensorimotor: This includes the acquisition of problem-solving behaviors relating to causality, means-end, action schemes, object permanence, imitation, and spatial relationships.
3. Preoperational: This involves more complex problem solving behaviors and levels of cognitive organization such as those in classification, conservation, and seriation.
4. Gross Motor: This area refers to motoric activities and coordination using the larger muscles necessary for balance and movement through space.
5. Fine Motor: This area refers to those activities dependent upon the muscles used for precise movement and manipulation.
6. Socioemotional: This includes a constellation of diverse facial, gestural, postural, vocal, and intonational responses for interacting with the social environment.
7. Self-help: This refers to a broad set of generalized responses leading to independent functioning across environments. (p. 126)

Instructional Strategy

The operational model used by an intervention program will be determined by many variables, including the ones specified that relate to the selection of materials. Daily routine will be determined in part by the population being served, the setting in which service is provided, and the age of the children. With these variables in mind Bricker (1982) has proposed two general operational models of service provision, one for a center-based program and one more suited to a home-based service delivery model. Table 6–4 presents these two operational models. Although variations in daily routine are possible, the basic approach toward structuring daily routine will include much of what is contained in the Bricker model. A host of additional concerns relative to center-based intervention such as arranging space in the center, feeding, diapering, sleep patterns, handling emergencies, communicating with parents, hiring and training staff, monitoring quality, and various other duties are covered in an excellent resource guide by Herbert-Jackson, O'Brien, Porterfield, and Risley (1977) for those interested in initiating center-based programs.

In summary, Karnes (1969) described a variety of specific suggestions for those involved in the actual provision of early intervention activities. These would be helpful for all providers to keep in mind as stimulation activities are initiated and sustained. To make any program of early intervention a success the following suggestions should be considered:

1. Start on easy activities to bolster the babies' confidence, then try the more challenging ones.
2. Convey your enthusiasm and be encouraging.
3. As you progress through a program of early intervention keep in mind developmental milestones so that the child's performance can be accurately judged.
4. Be attentive to each child's rate of growth. Modify activities to meet the individual needs of the children in the program.
5. Be a competent planner. Plan daily or weekly to ensure more uniform progress toward developmental goals.
6. Remove as many distractions as possible from the teaching environment.
7. Repeat directions or demonstrate the activity to be worked on several times for the child.
8. Once a child learns a new skill encourage the frequent use of that skill. Practice a new skill learned frequently.
9. Inform parents and others of progress the child is making, thus increasing the probability of the child using the skill in a variety of settings.

Evaluation

A critical part of any ongoing infant intervention program is regular evaluation of the progress evidenced by the children, which ultimately

Table 6-4.　Operational Models for Home Based and Center Based Early Intervention Programs

Center Based	Home Based
Arrival routine (bathroom time, talking with parents)	Arrival (greeting parents and child)
Group activities in which some general task is targeted	Discussion with parents of child's weekly progress
Snack or rest time	Individual work with child
Small group or individual training	Assessment of work with child
Rearrangement of small group or individual training	Demonstration of new activity to be conducted by parents
Group Activity	
Closing Routine	Departure

Note: From Finding and Educating High Risk and Handicapped Infants (p. 125) by C. Ramey and P. Trohanis (Eds.), 1982, Baltimore: University Park Press. Copyright 1982 by University Park Press. Reprinted by permission.

reflects on the success of the program itself. The obvious desired outcome of any intervention efforts, regardless of the model employed, is increased child performance. Therefore, questions must be addressed: What are the effects of specific materials on the child's performance? Are the facilities adequate for learning? Is there a need for additional or different staff? Is the curriculum appropriate? How effectively is the staff communicating with the parents? Is the progress that is evidenced by the children above that that would normally be anticipated as a result of maturation? Each of these areas are important considerations for those involved in early childhood intervention. Although there are many specific evaluation strategies that can be used, several evaluation principles are important.

The purpose of evaluation is to provide information that will contribute to better decision making, either for program improvement or for program accountability. This essentially means that evaluation is not conducted for its own sake but to assist educators who must make decisions about educational programs. Should this early childhood education program be continued as it is or should it be modified? Does the identification process work properly? Are parents informed about their rights under current federal and state legislation? These are all examples of important questions that need to be answered in the management of an early childhood education program. The function of evaluation is to assist in clarifying these questions and then to gather and analyze data that will help to provide answers.

Evaluation is a rational, systematic process that can usually be carried out by the same people who are implementing the program. Cronin (1979) listed five basic steps in the evaluation process.

1. Plan the evaluation design. Identify the evaluation questions to be addressed or the objectives to be measured; specify the procedures for answering these questions; specify when to collect the data and how it will be analyzed.
2.. Select or develop instrumentation.
3. Administer instrumentation or gather information.
4. Compile and analyze data or information.
5. Prepare a report or set of recommendations based on the results. Put the results in a format that enables them to be useful in answering the questions for which they were gathered. (p. 34)

An example of an evaluation format provided by the state of Illinois (Cronin, 1979) is shown in Table 6–5. Specific evaluation questions, as well as ideas about when and how these questions are to be answered are included. The questions relate to service delivery and are not exhaustive. A similar format can be used to evaluate child identification procedures, staff development efforts, and other areas of program concern. The important point to recall is that evaluation is not an option but rather a critical component of any early intervention efforts.

SUMMARY

The current status of early intervention is the product of several forces that have facilitated and enhanced its role in education. Parental concern, research data, legislative intent, and societal pressure all have contributed to an enhanced interest in and the actual provision of early childhood services for children from birth. A careful review of controlled studies that have systematically measured the effectiveness of a variety of early childhood intervention programs reveals that early intervention does indeed lessen the effects of a precarious neonatal period and also improves the overall developmental status of children with handicapping conditions. An important ingredient in any early intervention program is parental involvement. Although a variety of models exist for the provision of early intervention services, as well as several strategies for use of staff, the objectives of developmental enrichment programs are to help overcome delays in the babies' developmental progress and to help parents understand the disabilities and their implications, accept and be responsible for increased participation in daily treatment, and face the disability in a positive way. As Soboloff (1979) stated: "It can no longer be accepted that treatment

Table 6-5.   Sample Evaluation Questions Relative to Service Delivery

Questions	When and How
1. Has a full continuum of services been implemented in the program?	Documentation to be collected annually and summarized in a descriptive fashion
2. Is the learning environment adequate, or can it be improved?	Documentation to be collected annually or every 2 years
3. Have procedures for establishing parent involvement been implemented?	Documentation to be collected annually and compiled in a descriptive fashion
4. How effective is the parent involvement component of the program?	Documentation to be collected annually (numbers and percentages of parents responding favorably should be reported)
5. Is there evidence that the content of the curriculum is developmentally relevant?	Documentation delineated at the start of the program and periodically revised
6. Is there evidence that the instructional strategy and curriculum are resulting in the attainment of desired skills?	Documentation collected at the conclusion of each unit
7. Is there evidence that the staff is being utilized effectively?	Documentation collected annually and changes made as needed
8. Is there evidence that the overall program is making a significant difference in the achievement of the children?	A pretest/posttest design used annually

for these children does not begin until three years of age. From our own experience, we feel that early stimulation benefits not only the child, but also the parents and the entire family" (p. 424). It is to this goal that practitioners direct early intervention efforts.

REFERENCES

Beckwith, L., Cohen, S., Kopp, C., Parmelee, A., and Marcy, T. (1976). Caregiver-infant interaction and early cognitive development in preterm infants. *Child Development, 47,* 579.

Bricker, D. (1982). Program planning for at risk and handicapped children. In C. Ramey and P. Trohanis (Eds.), *Finding and educating high risk and handicapped infants.* Baltimore: University Park Press.

Caldwell, B., and Richmond, J. (1964). Programmed day care for the very young child: A preliminary report. *Journal of Marriage and the Family, 26,* 481.

Cronin, J. (1979). *Early childhood education for the handicapped.* Springfield, IL: Illinois State Board of Education.

Field, T. (1980). Teenage, lower-class, black mothers and their preterm infants: An intervention and developmental follow-up. *Child Development, 50,* 426.

Goldfarb, W. (1943). The effects of early institutional care on adolescent personality. *Journal of Experimental Education, 12,* 106.

Gray, S. (1977). *The family-oriented home visiting program: A longitudinal study.* Nashville: Peabody College.

Guralnick, M., and Bennett, F. (Eds.). *The effectiveness of early intervention for at-risk and handicapped children.* New York: Academic Press.

Herbert-Jackson, E., O'Brien, M., Porterfield, J., and Risley, T. (1977). *The infant center.* Baltimore: University Park Press.

Jones, G. (1985). *Seventh annual report to Congress on the Implementation of the Education of the Handicapped article.* Washington, DC: Division of Education Services Special Education Programs, U.S. Department of Education.

Karnes, M. (1969). *Investigations of classroom and at-home interventions: Research and development program on preschool and disadvantaged children* (Final Rep. No. 5-1181). Washington, DC: Bureau of Research, Office of Education, U.S. Department of Health Education and Welfare.

Keister, M. (1970). *The good life for infants and toddlers.* Washington, DC: National Association for the Education of Young Children.

Leib, S., Benfield, G., and Guidubaldi, J. (1980). Effects of early intervention and stimulation on the preterm infant. *Pediatrics, 66,* 83.

Levenstein, P. (1971). *Mothers are early cognitive trainers: Guiding low income mothers to work with their preschoolers.* Paper presented at the meeting of the Society for Research in Child Development, Minneapolis.

Mallory, A. (1985, November 6). Study shows benefits of early learning. *St. Louis Post Dispatch,* p. 7.

McCarthy, J. (1980). Early intervention and school programs for preschool handicapped children. In E. Sell (Ed.), *Follow-up of the high risk newborn: A practical approach.* Springfield, IL: Charles C. Thomas.

Palmer, F. (1976). *The effects of minimal early intervention on subsequent I.Q. scores and reading achievement* (Research Rep.). Washington, DC: Educational Commission of the States.

Powell, L. (1974). The effect of extra stimulation and maternal involvement on the development of low-birth-weight infants and on maternal behavior. *Child Development, 45,* 106.

Provence, S. (1974). Early intervention: Experiences in a service-centered research program. In D. Bergsma (Ed.), *The infant at risk.* New York: Intercontinental Medical Books.

Ross, G. (1984). Home intervention for premature infants of low-income families. *American Journal Of Orthopsychiatry, 54,* 263.

Scarr-Salapatek, S., and Williams, M. (1973). The effects of early stimulation of low birth weight infants. *Child Development, 44,* 94.

Schaefer, E., and Aaronson, M. (1972). Infant education research project: Implementation and implications of the home-tutoring program. In R. Parker (Ed.), *The preschool in action.* Boston: Allyn and Bacon.

Skeels, H., and Dye, H. (1939). A study of the effects of differential stimulation on mentally retarded children. *Proceedings of the American Association of Mental Defectives, 44,* 114.

Soboloff, H. (1979). Developmental enrichment programs. *Developmental Medicine and Child Neurology, 21,* 423.

Spitz, R. (1945). Hospitalism. *Psychoanalytic Study of the Child, 1,* 53.

Trohanis, P., Cox, J., and Meyer, R. (1982). A report on selected demonstration programs for infant intervention. In C. Ramey and P. Trohanis (Eds.), *Finding and educating high risk and handicapped infants.* Baltimore: University Park Press.

Williams, M., and Scarr,S. (1971). Effects of short-term intervention on performance in low birth weight disadvantaged children. *Pediatrics, 47,* 287.

Chapter 7

Delivery of Services

Statements made in earlier chapters alluded to the fact that an increasing number of practitioners representing a variety of disciplines are involved in the provision of services, either direct or indirect, to high-risk infants. The actual number of professionals involved would be impossible to determine. The services provided by these practitioners are geared toward children during infancy and the preschool years as well as during the elementary school years. What types of services are these professionals providing? What type of academic or educational preparation do they have? How have they alerted other professionals and the community to their availability? How have they kept current on the subject of high-risk infants? What do they see as needed areas of future research with this population of children? What specific duties do they perform? And finally, what additional resources are available to them as they provide clinical services? These questions relate to who the practitioner is and what the practitioner is currently doing or should be doing with this unique population of children. These concerns and others are addressed in this chapter.

THE HIGH-RISK INTERVENTION TEAM

To gain a more complete understanding of the services provided for high-risk infants, familiarity with the various members of the team of professionals working with this population would be most helpful.

Although team makeup may vary from setting to setting, the disciplines
that are usually represented include the social worker, physical therapist, speech-language pathologist, occupational therapist, developmental
psychologist, early childhood educator, neonatologist, and developmental pediatrician. Each of these disciplines may play varying roles in
the actual provision of services to the high-risk infant.

Occupational and Physical Therapists

The roles of occupational and physical therapists who work with populations of young children have merged in some settings. Although settings do exist in which occupational and physical therapists function
separately with pediatric populations, in the provision of services to at-
risk infants their services often overlap. Each of these professions is
concerned primarily with the child's strengths and problem areas in
gross and fine motor development and sensory skills. The evaluation
and treatment of motor disorders overlaps with the child's total development, and, therefore, physical and occupational therapists work
closely with other professionals providing services to the at-risk population. Each of these professionals is trained specifically to detect and
treat disorders of both fine and gross motor functioning. Familiarity
with normal motor development as well as with common or significant
deviations from what should be the normal pattern of development
allows the occupational and physical therapists to contribute to a significant degree to the team effort directed toward the child. These therapists are trained to evaluate and take into consideration muscle tone,
postural reactions, sensory skills, and functional motor skills. Once
deviations are detected, they are equipped to provide a course of treatment designed to alleviate the effects of motor dysfunction. The therapist may work with a child either in a one-on-one format or in small
groups. The treatment may take place in the home or in a hospital or
school setting. Generally, the program of treatment directed toward the
child with motor dysfuction is individualized to meet the specific needs
of the child. With younger populations of children physical and occupational therapists are involved to a great degree with parents. They
may design a program of treatment that is to be administered, in large
measure, by the parents. Occupational and physical therapists are
invaluable members of the high-risk infant team. Their services should
be highly valued by the other team members. Physical therapists
receive an undergranduate education in physical therapy from a training program certified by the American Physical Therapy Association.
Graduate education is also available in physical therapy. In addition,
physical therapists are licensed by each state. The passing of an exami-

nation is one of the requirements for licensure. Occupational therapists currently are not licensed in all states. However, the National Occupational Therapy Association administers a national examination in occupational therapy. After passing the examination the therapist is designated as a registered occupational therapist. A minimum of an undergraduate education in occupational therapy is required.

The Social Worker

The social worker is trained to plan for and provide services to individuals that will increase or restore their capabilities for social functioning. The social worker's goal is to improve social capability on all levels (West, 1978). Many social workers have received training in family counseling also and function quite well in that capacity. Social workers have knowledge of human development and behavior, social welfare systems and institutions, social and economic factors, and the availability of supportive services for children and their families. On the interdisciplinary team the social worker may serve as a case coordinator or as the main investigator in gaining historical data for a particular infant. All members of the team need background data on the child and family and information on the family's attitude toward the child and capacity to provide for the special needs of the child. The social worker is in the best position to gain such information. The family of the high-risk infant faces a unique set of circumstances that increase family stress (see Chapter 4), and the social worker is in a position to anticipate these after the child returns home. The continuation of services to the family over time, with special emphasis on family adjustment, would be a prime interest of the social worker. In addition, aiding the family in handling financial stress due to a prolonged hospital stay for the infant would appear to be valuable to parents. Social workers must a have minimum of a graduate degree in social work to be certified by the American College of Social Workers. In addition, the passage of a national examination is necessary to receive full certification.

The Speech-Language Pathologist and the Audiologist

The speech-language pathologist and the audiologist have a valuable role to play in terms of both direct and indirect service to the high-risk infant. One of the most frequently mentioned areas of concern for developmentally delayed children is communication. Follow-up studies of high-risk infants and other groups of delayed children consistently reveal that communication skills are generally impaired (see Chapter 3). Speech-language pathologists and audiologists are often referred to as communication specialists. They perform services, both diagnostic and therapeutic, in a variety of settings. These include public schools, colleges and universities, community speech and hearing centers, military institutions, hospitals, and private practice settings. Although the direct provision of services to the at-risk infant by the speech-language pathologist may be limited at first, valuable information can be shared with parents about the normal course of speech and language development. Because communication skills are such an integral part of social and academic performance, the parents can be appraised of activities they can perform that may serve to enhance speech and language development. As the child matures and is receiving systematic follow-up assessments the speech-language pathologist will provide important input on speech and language development as well as direct therapeutic intervention if indicated. The minimum educational requirements for certification by the American Speech-Language-Hearing Association include a master's degree in speech pathology or audiology. The speech-language pathologist and the audiologist also serve a 12-month clinical fellowship year in which close supervision by a certified professional in speech pathology or audiology is provided, thus ensuring high levels of professional expertise.

The Early Childhood Education Specialist

The term early childhood education specialist (ECES) refers to a variety of academic disciplines that share a common interest in the infant and the preschool child. Some of these areas include studies in human growth and development, child life, developmental psychology, preschool programs for handicapped children, special education, curriculum design, and family life. Perhaps the best way to describe the ECES is as a professional whose major interests and skills lie in the field of applied developmental psychology with emphasis on early childhood development, early childhood education, and the relationship of these two areas to early intervention programs with at-risk infants and young children (Allen, 1978). There is a growing trend toward professional certification and specified degree requirements for those interested in early childhood education; however, not all states have moved in this direction at present. An increasing number of universities are providing degree programs to meet the demands for persons specifically trained in early childhood education.

A valuable asset possessed by the ECES is interdisciplinary training. This becomes increasingly important as efforts are made to integrate developmentally delayed children into regular preschool programs in line with the spirit of U.S. Public Law 94–142. As a member of the high-risk infant team the ECES is in a position to provide valuable input for professionals working with these infants. A thorough knowledge of growth and development and familiarity with the results of stimulus deprivation and intervention strategies are important skills possessed by the ECES. The ECES's role may include the provision of input to other professionals or the direct provision of services in one of several ways. These include early identification, assessment, intervention and prevention, transition to other school programs, and systematic follow-up efforts. The ECES may assume a number of responsibilities on the interdisciplinary team that focuses its efforts on the high-risk or young handicapped child. The ECES is a necessary component of an early identification and intervention program and performs a valuable service to parents and professionals alike.

Educational and Developmental Psychologist

Both the educational and the developmental psychologist have valuable contributions to make to the overall services provided to young children who are displaying developmental delays or who are at risk of doing so. The developmental psychologist is less apt to be involved with direct service to individuals and is more likely to be employed in an academic setting or in consultation with several possible organizations. The developmental psychologist is knowledgeable about general principles of how and why changes in behavior occur and what variables relate to change (La Veck, 1978). The educational psychologist is most likely to be trained in educational programming. Educational psychologists are often equipped to diagnose specific learning problems in school-age children. Many educationaal psychologists as well as developmental psychologists have assumed an expanded role both in diagnosis and intervention strategies for young handicapped children.

The actual activities engaged in by the psychologist on the interdisciplinary team may depend more on the setting in which the activities are performed than on the psychologist's individual academic background. Direct time spent with children and parents will vary from setting to setting. The psychologist may assume two basic roles as a member of the team. The first is that of participant in the ongoing services rendered to a child. This usually involves the sharing and comparing of observations about an infant that may be outside the specific domain of any single discipline. The second major role is as a provider of services unique to the discipline of psychology. These may include behavior management, counseling, and educational planning. The most familiar role, however, may involve the administration and interpretation of psychological tests. Another area in which service is rendered by the psychologist is that of communicating with parents and helping them to better understand and accept the unique needs of their children. The psychologist may be in the best postition to interpret diagnostic data relative to infant performance and to communicate these results to parents and the entire team. The minimum requirements for a psychologist include a graduate degree in psychology, with special emphasis in developmental or educational psychology. Licensure requirements vary from state to state and may depend, in part, on the setting in which the psychologist is employed. State and national examinations may be required for certification or licensure. An internship of varying length may be an additional requirement for appropriate certification, thus ensuring a high level of professional expertise.

Medical Personnel

Physician input for those working with young at-risk children is an essential part of the overall provision of services. The greater the deviance that a child shows from normal developmental patterns the greater is the likelihood that there is a medical reason for the problems. In general the neonatologist and pediatrician will be the first physicians to be involved in the provision of medical care for the at-risk infant. Once the child is released from the NICU, primary medical care will be provided by the pediatrician. Pediatricians must know a great deal about growth and development and the effects of diseases on children. In many instances the pediatrician may consult with other medical specialists. The more complex the child's medical problems the more specialists the child is likely to see. In many settings the pediatrician serves as the coordinator for these specialists. Some of the medical specialists to whom a child might be referred include the opthamologist, otolaryngologist, orthopedist, pediatric neurologist, psychiatrist, geneticist, and physiatrist. The pediatrician's role is paramount in providing primary medical care for the child as well as in helping the parents fully understand the information gained through referral to any of a number of medical specialists.

An additional member of the team might be the pediatric nurse. The nurse is quite familiar with the specific characteristics of the child because of the prolonged contact between the nurse and infant in the NICU. If the team functions in a hospital setting, the input provided by pediatric nurses can be a valuable source of information. In some settings dismissal decisions are made by the neonatologist and the nurse, with the nurse having equal say about the child's readiness to go home.

Team Management

An additional consideration that relates to the team concept of service provision is the manner in which the team performs its duties. A team that works well together must make a variety of decisions that relate to philosophy and the sharing of team responsibilities. Additional concerns relate to answering the question, How are we actually going to provide services to at-risk children? These decisions relate in large measure to team leadership. In the past it was assumed that the best leadership for teams of this nature could be provided by a medical director. In actual practice today, however, this is not usually the case. Many early intervention teams are headed by nonmedical professionals. This includes those teams that may be providing services within a medical setting.

One concept of team functioning that has gained wide acceptance is the case manager system. The rationale behind the case manager system is the realization that the team approach implies that a group of people are dealing with an individual child; thus, somebody has to "be in charge" of each case (Holm and McCartin, 1978). The professional who assumes the role of being in charge for a particular child is known as the case manager. The case manager may make initial contact with the parents and, based on referral information and data gained from the parents, assigns various members of the team to assess and work with the child. The assumption is that all members of the team may not need to see each child. Thus, the case manager, in combination with the team members who do see the child, arrives at a final disposition for each child. The decision reached may involve referral for immediate early intervention, additional assessment by other team members, or simply sending the child home to be reevaluated in 3 to 6 months. If the decision reached includes the need for additional assessment or intervention, the case manager arranges these appointments and sees that all concerned are aware of the recommendations. Follow-up appointments are also arranged by the case manager. If several members of a team are assigned to see a child, then it is the case manager who schedules a staffing in which input from all professionals is gained and a final disposition is arrived at.

One helpful suggestion is that it is usually best to try to match the professional expertise of the case manager to the primary nature of the child's problem. For example, if the child referred is 8 months of age, and the primary concern is that of delayed motor skills, case management might be assumed by the physical or occupational therapist. The case manager system is a valuable means of organizing service delivery when a team approach to evaluation and intervention is used. If the number of professionals interacting with an infant is low, then alternative styles of service delivery may be better suited to a particular service model.

SETTINGS FOR SERVICE DELIVERY

Medical Settings

Services to high-risk infants are being provided in a variety of settings today. Perhaps one of the first that comes to mind is the medical facility. As has been pointed out, neonatal intensive care nurseries have proliferated nationally in the past 25 years. Large medical facilities that house these nurseries may also include an array of support personnel who are involved in the provision of services. These may include all or most of the disciplines specified previously. In most instances, however, the actual provision of ongoing developmental stimulation over time will not emanate from the medical facility. That is not to say that the medical facility may not be involved in longitudinal research activity, or be available for medical consultation should the need arise. Rather, the large medical setting may provide regular reassessment of infants who have been patients in the NICU and refer to other settings those infants in need of long-term monitoring and follow-up.

Practitioners who are currently employed in medical settings should alert themselves to the degree to which both evaluative and follow-up activity with high-risk infants is taking place. If the overall mission of the facility is compatible with what is involved in the provision of long-term services for high-risk infants, then services may be expanded. Later in this chapter direction is given to the practitioner on how to alert members of the medical community to the need for ongoing services to the high-risk infant.

Public Education Settings

As specified in the previous chapter, an increasing number of states are mandating the provision of special services to children at younger and younger ages, with several states requiring the provision of special services from birth. Michigan, for example, currently mandates the provision of services to young developmentally delayed children at birth and extends the mandate until the individual is 25 years of age (see Tables 6–1 and 6–2). This encompasses an age range in need of unique educational experiences for which public education is not accustomed. As state legislators lowered the age for which special services were available, local school districts across the United States were faced with a difficult problem. No trained professionals were currently in public education settings who had been specifically prepared to provide intervention and early identification services to children below the customary age for starting school. Because of this dilemma, many school districts contracted with local private agencies to provide services for children at younger ages. As mandates were written that lowered the age at which special services were available, the new legislation allowed local school districts to contract for early intervention services that the school districts themselves were unable to provide. In time, however, school districts, for the most part, began hiring personnel who had expertise with younger handicapped children and began providing their own early childhood education programs.

There are a variety of models used by school districts in the provision of early childhood services. Information presented in the previous chapter describes these in greater detail. Basically, however, early childhood education services for handicapped children under the age of 5 years are either center- or home-based. Prekindergarten classes may be offered for those children with a high-risk history as a means of better preparing them for enrollment into regular classrooms. These usually are initiated when the child is 3 years of age. Prior to 3 years of age services are generally home-based. A variety of infant enrichment curriculum programs have become available in the past decade to meet the local school district's need for programming and curriculum for children under the age of 5 years who have special needs. These provide systematic and structured intervention activities for children under age 5 and cover all areas of development (social, cognitive, motor, and communication). Appendix C lists a variety of materials that provide input for infant intervention programming. In many states that are primarily rural and made up of smaller school districts a severe hardship exists for a school district that must by law provide services for a small number of young handicapped children. One solution to this has been the formulation of special education agreements between districts to share the costs for service provision. The state of Iowa, for example, has formed Area Education Agencies (AEA), which provide all special services for a group of local school districts. The location of special classrooms are strategically placed in the area covered by the AEA so that needed services are readily available to all children within the AEA.

In most instances services that are available to young developmentally disabled children through the public schools are provided in a transdisciplinary manner. The transdisciplinary approach allows for the training of staff by other professionals not readily available, thus increasing the data base and service provision skills of the entire early intervention team. A case manager approach is often used. It is the case manager's responsibility to coordinate all services provided for a particular child and to ensure that proper communication between all persons involved takes place. (For a complete discussion of the transdisciplinary approach see Chapter 6.)

The personnel involved in the provision of services through local school districts may not vary much from that described previously. In center-based models an early childhood education specialist may provide the actual instruction to both the parents and the child. The teacher would have available the input from any or all of the other professionals discussed previously, but most likely on an itinerant basis. It would be cost prohibitive in most instances for a school district to provide a full-time speech-language pathologist for each classroom working with young developmentally delayed children. The professionals previously mentioned are available in the school setting to provide input to both teachers and parents as needed. Periodically, the entire array of professionals working with a child will gather to discuss progress, to reevaluate child performance and to formulate future treatment goals. This is all in accordance with U.S. Public Law 94–142 (see Chapter 6), which specifies regular updating of educational programming. Public school settings have undergone a great deal of change in the past 15 years relative to their expertise in the provision of services to young developmentally delayed children. As additional states mandate the provision of services to younger and younger children, local school districts will become, and already are in many communities, the primary resource for parents of preschool developmentally delayed children or those children at risk for developing developmental delay.

Private Agencies

Services to young developmentally delayed children were first available in many instances through private agencies or agencies funded by federal funds but not part of the local school district. Recall that in 1968 Public Law 90–538, The Federal Handicapped Children Early Education Assistance Act, was passed by the U.S. Congress. This act allowed for the establishment of model demonstration centers nationally to alert professional and local communities to the unique needs of young handicapped children. The centers also were mandated to serve as training centers for other professionals who showed initial interest in the provision of services to young handicapped children. These model demonstration centers fostered in many communities the establishment of a variety of child development centers. Although the primary population worked with in these centers varied greatly, the need to establish early intervention centers soon became obvious. The models of service provision in private centers varied greatly also, as did primary funding sources. In some instances fees were waived completely or determined by family income and based on a sliding scale. Other funding sources were federal and state, as well as research and demonstration grants.

As federal and state funds became harder to obtain because of spending restrictions, and as more and more school districts began providing services for students that they might previously have contracted services for, private agencies found themselves competing for fewer and fewer available dollars. The results have been both positive and negative: negative in that many agencies have been forced to close their doors and positive in that new avenues of service provision and funding have been explored. The private agency continues to play an important role in the overall spectrum of services available to young developmentally delayed children.

INITIATING SERVICES

Practitioners may find themselves employed in settings in which services to high-risk infants are possible but are not taking place. What steps can be taken to alert other staff and administrators to the need to provide early identification and intervention services? In other words, how does a practitioner go about initiating an early identification and intervention program in a setting in which one does not currently exist? The answer to that question is not a simple one and depends on several factors.

In Public Education Settings

One of the first considerations for the practitioner desirous of initiating services is the nature of the setting. In a public school setting restrictions on those who may be served are mandated by law. It is imperative that the practitioner be thoroughly familiar with state law governing special education. The age and populations for which services are mandated are of primary concern. Many states distinguish between mandatory ages and permissive ages. For example, it is possible for a state to mandate that children receive services at 5 years of age, but the law may permit the provision of services at younger ages, thus leaving decisions about serving youger children up to the individual school districts. In a situation of this nature the practitioner must assess the need in the community as well as the local school district's willingness to provide services to children below the mandated ages.

If the need is present, the practitioner must then begin to educate those in decision-making positions. The process of educating administrators and others concerned can take a varity of forms and can vary in length. The unique needs of high-risk infants as well as the developmental problems encountered by high-risk infants in both the preschool and school-age years can be stressed. The effectiveness of early intervention in reducing developmental delay, thus affording the child the opportunity to perform better in the elementary grades, should be pointed out. The data on early intervention presented in the previous chapter clearly demonstrate the efficacy of early case finding and intervention. This should be of interest to administrators who are concerned about efforts to prevent later school problems, which may incur greater involvement of special education personnel at a later date. Educational efforts of this nature may take a variety of forms, including the use of slide or tape presentations, films about high-risk infants, films describing normal infant development, videotape presentations, and presentations made by parents of high-risk infants. Putting those in decision-making positions in touch with current information on the need for early identification is mandatory. A listing of available materials of this nature can be obtained from Polly Morph Films Inc., 118 South Street, Boston, MA 02111. Another source of materials of this nature is university library holdings.

One advocacy source that the practitioner must use is the parents. The history of both state and federal legislation dealing with special education clearly demonstrates the effectiveness of parent groups in alerting legislators and administrators to populations of special children in need of services. Parents of young children with known mental and physical disabilities are aware of the difficulty of meeting the needs of their children. Parents of children who are at risk of displaying a developmental delay because of a high-risk history first need to be alerted to the potential of a delay in their child's development. Part of this process involves alerting them to state and federal mandates that cover the provision of services to handicapped or delayed children. They should be alerted to the fact that U.S. Public Law 94–142, which was described in Chapter 6, mandates the screening of children suspected of delay as soon as the delay is suspected. Although actual service provision is not mandated for children less than 3 years of age, screening and diagnostic services are included in the law for children from birth. Once this is accomplished, parents will generally lend support to local efforts to both identify and provide early intervention services for high-risk infants. Once again the concept of education becomes important.

How may parents be educated about the need for identification and intervention for high-risk infants? Community education must be a goal of the practitioner and can take a variety of forms. Certainly the media can help. Both radio and television public service announcements can be of assistance. Public speaking opportunities available in a community can be a valuable forum in which the practitioner can alert parents to the needs of high-risk infants. Identifying other professionals in a community who share an interest in early identification is also a valuable asset. One strategy that can be used to alert parents of developmental concerns is a developmental profile or checklist. Profiles of this nature alert parents to normal infant and child developmental milestones and inform parents of whom to contact in the event that concerns exist about their child's development. Developmental checklists of this nature can be placed in locations frequented by parents such as physician offices, dental offices, preschools, and hospitals, and they can even be made available to parents through the mail. Providing parents with information of this nature is a valuable means of alerting them to normal development and thereby alerting them and enlisting their help in identifying delayed development.

Although the preceding suggestions are directed initially toward practitioners in public education settings, they are applicable regardless of employment setting. Grass roots efforts of this nature are quite effective in alerting school administrators, the community, parents, other professionals, and legislators that a need exists for the provision of services for a population of children who have not previously been served.

In Medical Settings

Although the number of intensive care nurseries has expanded rapidly in the past decade, unfortunately the presence of systematic high-risk infant follow-up and early intervention programs in hospitals with neonatal intensive care nurseries has not kept pace. It is entirely possible for a practitioner to be employed in a hospital setting that contains a NICU but that is not involved in systematic follow-up and early intervention efforts once the child is dismissed from the unit. How does the practitioner in a setting such as this initiate services to high-risk infants once they are discharged from the hospital?

Once again the key concept is the solicitation of support from those in a position to authorize a program of evaluation and intervention. Pointing out the need for special attention to the high-risk population is of paramount importance. The use of a high-risk registry may help. This concept is not new. Basically, it involves establishing a set of criteria that are used to identify those infants who should be the recipients of systematic follow-up activity. The actual manner in which a high-risk registry is used may vary from state to state. The registry may be used to identify mothers prenatally who because of age, educational, medical, or other factors may be at risk of delivering a premature infant. In the case of the high-risk infant who is unanticipated by the mother or health care professionals, upon dismissal from the NICU the child may be placed on a registry and followed locally by community health nurses or other professionals to which the registry is disseminated. The registry thus allows for a systematic way of alerting the appropriate persons of the presence of a high-risk infant in a particular home setting. Of course the parents may choose not to participate in follow-up activity, but at least local professionals are alerted to the presence of the child in the community. Physicians are quite familiar with the concept of a risk registry as they use it in a variety of other medical contexts.

Laney (1985) presented a strategy to alert physicians to the need for early identification and intervention for communicative disorders. The principles presented by Laney are equally applicable to efforts designed to alert physicians to the need for follow-up and intervention for high-risk infants. Physicians, both family practitioners and specialists, are in perhaps the best position in which to refer a child suspected of delay for developmental assessment and possible early intervention. The physician is usually the first professional consulted by parents if they have concerns about their child's development. Even for the child with a known high-risk history, the physician can play a critical role in encouraging parents to participate in follow-up efforts.

The program described by Laney contains two basic parts with several sections under each major heading. The first major step is that of gaining access to physicians and then facilitating their awareness of the unique needs of high-risk infants. Gaining access is to be geared toward both individuals and service delivery systems. The practitioner may choose to express the need for follow-up of high-risk infants either on an individual basis or a small group basis. The practitioner should be alert to opportunities present in the medical setting that facilitate access of this nature. Gaining access to service delivery systems that currently do not serve the high-risk population can take a variety of forms and may involve efforts directed toward well baby clinics, state institutions that serve young developmentally delayed children, and any existing format in which infants receive regular medical evaluation. Once access to individuals and systems is obtained, the next step is facilitating awareness of the unique needs of the high-risk infant. Enhancing awareness of the need to provide follow-up and intervention for high-risk infants must be directed toward the specific audience the practitioner is interested in. Activities such as lecturing to medical students, participating in rounds with physicians, volunteer work in the intensive care nursery, and providing printed material can be valuable aids in increasing the awareness of target audiences. Additional strategies include making regular visits to physicians' offices to further enhance their awareness of the need. Up to 75 percent of all pediatricians do not systematically evaluate the developmental performance of their patients (Shonkoff, Dworkin, and Leviton, 1979). Time constraints and lack of awareness and training contribute to this. The practitioner may suggest that a regular schedule of developmental assessments be established for any of the patients for whom skill acquisition is in doubt. These assessments may be conducted by the practitioner in the physician's office and may serve to alert both the physician and the parents of patients seen to the need for developmental follow-up of this nature. As the practitioner becomes aware of specific high-risk infants who are displaying delay, it may be possible to accompany the child to its normal physician appointment and demonstrate to the parents and physician alike simple screening activities. The effectiveness of early intervention as well as community resources for such intervention can be stressed. Consistent efforts of this nature reap great benefits relative to enlisting the support of physicians and others who are in a position to aid in establishing services for the high-risk population.

An example of the benefits of implementing the strategies described here has been provided by L. Hopkins (personal communication, January 13, 1986). As the mother of twins, Hopkins, a speech-language pathologist, became interested in other children in the local NICU who were not being systematically followed or receiving early intervention efforts. She approached her pediatrician about her concerns (gaining access) and over time educated him on the unique needs of high-risk infants (facilitating awareness). The physician's response was to approach the board of the local hospital with a proposal that would allow Mrs. Hopkins access to the NICU for assessment and intervention efforts. These efforts are currently under way. Grass roots activity of this nature can be a potent force in establishing new delivery systems designed to meet the unique needs of the high-risk infant.

An additional source of help to the practitioner desirous of initiating services to high-risk infants is provided by state developmental disabilities councils. These councils had their beginning in 1963 when U.S. Public Law 88–164 was signed into law by John Kennedy. The overall mission of the councils, which are present in every state, is to plan, advocate for, and advise on the needs of the developmentally delayed population within each state. Practitioners would be wise to acquaint themselves with the workings of the council in their representative state. Although councils use their federally allocated funds differently, many councils award grants to initiate services to populations of developmentally delayed persons. There has been attention directed by these state councils toward the needs of the high-risk population as evidenced by grants awarded for the implementation of service delivery systems.

KEEPING CURRENT

Coursework on the graduate and undergraduate level geared specifically toward the high-risk infant is virtually nonexistent. A notable exception is the interdisciplinary infant specialist graduate program recently developed by Rutgers University and the University Affiliated Facility of the University of Medicine and Dentristry of New Jersey. This program is intended for students from disciplines including speech-language pathology, special education, psychology, physical and occupational therapy, early childhood education, nursing, and social work. Coursework will be offered in infant development, handicapping conditions, interdisciplinary assessment, and intervention approaches. The program is designed to prepare students to work with high-risk and handicapped infants and their families.

Most practitioners, however, have equipped themselves by extensive personal effort to gain a broad base of information about high-risk infants. Although several academic disciplines include coursework on infant development, developmental psychology, and parent-child relationships, the newness of neonatology and the relatively recent awareness of the fact that an increasing number of infants are surviving precarious neonatal periods accounts, in part, for the lack of formal coursework in this area. How then does the practitioner gain access to data geared toward the at-risk infant? Several avenues exist. First and foremost is the academic preparation provided by the practitioner's chosen discipline. The disciplines addressed throughout this text provide various degrees of input and information about human development. Elective coursework is possible in areas of interest that relate directly or indirectly to various aspects of at-risk infants. An additional source of information, and an invaluable one, is familiarity with publications (journals, texts, and otherwise) that direct effort, both didactic and research, toward high-risk infants. Appendix C provides a list of potential sources. An additional source of information is provided by Parents of Premature and High-Risk Infants International (PPHRI), an organization formed in 1982. The organization was formed by parents and perinatal professionals from across the United States. Its purpose is to provide information, referrals, and support to parent groups, families, and professionals concerned with infants who required special care at birth. PPHRI is affiliated with the National Self-Help Clearinghouse, The Graduate School and University Center of the City University of New York, 33 West 42nd Street, New York, NY 10036. Multiple publications and notices of national and local conferences are provided by PPHRI on request.

Talking with other practitioners and attending conferences and continuing education activities can also be of valuable help to the practitioner. An inquisitive mind, an insatiable appetite to learn, and the energy to feed that appetite are all indispensible attributes for the practitioner in need of greater education and information about high-risk infants.

THE FUTURE

Medical technology is making rapid progress in enhancing the survival chances for smaller and smaller infants. There is no reason to assume that this trend will not continue. In conjunction with this, on both a national and international basis, an increasing number of professionals are directing their attention—research, educational, legal, legislative, and humanitarian—toward the needs of the mentally retarded and developmentally delayed. Activities of this nature can serve, in part, to enhance societal awareness of the needs of all handicapped persons, including the unique set of circumstances surrounding the high-risk infant who may or may not display subsequent development deviance. The results of this trend will be several.

First, the need for specifically trained personnel will be realized. Academic training will be encouraged to include increased coursework on the preschool handicapped child. Five and 10 years ago coursework directed toward 2- to 5-year-old developmentally delayed children was scarce. Today it is commonplace. Coursework directed toward the birth to 2-year-old age range is clearly lagging behind the need. It is only when there are a sufficient number of professionals who are familiar with the needs of the high-risk infant that society as a whole can be better informed, thus enhancing services to this population. Efforts across the United States and internationally need to be directed toward mandating the provision of special services to young at-risk children.

Second, increased research activity will continue to be directed toward the high-risk infant. In any field of study description generally precedes comparative research activity. This is true relative to the short- and long-term results of a precarious neonatal history. Initial data described the infants, but did not follow them over long enough periods of time to carefully relate later sequelae to neonatal factors. Although professionals in the past 15 years have witnessed an increased interest in the long-term results of neonatal disease, medical technology has made survival of previously nonviable infants possible, thus introducing new populations of infants in need of systematic study. It is inevitable that research endeavors will be directed toward these survivors. Specific areas in need of detailed systematic study include the following:

1. The impact on specific skill areas of a high-risk history
2. The effectiveness of various early intervention models
3. The effects of the NICU environment on developmental performance
4. The nature of care (intervention) in the NICU and the results on later development
5. Parental response to the high-risk infant

Third, increased service provision will result. Tables 6–1 and 6–2 specify the ages at which special services are available state by state. It is clear that some states lag behind in recognizing the need for early assessment and intervention efforts. Local efforts, in which practitioners will participate, will result in increased awareness on the part of those states not fully providing for young developmentally delayed children. Practitioners can provide invaluable direction to advocacy groups who are organizing grass roots efforts to initiate services to populations not presently receiving them.

Fourth, the infants themselves and their families will be better served. Even a casual glance at the history of service provision to select groups of handicapped persons reveals that enhanced awareness of need leads to increased interest, which ultimately results in expanded services. At present the status of services to at-risk infants is in a transitional stage. Enhanced awareness has taken place to various degrees in the United States and internationally. Increased interest on the part of a comparatively small group of professionals has resulted. The transition from increased interest to expanded services is the present state of affairs. This is a process that takes time, as evidenced by the evolution of services to other groups. As this process unfolds, the quality and quantity of services to at-risk infants will increase. Efforts designed to expand services to any group of developmentally delayed persons must be made in light of shrinking state and federal dollars. Competition for those dollars is keen, thereby amplifying the need for all involved to be equipped and ready to assist in the process of pointing out the need for service provision.

SUMMARY

An exciting and challenging set of circumstances exists today for the practitioner interested in the high-risk infant. Increased numbers of infants surviving a difficult neonatal period serve as testimony to the efforts put forth by the medical community. The result for the practitioner has been increased numbers of children at risk for developmental delay. The practitioner's goal therefore must be the early identification of developmental delay and the provision of aggressive early intervention when indicated. In areas where services are not available the practitioner can serve as a catalyst in generating interest. Parents, administrators, legislators, physicians, practitioners, and, most importantly, the children will benefit immeasurably from these efforts. The purpose of this text is to aid in the process.

REFERENCES

Allen, K. (1978). The early childhood specialist. In K. Allen (Eds.), *Early intervention: A team approach.* Baltimore: University Park Press.

Holm, V., and McCartin, R. (1978). Interdisciplinary child development team: Team issues and training in interdisciplinariness. In K. Allen (Eds.), *Early intervention: A team approach.* Baltimore: University Park Press.

Laney, M. (1985). *Communication screening and assessment in pediatric populations.* Miniseminar presented at the Annual Convention of the American Speech-Language-Hearing Association. Washington, DC, November.

La Veck, B. (1978). The developmental psychologist. In K. Allen (Eds.), *Early intervention: A team approach.* Baltimore: University Park Press.

Shonkoff, J., Dworkin, P., and Leviton, A. (1979). Primary case approaches to developmental disabilities. *Pediatrics, 64,* 506.

West, M. (1978). The social worker specializing in handicapped children. In K. Allen (Eds.), *Early intervention: A team approach.* Baltimore: University Park Press.

Appendix **A**

Glossary of Terminology for Clinician-Educators Working With High-Risk Infants

Enhanced communication between medical and allied health professionals is of great importance. The role of the clinician-educator with high-risk infants is a relatively new area of service provision. An increased number of practitioners are now afforded hands on exposure to high-risk infants. The full role to be played by the clinician-educator in assessment, treatment, and research has yet to be established and varies from setting to setting. In addition, public education mandates in many states require service provision to persons from birth through 21 years of age. Hence, an increasing number of clinician-educators are involved to one degree or another with at-risk infants.

For the clinician to be a valuable member of the early identification and treatment team an understanding of terminology peculiar to the at-risk population is essential. Information of this nature is not generally provided as part of graduate training programs. It is the purpose of this glossary to list and define some of the more frequently used terms. Improved overall communication with physicians, parents, nurses, and others will serve to enhance the scope and role of the speech-language pathologist, early childhood educator, developmental psychologist, and other professionals with this unique population of patients being served.

Apgar score: A system of scoring an infant's physical condition at 1 minute and 5 minutes after birth. Heart rate, respiration, muscle tone, color, and response to stimuli are scored as 0, 1 or 2. The maximum total score for a baby is 10. Those with low scores require immediate attention if they are to survive. The Apgar score remains the simplest and best way to evaluate the condition of an infant at birth. If the score is 8 to 10 at 1 or 5 minutes of age, the infant usually does not require active resuscitation; if the score is 2 or less at 1 minute or less than 5 at 5 minutes of age, the infant requires resuscitation. An ominous sign is a 5-minute Apgar score that is much lower than the 1-minute Apgar score (Apgar, 1953). Table A–1 presents a complete Apgar evaluation scoresheet.

Table A-1. The Apgar Score

Sign	Score		
	0	1	2
Heart rate	Absent	Less than 100 beats/min	More than 100 beats/min
Respiratory effort	Absent	Weak Cry	Strong cry
Muscle tone	Limp	Some flexion	Good flexion
Reflex irritability	No response	Some motion	Good motion
Color	Blue or pale	Body pink, extremities blue	Pink

Apnea: Apneic spells in small babies are related to the irregular respiratory pattern known as periodic breathing. Periodic breathing occurs in 25 to 50 percent of premature infants. The pattern usually consist of periods of apnea lasting from 5 to 10 seconds. Periods of apnea that last more than 20 seconds are termed apneic spells. At least 25 percent of the infants in an intensive care nursery will demonstrate such spells.

Babinski reflex: A reflex is normally present in infants less than 6 months of age. Normally, when the lateral aspect of the sole of the relaxed foot is stroked, the large toe is flexed. If the toe extends instead of flexes and the other toes spread out, the Babinski reflex is present. The Babinski reflex is measured in infants as part of a routine assessment of general neurological function.

bagging: Bag and mask ventilation is a short-term substitute for ventilation with a respirator. It is most commonly used during resuscitation and is of help prior to establishing the need for mechanical ventilation. It is frequently used for the management of infants with recurrent apnea.

bililight (phototherapy): A light source used to reduce bilirubin levels in infants with hyperbilirubinemia. Phototherapy is the term used to refer to the treatment for this condition. Cremer, Perryman, and Richards (1958) observed that exposure to sunlight or blue fluorescent light produced a reduction in serum bilirubin concentration. In the United States it has been estimated that 90,000 infants annually will receive phototherapy. Treatment in this method has received great acceptance. Research studies have shown phototherapy to be highly effective as a means of preventing or treating moderate hyperbilirubinemia.

birth asphyxia: Asphyxia occurs when the process of respiration fails. The infant is particularly vulnerable to asphyxia during labor and delivery and immediately after birth. There are four basic mechanisms for asphyxia: (1) fetal asphyxia from interruption of umbilical blood flow, such as occurs with cord compression during labor; (2) fetal asphyxia from failure of oxygen exchange across the placenta because of placental separation, as in abruption; (3) fetal asphyxia due to inadequate oxygen supply to the mother; and (4) neonatal asphyxia from failure to inflate the lungs, which may occur as a result of airway obstruction, excessive fluid in the lungs, or weak respiratory effort.

blood gases: Measurement of blood gases is routinely performed for the infant in the intensive care nursery. The purpose of these measures is to monitor blood oxygen levels. After placental separation oxygen exchange is assumed by the infant's lungs. A suffecent level of oxygenation is needed to insure adequate functioning. Blood gas monitoring is the method of choice for measuring oxygenation.

Brazelton Scale: The Brazelton Scale, used to measure neurological adequacy, focuses on 20 reflex measures and 26 behavioral responses to environmental stimuli. Estimates of the infant's vigor and attentional excitement are made. Assessment is made of motor activity, tone, and automatic responsiveness as the infant changes state. The infant's state of consciousness is paramount in interpreting responses to various types of stimuli. For a full description of the scale see Brazelton (1973).

bradycardia: A slowing of the fetal heart rate. This may occur during labor and delivery. It may be associated with perinatal asphyxia (hypoxemia). Central nervous system damage may ensue from the results of reduced blood flow and fetal oxygenation.

bronchopulmonary dysplasia (BPD): A disease process that may occur in infants during respiratory therapy for acute hyaline membrane disease or other respiratory diseases (Northway, Rosen, and Porter, 1967). Chronic pulmonary changes are noted instead of rapid improvement following the acute initial disease. The pathologic changes of BPD represent damage to the alveolar and bronchial epithelium. Overall incidence of BPD has been reported to be 10 to 15 percent, with incidences of 20 to 38 percent in infants of very low birth weight (Tooley, 1979).

continuous positive airway pressure (CPAP): A gas pressure greater than atmospheric pressure that is applied continuously to the airway during spontaneous breathing. The major use of CPAP has been with infants suffering from hyaline membrane disease who do not require assisted ventilation.

cyanosis: Slightly bluish, grayish, slatelike or dark purple discoloration of the skin. This condition is due to a deficiency of oxygen and an excess of carbon dioxide in the blood caused by interference of entrance of air into the respiratory tract. It may also be associated with a variety of cardiac problems that result in reduced blood flow and oxygenation in the fetus.

gavage feeding: A method of feeding used when an infant is unable to nipplefeed for whatever reason. Gavage feedings may also be used to supplement nipple feedings if the infant tires easily. Both oral and nasal gavage feedings are used, depending on the particular needs of the infant. Gavage tubes are normally removed after the feeding.

gestational age: The period of intrauterine development from conception to birth. The World Health Organization has set the dividing line between preterm and term birth at 37 weeks. Thus, infants born before 38 weeks are considered preterm, those born between 38 and 42 weeks are term, and those born 42 weeks or later are considered to be postterm.

grunting: An audible expiratory grunt or cry during the first few hours of life. It is a reflection of forcing expired air past the partially closed glottis. As time progresses more and more physical effort is required by the infant to maintain satisfactory respiration. The presence of grunting is often indicative of impending hyaline membrane disease.

hyaline membrane disease (HMD):   Newborn infants are susceptible to a variety of forms of respiratory distress. The most common of these is HMD. Thirty percent of all neonatal deaths in the United States and 50 to 70 percent of deaths among premature infants are associated with HMD. Degree of susceptibility depends more on the stage of lung maturation than on precise gestational age. There are other infants with progressive respiratory difficulties in the first 24 to 48 hours of life who display symptoms similar to HMD, but who do not have HMD. This is known as Type II respiratory distress syndrome (RDS). Infants with Type II RDS respond nicely to appropriate treatment.

hyperbilirubinemia: A condition in which elevated serum bilirubin levels are present in an infant. Levels of bilirubin that are considered appropriate depend, in part, on the weight of the infant. Increased levels of bilirubin can result in jaundice, and if levels are exceedingly high, kernicterus may result. If bilirubin levels approach a level at which kernicterus may result, exchange transfusion, phototherapy, or drug therapy may be administered. The latter form of treatment is too slow for the already jaundiced infant and is most effective as a preventive measure. See also, *jaundice* and *kernicterus.*

intrauterine growth retardation (IUGR):   Failure of the fetus to grow sufficiently within known parameters and expectations. Fetal head size, as measured by ultrasound, is one method used to monitor fetal growth rate and differentially detect patterns of growth retardation. Fetal growth patterns are influenced by the inherent growth potential of the fetus and the growth support received by way of the placenta from the mother (Ounsted and Ounsted, 1973).

intubate: The establishment of an artificial airway to correct an airway obstruction. The choice of artificial airway pathway is dictated by the location of the obstruction. Both orotracheal and nasotracheal intubation are in general use for prolonged mechanical ventilation of term and preterm infants.

jaundice: A condition characterized by yellowness of the skin and whiteness of eyes, mucous membranes, and body fluids due to the presence of increased levels of bile (excess bilirubin) in the blood. At higher bilirubin levels a condition known as kernicterus may result. Physiological jaundice refers to transient hyperbilirubinemia in the newborn. Pathological jaundice is due to a pathological condition that prevents bilirubin levels from being controlled in a normal manner. The differential diagnosis of these types of jaundice is essential to the management of the infant displaying symptoms of increased bilirubin in the blood. See also, *kernicterus* and *hyperbilirubinemia.*

kernicterus: A condition caused by excessive levels of bilirubin in the blood (hyperbilirubinemia). Portions of the brain are infiltrated by a yellow pigment that results from increased bile in the blood. Higher morbidity levels are associated with kernicterus. In addition, associations between kernicterus and poor intellectual functioning and neurological status later in life are reported frequently in the literature.

mechanical ventilation: Infant respirators are now a common and essential part of any neonatal intensive care nursery. Several commercially designed respirators are available for use with infants. The use of a mechanical respirator for an infant displaying respiratory difficulties must be carefully monitored relative to pressure and oxygen level. Respiratory complications, both short-term and long-term, are possible when assisted respiration is employed. All nursery personnel must be familiar with the use of ventilatory support equipment, recognition of equipment malfunction, and use of monitoring procedures.

meconium aspiration: More mature infants who are stressed may pass meconium. This is rarely observed prior to 34 weeks gestational age. Meconium can thus be aspirated into the airway through initial respiratory effort on the part of the infant. The presence of meconium in the airway may result in pulmonary complications. These may range from mild respiratory distress to respiratory failure. Prompt suctioning of the airway in the presence of meconium aspiration can often prevent or reduce serious pulmonary complications.

meningomyelocele: An incomplete closure of the dorsal midline that results from a disturbance in normal fetal growth. A lesion results that leaves neural tissue exposed. The incidence of this disorder is approximately 1 in every 500 live births. The size and site of the lesion may vary. The diagnosis is usually made at birth. Head size must be monitored also because of an increased incidence of hydrocephalus. Long-term surgical intervention and supportive help is needed for these infants and their family.

Moro reflex (startle reflex):   A reflexive pattern of response on the part of the infant. The infant draws its arms across the chest in an embracing manner in response to stimuli produced by striking the surface on which the infant rests. The Moro reflex has also been described as a lateral extension of the upper extremities (with opening of hands) followed by anterior flexion and audible cry. This reflexive pattern is in response to a sudden dropping of the infant's head backwards in relation to the trunk (the dropping head should be caught by the examiner).

neonatal behavioral assessment (newborn maturity rating):   Both behavioral and maturity assessment strategies are available. Behavioral scales that measure motor, social, cognitive, and adaptive areas of performance are widely used. Maturity ratings refer to the determination of an approximate gestational age and are useful in determining potential risk status. (See Chapters 1 and 3 for a more complete discussion of behavioral and maturity assessment techniques.)

newborn nursery (level I, II, III):   Level I nurseries (for 85 percent of pregnancies) are equipped and staffed to look after normal, low-risk pregnancies, deliveries, and newborns only. They do, however, have the capability to deal with emergencies when aided by a predetermined contingency plan for support from the nearest level II or level III nursery. Level II nurseries (for 12 percent of pregnancies) are equipped and staffed as in level I but, in addition, are capable of providing services for pregnancies, deliveries, and newborns at moderate to high risk. Level III nurseries (for 3 percent of pregnancies) provide level I and II services but, in addition, are capable of managing ultra-high-risk pregnancies, deliveries, and newborns (Sawyer, 1981).

Ortolani's sign: A diagnostic sign indicative of a congenitally dislocated hip. Diagnosis in the newborn is made by demonstrating that the femoral head dislocates as the hip is adducted. This sign is present in the dislocated hip until 6 to 8 weeks of age and sometimes even longer. As the hip is adducted the examiner should be able to feel and see the sudden jerk that takes place as the hip dislocated.

placenta abruptio: A condition in which the placenta separates prematurely from the uterine wall. This is a serious condition that may result in spontaneous abortion.

placenta previa: A condition characterized by placental implantation in the lower portion of the uterus. The position of the placenta may completely cover the internal cervical opening, it may be just within the lower uterine segment, or it may partially cover the internal cervical opening.

pneumothorax: A collection of air or gas in the pleural cavity. Pneumothorax must be considered whenever there is an abrupt worsening of the respiratory or circulatory status of an infant at risk. Too much pressure being delivered to an infant who is receiving mechanical ventilation may result in pneumothorax. Diminished breath sounds, asymmetry of chest movement, deterioration of blood gases and a shift in heart sounds to one side are characteristic of pneumothorax, Immediate attention is needed for the infant with a pneumothorax.

radiant warmer: Overhead radiant heaters used to provide heat for an infant and still allow free access to the infant. The maintenance of a constant body temperature within a safe range is essential for the survival of an at-risk infant. Careful monitoring of the baby's temperature must be undertaken to ensure that neither hyperthermia nor hypothermia result. The provision of adequate warmth can cut mortality in small babies by 25 percent.

respiratory distress: See *hyaline membrane disease.*

seizures: Seizure activity in the neonatal period is not uncommon, but it does not usually represent a medical emergency, as may be more likely the case with older infants. Seizure activity, however, may be associated with significant illness, and the need to determine causation is important. Variation in the type of seizure activity is present in infants, with premature infants differing from full-term infants. Possible causes include perinatal complications, of which intrauterine insults are the most common; metabolic disturbances; infection; developmental disorders; and passive addiction to narcotics and barbiturates.

sepsis: The presence of a bacterial infection in the blood. The incidence of sepsis in the neonatal period is 1 case per 1000 live full-term births and 1 per 250 live premature births (Wientzen and McCracken, 1977). Once septicemia is suspected, suitable cultures are obtained and proper drug therapy is immediately initiated.

subdural hemorrhage: Neonatal subdural hemorrhage is in almost all instances the result of a traumatic lesion in the full-term infant. Major factors that contribute to subdural lesions are (1) the relationship of the size of the fetal head to the size of the birth canal, (2) rigidity of the birth canal, (3) the duration of labor, and (4) the manner of delivery (Volpe and Koenigsberger, 1981). The prognosis for infants with intracranial hemorrhage varies according to the nature of the hemorrhage and the factors leading to the hemorrhage.

tremor: An involuntary movement (quivering) of a part or parts of the body. In the neonatal period tremor activity is often associated with seizures. The treatment may vary, depending on the underlying cause of the seizures. See *seizures.*

REFERENCES

Apgar, V. (1953). A proposal for a new method of evaluation of the newborn infant. *Anesthesia Annals, 32,* 260.

Brazelton, T. (1973). *Neonatal behavioral assessment scale* (National Spastics Monograph No. 50). Philadelphia: J. B. Lippincott.

Cremer, R., Perryman, P., and Richards, D. (1958). Influence of light on hyperbilirubinemia of infants. *Lancet, 1,* 1094.

Northway, W., Rosen, R., and Porter, D. (1967). Pulmonary disease following respiratory therapy for hyaline membrane disease. *New England Journal of Medicine, 276,* 357.

Ounsted, M., and Ounsted, C. (1973). Fetal growth rate: Its variations and their consequences. *Clinics In Developmental Medicine, 46.* Spastics International Publications. Philadelphia: J. B. Lippincott.

Sawyer, P. (1981). The organization of perinatal care with particular reference to the newborn. In G. Avery (Ed.), *Neonatology, pathophysiology and management of the newborn.* Philadelphia: J.B. Lippincott.

Tooley, W. (1979). Epidemiology of BPD. *Journal of Pediatrics, 95,* 851.

Volpe, J., and Koenigsberger, R. (1981). Neurologic disorders. In G Avery, (Ed.), *Neonatology, pathophysiology and management of the newborn.* Philadelphia: J. B. Lippincott.

Wientzen, R., and McCracken, G. (1977). Pathogenesis and management of neonatal sepsis and meningitis. *Current Problems In Pediatrics, 8,* 12.

Appendix B

Hospital Discharge Summaries and Developmental Outcomes of Selected Infants

The purpose of this appendix is to familiiarize the practitioner with the normal course of events for the typical high-risk infant. Many practitioners have limited exposure to information of the type contained in the hospital discharge summary. Data of this nature can be of help to the practitioner in determining the schedule of reassessments as well in interpreting assessment results.

The data contained in this appendix were derived from hospital discharge summaries from infants enrolled in the Neonatal Follow-Up Program described by Rossetti (see Chapter 3). Birth history and hospital data have been summarized. Detailed laboratory data have been deleted. The developmental performance of these infants has also been summarized in a chronological manner.

CASE A

Birthdate: 5/23/85
Admission Date: 5/23/85
Discharge Date: 8/13/85
Admitting Diagnosis: Preterm appropriate for gestational age female, 30–31 weeks gestational age.

Hospital Course

A 1,077 g white female was delivered to a 19-year-old, Para I, Gravida II female with estimated due date of mid-August, with the last menstrual period in

193

November of 1984. Estimation of gestational age was placed around 30–31 weeks. The patient was delivered in the OB suite with forceps to protect the head. The birth was at 10:38 a.m. The mother had no meds during the pregnancy, was not on any alcohol, and did not smoke during the pregnancy. Apgars were 2 and 5 at 1 and 5 minutes, respectively. The heart rate dropped to 40–50 beats/min at 1 minute of age. The patient was intubated and the Apgars did increase, with the heart rate increasing also with bagging. The patient was transferred immediately, via helicopter, to a large perinatal center 100 miles away. Upon transfer x-ray studies showed severe respiratory distress syndrome, Type I–II. Condition upon dismissal to the perinatal center was improved. Prognosis was felt to be poor upon dismissal.

Information received from the NICU, where the patient was transferred, indicated the following sequence.

Date: 5/28/85. The patient's current medical problems included hyaline membrane disease, bilateral pneumothorax, and small size. Therapy consisted of a respirator at 34 percent oxygen level, rate of 32 per minute. Nutrition was supplied by total parenteral nutrition. The patient's weight was 890 g.

Date: 6/12/85. The patient continued to be hospitalized in the NICU to which she was transferred shortly after birth. Her medical problems included patent ductus arteriosus, respirator dependence following hyaline membrane disease and pneumothorax, pulmonary interstitial emphysema involving the entire left lung, and infiltrate of the right lung. Therapy consisted of a respirator at 26 percent oxygen level, rate of 42 per minute, and antibiotics. Nutrition was supplied by total parenteral nutrition. The patient's weight was 1,030 g.

Date: 6/24/86. The patient continued to be hospitalized at the referral NICU. Her medical problems included respirator dependence and pneumonia. Therapy consisted of a respirator at 35 percent oxygen level, rate of 13 per minute and continued antibiotics. Nutrition was supplied as total parental nutrition and liquids intravenously (IV). The patient's weight was 1,220 g.

Date: 7/14/85. The patient continued to be hospitalized at the referral NICU. Her current medical problems included resolving pneumonia, chronic lung disease, and congestive heart failure. Therapy consisted of hood oxygen and digoxin; she was no longer on antibiotics. Nutrition was supplied by parenteral nutrition and small gavage feedings. Her weight was 1,580 g. No date for discharge had as yet been set.

Date: 7/28/85. The patient continued to be hospitalized in the NICU. Her pulmonary problems were resolving somewhat. She was off the respirator and breathing room air. Her cardiac output continued to be decreased, with decreased left ventricular function. Nutrition was supplied as alternate oral and gavage feedings. Present weight was 1,980 g. The patient could be discharged to her local hospital at any time.

Developmental Course

The child was first seen in the neonatal follow-up clinic on 10/31/85. Her chronological age was 5 months and 8 days. Her performance on the Bayley

Scale of Infant Development (Mental Scale) placed her at the 2½ month level of performance. This represents relatively good developmental performance when correcting for prematurity. At the initial evaluation she did not display good head support, although she was starting to roll from her stomach to her back. The mother indicated that the infant was feeding poorly. The mother further indicated that after approximately 90 days in the NICU (the mother was able to visit the child once) she was having a difficult time adjusting to and caring for the child. The mother was provided with home stimulation materials and instructed to keep a developmental log. The infant was scheduled for a reevaluation approximately 3 months later.

The child was seen for a reevaluation on 1/30/86. Her chronological age at that time was 8 months and 7 days. The developmental log kept by the mother indicated that in November of 1985 the child began to coo and demonstrated more voluntary and purposeful vocalizations. On December 8 the mother indicated that the child laughed for the first time. One week later she began to roll from her back to her stomach. On January 10 she began to sit alone for short periods of time. She also began to support her weight when her arms were held by the parents. On January 17 the mother indicated that the child sat alone for 5 minutes. The results of the Mental Scale of the Bayley Scales indicated her performance level to be approximately at the 5½ month level. Once again this is indicative of relatively good performance when correcting for prematurity. The home stimulation program was updated and the child was scheduled for a reevaluation in 3 months. As of this writing the reevaluation date has not arrived. Prognostic statements for this child cannot be made with any certainty at present. The rate of catch-up growth she will or will not display in the next 12 months will be a strong indicator of the adequacy of developmental skill mastery.

CASE B

Birthdate: 12/5/80
Admitting Date: 12/5/80
Discharge Date: 4/3/81
Admitting Diagnosis: Preterm appropriate for gestational age male, 32 weeks gestational age.

Hospital Course

Case B was delivered via emergency cesarean section at 3:04 a.m. in a hospital 60 miles from the NICU. The NICU transport team was dispatched to transport the child to the NICU. Whe the transport team arrived, the infant had been intubated and bagging was in progress. External cardiac massage was also being administered. An umbilical venous catheter was inserted and IV fluids were being given. The infant was immediately placed on a respirator in preparation for transport. The child arrived at the NICU at 7:10 a.m. Apgar scores at 1 and 5 minutes were 3 and 4 respectively. Birth weight upon admission to the NICU was 1,850 g. Soon after arrival at the NICU the child required 100 percent oxygen, rate of 45 per minute. A heart murmur was noted on 12/6/80. The child was weaned from the mechanical ventilator, and on 12/14/80 the child was extubated and placed under an oxygen hood. The child underwent a double exchange transfusion on 12/17/80. Four additional double-volume exchange transfusions were required. Severe acidosis was detected on 12/23/80. Respiratory adequacy deteriorated and the baby was intubated again on 12/21/80 and a mechanical ventilator used. On 12/25/80 his condition deteriorated rapidly, and it was feared that he might expire because of respiratory difficulties encountered. Nutrition was provided through total parenteral nutrition, with fluids administered IV. His condition gradually improved, and he was fed through gavage minimal amounts of glucose and water. He was subsequently able to take a 24 cal/oz premature formula. On 2/26/81 he was extubated and placed under the oxygen hood at 90 percent oxygen level. Twenty-four hours later the oxygen level was reduced to 60 percent. On 2/27/81 x-ray studies revealed the onset of bronchopulmonary dysplasia. By 3/23/81 the child was on room air. The child was discharged from the NICU on 4/3/81. Weight on dismissal was 3,560 g.

Developmental Course

Case B was immediately enrolled in the neonatal follow-up program to monitor developmental progress and provide early intervention if required. The child lived approximately 70 miles from the follow-up program, so it was no small effort for the parents to transport the child for evaluation visits. The first assessment was performed on 4/30/81. The child's chronological age on that date was 4 months and 25 days. His performance on the Bayley Scale placed him at the 3 month level of functioning. This represents essentially adequate skill mastery when taking his degree of prematurity into consideration. Head support at that time was well established. Visual skills appeared to be appropriate. Good bilateral arm and leg movements were noted. He consistently searched for the source of auditory stimuli. He was at the beginning stages of reaching and grasping. The parents were provided with home stimulation materials and asked to keep a developmental log. A reevaluation was scheduled for 6 months.

The child was reevaluated on 11/5/81. His age on the date of assessment was 11 months exactly. His performance on the mental portion of the Bayley Scale placed him at the 10 month level of performance, thus some catch-up growth was present. The overall progress evidenced by the child was quite remarkable. He was pulling himself to the standing position, as well as starting to crawl. Good bilateral reach and grasp were noted. He actively scanned the environment. He was able to move around in the home with a walker. The parental log indicated that he was using some syllables, such as *mama* and *dada*. The mother also indicated that he was able to follow some simple commands in the home. No major developmental concerns were expressed at this time. The home stimulation program was updated, and he was scheduled for a reevaluation in 6 months.

Reevaluation was performed on 4/15/82. His age on that date was 16 months. It is apparent that he had made strong progress since the last evaluation. His performance on the Bayley Scale placed him at the 16 month level, thus catch-up growth was complete. He was quite active and verbalized freely during the evaluation. Motor skills appeared to be age appropriate. Receptive language skills likewise appeared to be age appropriate. No major concerns were expressed relative to his developmental adequacy. He was scheduled for a reevaluation in 6 months.

A reevaluation was performed on 10/21/82. His age at that time was 22 months. His performance on the Bayley Scale placed hime at the 22 month level. No areas of developmental concern were detected. Cognitive, motor, and language skills appeared to be age appropriate. It is apparent that the home stimulation provided by the parents was a significant aid to him in attaining developmental adequacy. The rate of catch-up growth observed over time and the adequacy of the latest performance were strongly indicative of essentially normal continued development. The family moved from the area shortly after this final evaluation; thus his present school performance is unknown.

CASE C

Birthdate: 6/5/81
Admission Date: 6/5/81
Discharge Date: 10/12/81
Admitting Diagnosis: Preterm appropriate for gestational age male, birth asphyxia, respiratory distress, birth weight 2,012 g.

Hospital Care

Case C was born on 6/5/81. Birth weight was 2,012 g. Apgars were noted to be 0 and 2 at 1 and 5 minutes, respectively. The baby was given oxygen by mask and was quite slow in crying initially. The baby was delivered in an out-lying hospital, and the NICU transport team transported the child to the NICU shortly after birth. Without bagging perfusion was reported to be poor, and the baby developed general duskiness and central cyanosis. The baby was intubated immediately upon arrival at the NICU. Heart rate was above 125 beats/min, with color remaining poor. After mechanical ventilation was initiated, the baby's color improved markedly. Initial neurological examination revealed a weak sucking reflex and an incomplete Moro reflex. Initial impressions after the baby's condition was stabilized in the NICU were of an infant appropriate for gestational age (33 weeks), with respiratory distress syndrome type I, who had suffered a moderate amount of birth asphyxia. On 6/20/81 the baby developed severe bronchopulmonary dysplasia. This condition remained essentially unchanged for approximately 120 days. On 6/21/81 the baby was transfused; his weight was 2,100 g. Five additional transfusions were required during the remainder of the hospital stay. By 7/13/81 the baby weighed 2,620 g. Weight gain after that point was slow. The infant was extubated on 7/23/81 and placed under an oxyhood at 30 percent oxygen. By 7/27/81 the baby was receiving 25 ml of infant formula every 3 hours. The baby developed a variety of infections during the hospitalizatiiion, which required aggressive antibiotic treatment. Weight increased slowly during the month of September. On 10/10/81 the patient was transferred to the routine nursery. The patient was dismissed to the care of his parents on 10/12/81. During the baby's extensive hospital stay the parents visited on one occasion and kept minimal contact with the neonatologist. Although the baby's condition on dismissal was much improved, prognosis was thought to be poor by the neonatologist. The child was referred to the neonatal follow-up program for regular evaluation of developmental progress.

Developmental Course

The parents were quite reluctant to return to the hospital for developmental follow-up. They finally did return on 6/10/82. This was approximately 9 months after the baby had been dismissed from the NICU, and 6 months later than initially scheduled. On initial developmental evaluation the child displayed delayed development across modalities. His chronological age was 12 months. His performance on the Bayley Scale placed him at the 6 month level of performance. This represented a significant developmental delay. Minimal arm and leg thrust was noted. The child showed reduced environmental interaction. His physical appearance was frail. Head support was not fully established. He was not sitting alone, rolling over, or crawling. Minimal reaching was noted. The mother reported that she did little if anything to assist the child in developing skills he did not possess. The parents were provided with an aggressive home stimulation program; however, their ability to carry it out was questioned at the time. The child was rescheduled for an evaluation in 60 day. Follow-up conversations with the parents revealed that they were not carrying out the program of home activities provided for them. In August of 1982 the baby died in the home setting.

Appendix C

Bibliography of Early Intervention, Curriculum, Textbook, and Parent Materials

TEXTBOOKS

Abbot, M. (1976). *Alternative approaches to educating young children.* Atlanta: Humanics Limited.

Abt Associates, Inc. (1971). *A study in child care.* Cambridge, MA: Author.
  I. *Findings.* Fitzsimmons, S. J., and Rowe, M. P. (coordinators).
  II-A. *Center case studies.* Ruopp, R. R. (coordinator).
  II-B. *System case studies.* Ruopp, R. R. (coordinator).
  III. *Cost and quality issues for operators.* Thompson, L. C. (coordinator).

Day Care and Child Development Council of America. (1972). *Alternatives in quality child care.* Washington, DC: Author.

Denenberg, V. (Ed.). (1970). *Education of the infant and young child.* New York: Academic Press.

Dittmann, L. L. (1967). *Children in day care with focus on health* (Children's Bureau Publication No. 444). Washington DC: U.S. Department of Health, Education, and Welfare.

Dittman, L. L. (Ed.). (1973). *The infants we care for.* Washington, DC: Association for the Education of Young Children.

Dyrud, G. (1971). *Play to learn.* Minneapolis: Augsburgh College.

Elardo, R., and Pagan, B. (Eds.). (1972). *Perspectives on infant day care.* Little Rock, AR: Southern Association on Children Under Six.

Evans, E. B., and Saia, G. E. (1972). *Day care for infants.* Boston: Beacon Press.

Evans, E. B., Shub, B., and Weinstein, M. (1971). *Day care: How to plan, develop, and operate a day care center.* Boston: Beacon Press.

Gordon, I. J. (1970). *Baby learning through play.* New York: St. Martin's Press.

Grotberg, E. H. (1971). *Day care: Resources for decisions* (Pamphlet 6106–1). Washington, DC: Office of Economic Opportunity.

Harrell, J. A. (1972). *Selected readings in the issues of day care.* Washington, DC: Day Care and Child Development Council of America.

Honig, A. S. (1972). *Infant development: Problems in intervention.* Washington, DC: Day Care and Child Development Council of America.

Hutchison, D. J., and Haynes, U. B. (in press). *Transdisciplinary: A team approach to service for the developmentally disabled.* Thorofare, NJ: Charles B. Slack.

Jew, W. (1974). Helping handicapped infants and their families: The delayed development project. *Children Today, 3,* 7–10.

Keister, D. J. (1973). *Who am I? The development of self-concept.* Durham, NC: Learning Institute of North Carolina.

Keister, M. E. (1970). *The good life for infants and toddlers.* Washington, DC: National Association for the Education of Young Children.

Keyserling, M. D. (1972). *Windows on day care: Report on the findings of members of the National Council of Jewish Women on day care needs and services in their communities.* New York: National Council of Jewish Women.

Louisiana Department of Public Welfare. (1972). *Program planning aids for day care centers.* New Orleans: Author.

Provence, S. (1971). *Guide for the care of infants in groups.* New York: Child Welfare League of America.

Saunders, M. M. (1971). *ABC's of learning in infancy.* Greensboro, NC: University of North Carolina.

Weber, E. (1970). *Early childhood education: Perspective on change.* Worthington, OH: Charles A. Jones Publishing.

Wurman, R. S. (Ed.). (1972). *Yellow pages of learning resources.* Boston: MIT Press.

EARLY INTERVENTION PROGRAMS

Appalachia Educational Laboratory. (1971). *Evaluation report: Early childhood educational program, 1969–70 Field Test* (Summary Rep., Division of Research and Evaluation). Charleston, WV: Author.

Bergstrom, J. L., and Gold, J. R. (1974). *Sweden's day nurseries: Focus on programs for infants and toddlers.* Washington, DC: Day Care and Child Development Council of America.

Bronfenbrenner, V. (1976). *A report on longitudinal evaluations of preschool programs: Vol. 2. Is early intervention effective?* (Publication No. OHD 76–30025. Washington, DC: Department of Health, Education, and Welfare.

Caldwell, B. M., and Richmond, J. B. (1968). The children's center in Syracuse, New York. In L. Dittman (Ed.), *Early child care: The new perspective.* New York: Atherton Press.

Family day care west: A working conference. (1972). Pasadena: Community Family Day Care Project of Pacific Oaks College.

Garber, H., and Hever, R. (1973). *The Milwaukee project: Early intervention as a technique to prevent mental retardation.* Madison, WI: Connecticut University National Leadership Institute-Teacher Education/Early Childhood Madison Regional Rehabilitation Research and Training Center in Mental Retardation.

Gordon, I. J. (1971). *A home learning center approach to early stimulation.* Gainesville: Florida University, Gainesville Institute for Development of Human Resources.

Gordon, I. J. (1972). *Child learning through child play, learning activities for two and three year olds.* New York: St. Martin's Press.

Rabinowitz, M. (1973). *The New Orleans model for parent-infant education.* (Available from Curriculum Specialist, Parent Child Developmental Center, 3300 Frehet Street, New Orleans, LA 70115.)

Reimmele, M. (1967). *Step by step: An informative and training guide for teacher, volunteers, and parents of handicapped children.* LaSalle, IL: United Cerebral Palsy Association, Seaton and Sons.

Peoria Association for Retarded Citizens and United Cerebral Palsy Association, Inc. (1967). *Replication of an inter-disciplinary approach for early education of handicapped children age 0–3 years.* LaSalle, IL: Seaton and Sons.

Segal, M. M., and Adcock, D. (1976). *From birth to one year: The Nova University Play and Learn program.* Fort Lauderdale: Nova University, Institute of Child Centered Education.

Segal, M. M. and Adcock, D. (1976). *From one to two years: The Nova University Play and Learn program.* Fort Lauderdale: Nova University, Institute of Child Centered Education.

Segner, L., and Patterson, C. (1970). *Ways to help babies grow and learn: Activities for infant education.* Denver: University of Colorado, John F. Kennedy Child Development Center.

Sparling, J. J. *The Carolina infant curriculum.* Chapel Hill: Frank Porter Graham Child Development Center.

Wiener, G. (1973). New Orleans: New Orleans Parent Child Development Center.

Willis, A., and Ricciuti, H. (1975). *A good beginning for babies: Guidelines for group care.* Washington, DC: National Association for Young Children.

Yurchak, M. J. (1975). *Infant-toddler curriculum of the Brookline Early Education Project.* (Available from 278 Kent Street, Brookline, MA 02146).

PARENT CURRICULUM

Badger, E. (1970). *Activities for infant stimulation or mother-infant games.* Mount Carmel, IL: Mount Carmel Parent and Child Center.

Badger, E. (1978). *Mothers training program: Educational intervention by the mothers of disadvantaged infants.* Champaign-Urbana: University of Illinois, Urbana Institute of Research for Exceptional Children.

Developmental Language and Speech Center, Grand Rapids, Michigan, *Teaching your child to talk: A parent handbook.* (Available from CEBCO/ Standard Publishing Co., 104 Fifth Avenue, New York, NY 10011).

Drezek, W. *Teachers as mothers: An innovative conceptual rationale for a program for multiply handicapped infants.* (Available from Infant Parent Training Program, 1226 East 9th Street, Austin, TX 78702.)

Drezek, W. (1976). *Infant-parent training program checklist* (Rev.). (Available from Infant-Child Training Program, 1226 East 9th Street, Austin, TX 78702.)

The El Paso Rehabilitation Center. (1974). *Mothers can help: A therapist's guide for formulating a developmental text for parents of special children.* El Paso: Guynes Printing.

Experience (Language Development Activities). Bill Wilkerson Hearing and Speech Center. Nashville: Author.

Frichtl, C., and Peterson, L. W. (1969). *Early infant stimulation and motor development.* Springfield, IL: Illinois State Department of Mental Health.

Furuno, S., and O'Reilly, K. (1972). *A family oriented enrichment program for handicapped infants.* Honolulu: Hawaii University, Honolulu School of Public Health.

Gordon, I. J. (1967). *A parent education approach to provision of early stimulation for the culturally disadvantaged* (Final Report). Gainesville: Florida University, Gainesville College of Education.

Gordon, I. J. (1969). *Reaching the child through parent education: The Florda approach.* Gainesville: Florida University, Gainesville Institute for Development of Human Resources.

Massachusetts Department of Mental Health, Division of Mental Retardation. (1973). *Home stimulation for the young developmentally disabled child.* (Available from Commonwealth Mental Health Foundation, 4 Marlboro Road, Lexington, MA 02173.)

Massachusetts Department of Mental Health, Division of Mental Retardation. (1974). *Exploring materials with your young child with special needs.* (Distributed by Commonwealth Mental Health Foundation, 4 Marlboro Road, Lexington, MA 02173.)

Montgomery County Public Schools. (1977). *The growing parent: The growing child: A parent education curriculum guide.* Rockville, MD: Author.

Painter, G. (1971). *Teach your baby.* New York: Simon and Schuster.

Parents as Resource Team. (1970). *Recipes for fun: Activities to do at home with children.* Winetka, IL: Author.

Parents as Resource Team (1972). *I saw a purple cow and 100 other recipes for learning.* Boston: Little Brown.

Parents as Resource Team (1972). *More recipes for fun.* Northfield, IL: Author.

Rabinowitz, M. (1973). *The New Orleans model for parent-infant education.* (Available from Curriculum Specialist, Parent Child Development Center, 3300 Frehet Street, New Orleans, LA 70115.)

Rabinowitz, M. (1973). *In the beginning: A parent guide of activities and experiences for infants from birth to six months: Book I.* (Available from Curriculum Specialists, Parent Child Center, 3300 Frehet Street, New Orleans, LA 70115.)

Segal, M. M. (1973). *You are your baby's first teachers.* Fort Lauderdale: Nova University.

Stinick, V. *Parent infant communication: A program of clinical and home training for parents and hearing impaired.* (Available from Dormac Inc., P.O. Box 752, Beaverton, OR 97005.)

CURRICULUM

Chapel Hill Training-Outreach Project. *A planning guide: The preschool curriculum.* Chapel Hill: Author. (Available from Kaplan School Supply Corp., 600 Jonestown Road, Winston-Salem, NC 27103).

Cooperative Educational Service Agency. *Portage guide to early education.* Portage, WI: Author.

Croft, D. (Ed.) (1973). *Recipes for busy little hands.* Cupertino: DeAnza College, Department of Nursery School Training.

Croft, H. (1972). *An activities handbook for teachers of young children.* Boston: Houghton Mifflin

The developmental activity file. (Available from Boston Center for Blind Children, 147 South Huntington Avenue, Boston, MA 02130.)

Drash, P., and Stolberg, A. (1977). *Acceleration of cognitive, linguistic, and social development in the normal infant.* Tallahassee, Florida: State Department of Health and Rehabilitative Services.

Educational Products Information Exchange Institute. (1972). *Early childhood education: How to select and evaluate materials.* New York: Author.

Forrester, B. J. (1971). *Materials for infant development.* Nashville: George Peabody College for Teachers, John F. Kennedy Center for Research on Human Development.

Friends of Perry Nursery School. (1972). *The scrap book: A collection of activities for preschoolers.* (Available from Friends of Perry Nursery School, 1541 Washtenaw, Ann Arbor, MI.)

Furfey, P. H. (Ed.). (1972). *Education of children aged one to three: A curriculum manual.* Washington, DC: The Catholic University of America (Available from School of Education Curriculum Development Center, 620 Michigan Ave., Washington, DC 20017.)

Honig, A. S. *Infant education and stimulation (birth to three years): A bibliography.* Champaign-Urbana: University of Illinois, College of Education Curriculum Laboratory. (Available from 1210 West Springfield Avenue, Urbana, IL 61801.)

Infant stimulation curriculum: The developmentally delayed infant education project. (1975). Columbus, OH: Ohio State University, The Nisonger Center for Mental Retardation and Developmental Disabilities. (Available from 1580 Cannon Drive, Columnbus, OH 43210)

Karnes, M. B. (1975). *The Karnes early language activities.* Champaign-Urbana: University of Illinois, Institute for Child Behavior and Development. (Available from Generators of Educational Materials Enterprises, P.O. Box 2339, Station A, Champaign, IL 61821.)

Karnes, M. B. (1975). *Small wonder.* Circle Pines, MN: American Guidance Service.

Koontz, C. W. (1974). *Koontz child developmental program: Training activities for the first 48 months.* Los Angeles: Western Psychological Services.

Krajicek, M. (1973). *Stimulation activities guide for children from birth to five years.* Denver: University of Colorado Medical Center, John F. Kennedy Child Development Center.

The National Collarborative Infant Project. (1986). *A program guide for infants and toddlers with neuromotor and other developmental disabilities.* New York: United Cerebral Palsy Assn.

Northcutt, W. H. (Ed.). (1971). *Education curriculum guide: Hearing impaired children: Birth to three years and their parents.* St. Paul: Minneapolis Public Schools, Minnesota State Department of Education.

Saunders, M. M., and Keister, M. E. (1971). *Curriculum for the infant and toddler* (A color slide series with script). Greensboro, NC: University of North Carolina, Infant Care Project, Institute for Child and Family Development.

Seefeldt, C. (1974). *A curriculum for child care centers.* Columbus, OH: Bell and Howell Co.

The Sewall Rehabilitation Center, Sewall Early Education Developmental Program (SEED). *Developmental activities for young children birth to three years.* Denver: Author.

Tronic, E., and Greenfield, P. M. (1973). *Infant curriculum: The Bromley-health guide to the care of infants in groups.* New York: Media Products, Inc.

Upchurch, B. (1971). *Easy-to-do toys and activities for infants and toddlers.* Greensboro, NC: University Press.

Yurchak, M. J. (1975). *Infant-toddler curriculum of the Brookline early education project.* (Available from 278 Kent Street, Brookline, MA 02146.)

Appendix D

Annotated Bibliography of Infant and Child Assessment Instruments

The material contained in this appendix was adapted from publications obtained from the Minnesota Department of Education, as well as the Illinois Department of Specialized Educational Services. The specific publications are listed below:

Smith, S., and Rudnall, R. (1982). *Early childhood assessment: Recommended practices and selected instruments.* (1982). Springfield: Illinois State Board of Education.

Bettenburg, A. (1985). *Instruments and procedures for assessing young children.* (1985). St. Paul: Minnesota Department of Education.

Test Name: Assessment in Infancy: Ordinal Scales of Psychological Development (1975)
Author(s): Ina C. Uzgiris and J. Hunt
Publisher: University of Illinois Press
Address: Box 5081, Station A, Champaign, IL 61820

Purpose/Description: The six ordinal scales measure the effects of infants' encounters with various kinds of circumstances in relation to cognitive development. This assessment tool uses Piaget's work and is based on the theory that development is a process of evolving new, more complex, hierarchical levels of organization, intellect, and motivation. Six individually administered scales have been developed to measure infant development. It is not necessary to present the scales in a single session or in sequence, nor is it necessary to administer all of the scales. It is necessary, however, to present situations appropriate for eliciting the critical actions for several consecutive steps on the scale in order to ascertain the infant's level of development. The populations examined in developing the scales ranged in age from 1 to 24 months.

Test Name: Attachment—Separation—Individuation Scale (ASI)
Author(s): B. Mosey
Publisher: The Family Centered Resource Project—Outreach
Address: 3010 St. Lawrence Avenue, Reading, PA 19602, (215) 779-7111

Purpose/Description: The purpose of the ASI is to provide informal evaluation of the social and emotional interactions between infant and parents. The evaluator asseses three parameters: (1) the infant's attachment-separation-individuation-oriented behaviors, (2) the parent behaviors in relation to encouragement and discouragement of the child's behaviors, and (3) the parent-child interaction. No quantifiable score is obtained, but a rating score is developed to identify where parent and child are on the continuum of attachment-separation-individuation development. Administration takes up to 1 hour, depending on the age of the child. The scale is designed for subjects ranging in age from infancy to 3 years.

Test Name: Battelle Developmental Inventory (BDI) (1984)
Author(s): J. Newborg, J. Stock, and L. Wnek
Publisher: DLM Teaching Resources
Address: One DLM Park, Allen, TX 75002

Purpose/Description: One of the primary functions of the Battelle Developmental Inventory (BDI) is to identify children who are handicapped or delayed in several areas of development. The BDI includes a screening test that can be used to identify those areas of development in which a child needs comprehensive assessment with the complete BDI. The BDI is a standardized, individually administered assessment battery of key developmental skills. It consists of a screening component and a full battery. The full BDI consists of 341 test items grouped into five domains: personal-social, adaptive, motor, communication, and cognitive. Each domain is contained in a separate test booklet. The BDI screening test consists of 96 of the 341 items. Each item is presented in a standard format that specifies the behavior to be assessed, the materials needed for testing, the procedures for administering the item, and the criteria for scoring. Data are collected through presentation of a structured test format, interviews with parents and teachers, and observations of the child in the natural setting. The instrument can be administered to children ranging in age from birth to 8 years. Modifications are suggested for children with motor, visual, and auditory impairments.

Test Name: Bayley Scales of Infant Development (1969)
Author(s): N. Bayley
Publisher: Psychological Corporation
Address: 304 East 45th Street, New York, NY 10017

Purpose/Description: The Bayley Scales assess developmental status in infants and young children. The instrument consists of two scales. The

Mental Scale (163 items) measures (1) sensory-perceptual acuities and discrimination; (2) early acquisition of object constancy and memory, learning, and problem-solving ability; (3) vocalizations and the beginning of verbal communication; and (4) early evidence of the ability to form generalizations and classifications. The Motor Scale (81 items) measures the degree of and control of the body coordination of the large muscles, and finer manipulatory skills of the hands and fingers. The Infant Behavior Record, which consists of 30 ratings, is completed after the scales have been administered and on the basis of the examiner's observation. The Scales can be administered to children ranging in age from 2 to 30 months.

Test Name: Bracken Basic Concept Scale (BBCS) (1984)
Author(s): B. A. Bracken
Publisher: Charles E. Merrill
Address: Bell & Howell Company, Columbus, OH 43216

Purpose/Description: The Bracken Basic Concept Scale allows for an in-depth assessment of an individual child's conceptual knowledge. A screening version of the scale is also available to identify which children may benefit from a more intensive diagnostic assessment. The BBCS measures 258 concepts divided into 11 categories or subtests. The 11 categories are colors, letter identification, numbers/counting, comparisons, shapes, direction/positon, social/emotional, size, texture/material, quantity, and time/sequence. The BBCS yields the following scores: (1) the first 5 listed subtests are combined for a School Readiness Composite Standard Score; (2) the remaining 6 subtests have individual scores; and (3) a composite score that is a total of the standard scores for the 11 subtests. A 30-item screening test is also available, which is intended to be used primarily with kindergarten and first-grade children. The test format requires that the examiner read a statement and the child respond by pointing. No verbal responses are required. The Diagnostic Scale of the BBCS is appropriate for children between the ages of 2 years, 6 months and 7 years, 11 months. The BBCS Screening Test is appropriate for children ages 5 to 7 years.

Test Name: California Preschool Social Competency Scale (1969)
Author(s): S. Levine, F. F. Elzey, and M. Lewis
Publisher: Consulting Psychological Press, Inc.
Address: 577 College Avenue, Palo Alto, CA 94306

Purpose/Description: This scale is designed to measure the adequacy of interpersonal behavior and degree of social responsibility in children ages 2 to 5 years. The behaviors included are situational. They were selected in terms of common cultural expectations to represent basic competencies to be developed in the process of socialization. The scale contains 30 items. Each item consists of four descriptive statements, given in behavioral terms, and represents various degrees of competency. The examiner must have had considerable opportunity to observe the child in a variety of situations prior to completion of the scale. The scale was designed for use with children ranging in age from 2½ to 5½ years of age.

Test Name: Carolina Developmental Profile (CDP) (1975)
Author(s): D. L. Lillie and G. L. Harbin
Publisher: Kaplan School Supply Corporation
Address: 600 Jonestown Road, Winston-Salem, NC 27103

Purpose/Description: The CDP is an individually administered criterion-referenced test consisting of a test booklet with instructions included on the inside cover and a profile on the back cover. The CDP covers developmental abilities in six areas: gross motor, fine motor, visual perception, reasoning, receptive language, and expressive language. The Carolina Developmental Profile is designed to be used with the Developmental Task Instruction System. In this system, the goal is to increase the child's developmental abilities to the maximum level of proficiency to prepare the child for the formal academic tasks that will be faced in the early elementary school years. The profile is designed to assist the teacher in establishing long-range objectives to increase developmental abilities in six areas. The purpose of the checklist is not to compare or assess the child in terms of age-normative data. The CDP can be used children ranging in age from 2 to 5 years.

Test Name: Cognitive Observation Guide (COG)
Author(s): B. Mosey
Publisher: The Family Centered Research Project—Outreach
Address: 3010 St. Lawrence Avenue, Reading, PA 19606, (215) 779-7711

Purpose/Description: The COG is designed to provide a conceptual and behavioral framework for the assessment and facilitation of cognitive skill in young children. The COG is an informal criterion-referenced observation guide for assessing cognition. The COG is composed of 24 subskills with behavioral indicators arranged by age level. Each item or behavioral indicator is scored individually. Results are informal and indicative of the child's progress toward developing specific cognitive skills. It is designed for use with subjects ranging in age from birth to 2 years.

Test Name: Denver Developmental Screening Test (DDST) (1968, 1970, 1973)
Author(s): W. K. Frankenburg, J. B. Dodds, and A. W. Fandal
Publisher: William K. Frankenburg and Josiah B. Dodds
Address: Ladoca Project and Publishing Foundation, Inc., East 51st Avenue and Lincoln Street, Denver, CO 80216

Purpose/Description: The DDST was designed and standardized as a simple, useful tool to aid in the early discovery of children with developmental problems. It is a screening instrument and is not intended to result in diagnosis of specific problems. The DDST is an individually administered screening test of development with 105 items arranged in four sectors: personal-social, fine motor-adaptive, language, and gross motor. The test can be administered to children ranging in age from 2 weeks to 6 years.

Test Name: Developmental Activities Screening Inventory (DASI) (1977)
Author(s): R. F. DuBose and M. B. Langley
Publisher: Teaching Resources
Address: 50 Pond Park Road, Hingham, MD 02808

Purpose/Description: The main purpose of the authors was to design an easily administered screening test that could be used with preschool handicapped children. The test has a nonverbal design so that children with auditory impairments or language disorders would not be penalized by their handicap. The test has modifications for the visually impaired. The DASI kit is equipped with a carrying case, an instructor guide, and educational materials for administering the test. Everyday objects, necessary for administrations, are not included. Scoring sheets are. The DASI is an informal, individually administered test. The tasks are presented to the child through demonstration, and the child's response is observed and recorded on a checklist score sheet. Areas that are measured include fine motor coordination, cause-effect and means-end relationship, association, number concepts, size discrimination, and seriation. The DASI is designed as an informal screening measure for children functioning between the ages of 6 months and 60 months.

Test Name: Developmental Indicators for the Assessment of Learning, Revised (DIAL-R) (1983)
Author(s): C. D. Mardell-Czudnowski and D. Goldenberg
Publisher: Childcraft Education Corporation
Address: 20 Kilmer Road, Edison, NJ 08818

Purpose/Description: DIAL-R is an early childhood screening test that is intended to assist in the identification of children who may have special education needs. The DIAL-R can be used to determine if further assessment or diagnosis of a child needs to be completed in accordance with state and federal mandates for serving young handicapped children. The authors also indicate that the DIAL-R can be used in the regular classroom to identify students' strengths and weaknesses as the first step in programming or curriculum development. The DIAL-R was revised in 1983 and is considered to be an improved version of the original DIAL screening instrument. It is a team-administered individual assessment of early childhood development. The basic format and procedures of the original DIAL are maintained on the DIAL-R, and it assesses the following areas: motor, concepts, and language. The norms have also been extended to include children from 2 to 6 years of age. It includes separate norms for white and nonwhite populations.

Test Name: The Developmental Profile (1972)
Author(s): G. Alpern and T. Boll
Publisher: Psychological Development Corporation
Address: P.O. Box 3198, Aspen, CO 81611

Purpose/Description: The Developmental Profile is an inventory of skills that has been designed to assess a child's development from birth to preadolescence. The Developmental Profile consists of 217 items arranged into five scales. All scales have the items arranged into age levels. The age levels proceed in 6-month intervals from birth to 3½ years and proceed thereafter by year intervals. Year intervals describe children 6 months from both sides of the year norms (e.g., 6-year level covers ages 5½ to 6½ years). The profile is administered in an interview format with a rater who knows the child well. The rater might also self-administer the test. The scale can be used with children ranging in age from birth to 12 years. The authors indicate that the scale can be used for assessing handicapped children. However, some revisions must be made with test administration procedures.

Test Name: Diagnostic Inventory of Early Development (Brigance) (1978)
Author(s): A. H. Brigance
Publisher: Curriculum Associates
Address: 5 Esquire Road, North, Billerica, MA 01862, (800) 225-0246

Purpose/Description: The Brigance inventory was designed to simplify and combine the processes of assessing, diagnosing, recordkeeping, and instructional planning for young children. The author claims that the instrument serves as an assessment instrument, an instructional guide, a recordkeeping tracking system, a tool for developing and communicating IEP, and as a resource for training parents and professionals. The individually administered inventory includes 98 skill sequences, from birth through the developmental age of 6 years, for the following areas: psychomotor, self-help, speech and language, general knowledge and comprehension, and early academic skills. It is criterion-referenced but is considered by the author to be norm-referenced because the age ranges for each skill were validated from several resources that list normative data. During administration the inventory booklet is opened to an assessment procedure, and the printed material for the examiner is in the correct position for reading with the visual material facing the child. The author recommends that the materials provided by the examiner to assess the child be familiar to the child and commonly found in the home or school. The inventory was designed to be used in programs for infants and children below the developmental age of 7 years.

Test Name: The Early Intervention Developmental Profile (Developmental Programming for Infants and Young Children) (Vols. 1–3, 1977; Vols. 4 and 5, 1981)
Author(s): D. S. Schafer and M. S. Moersch
Publisher: The University of Michigan Press
Address: 615 East University, Ann Arbor, MI 48106

Purpose/Description: Volumes 1, 2, 4, and 5 enable the educator or therapist to develop comprehensive and individualized developmental programs by translating comprehensive evaluation data rendered by the profile into short-term behavioral objectives that form the basis of daily activities planned to facilitate emerging skills. Volume 3, a comprehensive collection of sequenced activities, enables parents and professionals to select appropriate activities that will blend into the family's daily routine (birth to 36 months). Assessment and Application, Volumes 1 and 4, and The Early Intervention Developmental Profile, Volumes 2 and 5, make up the assessment portion of the program. This assessment instrument is made up of six scales that provide developmental milestones in the following areas: perceptual/fine motor, cognition, language, social/emotional, self-care, and gross motor development. The profile contains 487 items and yields information for planning comprehensive developmental programs for children with various handicaps who function below the 72-month level. The five volume program has been designed for children ranging in age from birth to 72 months.

Test Name: Flint Infant Security Scale (1974)
Author(s): B. M. Flint
Publisher: Guidance Center
Address: Faculty of Education, University of Toronto, Toronto, Canada M4W 2K8

Purpose/Description: The Flint Infant Security Scale is designed to assess the mental and emotional health of children from 3 months to 2 years of age. Applications to pediatric examinations, preadoptive placements, and implications for intervention therapies are provided. The scale has a total of 72 items descriptive of infant-toddler behavior. These items describe a range of behavior and encompass a variety of life experiences. Through an interview with the mother and objective descriptions of the child's observed behavior while in the same room during the interview, security ratings or scores are obtained in the following eight areas: eating, unfamiliar situation, sleeping, toileting and bathing, physical experiences, changing environment, socializing, and playing. The rating choices are: "Secure" versus "Deputing Agent and Regression." The former is a positive, healthy or age-appropriate rating, and the latter is a negative, unhealthy, and age-inappropriate rating.

Test Name: Functional Profile (1981)
Author(s): Peoria 0–3 Program, Allied Agencies Center
Publisher: Materials Coordinator, The Peoria 0–3 Outreach Project
Address: 320 East Armstrong Avenue, Peoria, IL 61603

Purpose/Description: The Functional Profile is designed to determine an approximate level of functioning and to plan a program suited to the child's individual needs. The profile is a checklist of 481 developmental skills and social traits that normal infants and young children usually demonstrate at certain age levels. There are seven categories: social, cognitive-linguistic-verbal, gross motor, fine motor, eating, dressing, and toileting. Within each category, the tasks are separated into age groups in months and are arranged according to level of difficulty. The same form is used repeatedly for a given child. Basal levels and ceilings are established in the usual manner. The child's performance is rated either Yes or No, the behavior being present or absent. The child is said to be functioning at the highest level at which one more than half of the items are passed. Functioning levels are plotted on a graph to provide a visual representation of the child's skills. The profile is designed for use with children ranging in age from birth to 6 years of age.

Test Name: Gesell Developmental Schedules (1940)
Author(s): A. Gesell
Publisher: Nigel Cox
Address: 69 Fawn Drive, Cheshire, CT 06410

Purpose/Description: The Gesell Developmental Schedules were developed and organized to provide an adequate developmental diagnosis. The diagnosis requires an examination of the quality and integration of five domains of behavior. The Gesell Developmental Schedules are individually administered and assess five domains of behavior: adaptive, gross motor, fine motor, language, and personal-social. The materials required for the developmental examination are contained in a kit, but no manual is provided. The user will need to refer to *Developmental Diagnoses* (Knobloch and Pasamanick, 1974) for a discussion of the schedules and assessment procedures. The schedules are designed for children ages 4 weeks to 6 years.

Test Name: Griffiths Mental Developmental Scales (1954)
Author(s): R. Griffiths
Publisher: Test Center, Inc.
Address: Snug Harbor Village, 7721 Holiday Drive, Sarasota, FL 33581

Purpose/Description: The Griffiths Scales were designed to measure trends of development that are indicative of mental growth in young children (standardized measure of intelligence). They are divided into two levels: birth to 2 years, which is described in the book *The Abilities of Babies,* and 2 to 8 years, which is described in *The Abilities of Young Children.* Five scales are used in evaluating the birth to 2-year-old child: locomotion, personal-social, hearing and speech, eye and hand coordination, and performance. A sixth scale, practical reasoning, is added for children ages 3 to 8 years. A developmental age and developmental quotient can be computed for each scale as well as an overall mental age and intelligence quotient.

Test Name: Hawaii Early Learning Profile (HELP) (1979)
Author(s): Enrichment Project for Handicapped Infants (S. Furuno, Director)
Publisher: VORT Corporation
Address: P.O. Box 11132, Palo Alto, CA 94306

Purpose/Description: The HELP was developed to assist in planning individualized programs for children with a wide range of handicaps and diagnoses. It provides a comprehensive visual picture of the child's functioning levels and focuses on the whole child (i.e., building strengths as well as helping work on areas of weakness). The HELP is divided into the HELP Charts and the HELP Activity Guide. The chart provides a comprehensive visual picture, and the skills are developmentally sequenced in small incremental steps, arranged in a horizontal continuum. The guide corresponds with the developmental steps and assists in planning and task analysis to develop the appropriate skills. Both the chart and guide provide a month-to-month sequence of normal developmental skills in six areas: cognitive, expressive language, gross motor, fine motor, self-help, and social-emotional. The profile is intended for use with children from birth to 36 months.

Test Name: Home Observation for Measurement of the Environment (HOME) (1978)
Author(s): B. M. Caldwell
Publisher: Child Development Research Unit
Address: University of Arkansas at Little Rock, 33rd and University Avenue, Little Rock, AR 72204

Purpose/Description: Two separate instruments have been designed to sample certain aspects of the quantity and quality of social, emotional, and cognitive support available to a young child within the child's home. One instrument measures these aspects for children from birth to age 3 years. The second measures these aspects for children from ages 3 to 6. The inventory for children ages birth to 3 contains 45 items; the inventory for 3 to 6-year-old children contains 55 items. The original intent was that all items would be based on direct observation of the interaction between caretaker (usually the mother) and the child. However, an examination of the item pool suggested that many important areas of experience for the infant and preschooler were excluded with this restriction on item selection. Therefore, succeeding versions of the inventory included items requiring an interview format. Such items make up about one third of the total number for the birth to 3 years inventory and about two-thirds of the total number for the 3 to 6 years inventory. The present version of each of the inventories requires a home visit of about one hour's duration at a time when the child is awake. The instructional manuals provide a description of items, definitions, guidelines for conducting the interviews, and recommendations for reducing subjectivity on scoring. The inventory for infants can be used for children from birth to 3 years of age. The preschool version is intended for children ages 3 to 6 years.

Test Name: Indiana Preschool Developmental Assessment Scale (IPDAS) (Indiana Home Teaching System for Parents and Handicapped Preschoolers) (1976)
Author(s):   Primary authors: B. Bateman, J. Henn, J. Wilke, R. Wilson, C. Maslen, and W. A. Bragg
Publisher: Developmental Training Center
Address: 2853 East Tenth Street, Bloomington, IN 47401

Purpose/Description: The purpose of the total program (IHTS) is fourfold: (1) to provide a comprehensive model for the home delivery of educational services to handicapped preschool children, (2) to provide an assessment instrument applicable to preschool handicapped children, (3) to develop a corresponding home teaching curriculum and related materials for parental use with the preschool handicapped child, and (4) to provide technical assistance to administrators and professional and paraprofessional service providers at the preschool level. The purpose of the assessment is to develop a well-defined profile describing the level of the child's developmental functioning in the motor, personal autonomy, communication, and preacademic areas. This profile will be used to formulate an appropriate educational program for the child to be carried out, generally, by the parents under the guidance of a key staff member. The scale is intended for use with children ranging in age from birth to 6 years.

Test Name: Infant Intelligence Test (1940–1960)
Author(s):   P. Cattell
Publisher: The Psychological Corporation
Address: 304 East 45th Street, New York, NY 10017

Purpose/Description: As of October 1937, the author was unable to find a single published test for infants that contained definite and precise directions for scoring, comparable to those for children of school age. The

Infant Intelligence Scale was constructed to be as free as possible from the limitation of existing infant tests at that time. The scale consists of five items at each month from 2 to 12 months. From 12 to 24 months, five items are presented at 2-month intervals. From 24 to 30 months, five items are presented at 3-month intervals. Two thirds of the manual is devoted to the administration of test items. Each item is presented on a separate page. The directions include the material to be used, the procedures to be followed, and the scoring system to be applied. The majority of the items include a photograph that illustrates a young child responding to the task. The materials and examination forms used to administer the tests are contained in a small suitcase. The publisher has attempted to organize the case of materials in a manner that facilitates the administration process. The scale's items range developmentally from 2 to 30 months.

Test Name: Koontz Child Developmental Program Training Activities for the First 48 Months (1974)
Author(s):   C. W. Koontz
Publisher: Western Psychological Services
Address: 12031 Wilshire Boulevard, Los Angeles, CA 90025

Purpose/Description: The Koontz instrument was designed to evaluate, monitor progress, and plan suitable activities for infants. Evaluation is achieved by matching the behavior of a child in a normal setting with a list of graded observable performance items. Progress is recorded in relation to the performance items, and activities are suggested that are designed to reinforce the performance items. Four functional areas of development are considered: gross motor, fine motor, social, and language. There is a possible total of 550 performance items. Activities associated with each level and each area are designed to strengthen the performance of the items. Other pertinent information corresponding to the levels and the areas is included in the activity section. The program is designed for children aged 1 to 48 months.

Test Name: Learning Accomplishment Profile: Diagnostic Edition (LAP-D) (Revised) (1977)
Author(s):   D. W. LeMay, P. M. Griffin, and A. R. Sanford
Publisher: Kaplan School Supply Corporation
Address: 600 Jonestown Road, Winston-Salem, NC 27103

Purpose/Description: The LAP-D sees as a major educational objective the determination of the individual child's mastery level in each of the five skill areas included in the instrument. It is anticipated that the accurate and reliable assessment of the child's developmental level should translate into an effective instructional program, providing the foundation in which sound instructional programs can be grounded. The LAP-D consists of 323 items organized according to five scales and 13 subscales: fine motor (manipulating and writing), cognitive (matching and counting), language/cognitive (naming and comprehension), gross motor (body movement and object movement), self-help (eating, dressing, grooming, toileting, and self-direction). The items within each subscale are arranged in an ascending order of complexity and in a task-analytic manner. Each item describes the behavior to be observed, the procedure to be followed in eliciting the desired responses, and the criteria against which success is measured. Developmental ages are provided for each item. At 6-month intervals the developmental ages serve as indicators of the appropriate starting point for the assessment. The LAP-D kit contains a loose-leaf easel. The easel contains the procedures for administering the test, a list of the behaviors to be observed, critiera for evaluating the child's performance, and picture cards and matching cards located in pockets adjacent to the particular items. A variety of colorful materials are also included in the kit. All of the materials necessary for complete assessment (with the exception of food items for the self-help section) are provided. Behaviors assessed with the LAP-D range from a developmental age of 6 to 72 months.

Test Name: Learning Accomplishment Profile for Infants (Early LAP) (Revised) (1975, Revised 1978)
Author(s):   M. E. Glover, J. L. Preminger, and A. R. Sanford
Publisher: Kaplan Press
Author(s):   P.O. Box 15207, 600 Jonestown Road, Winston-Salem, NC 27103

Purpose/Description: The Early LAP is a criterion-referenced assessment that provides a simple profile of the overall development of children from birth to 3 years. The Early LAP is a revision of the 1975 Learning Accomplishment Profile for Infants. It contains six developmental skill areas: gross motor, fine motor, cognitive, language, self-help, and social-emotional. There are 412 items, which were taken from previously developed instruments. The bibiliography lists 19 sources. Items are stated as behavioral objectives. Developmental ages are provided. It is individually administered. The instrument is intended for use with children from birth to 36 months.

Test Name: McCarthy Scales of Children's Abilities (1972)
Author(s):   D. McCarthy
Publisher: The Psychological Corporation
Address: 7955 Caldwell Avenue, Chicago, IL 60648

Purpose/Description: The McCarthy Scales of Children's Abilities were designed to evaluate children's general intellectual level as well as their strengths and weaknesses in a number of ability areas. This individually administered test consists of 18 subtests that make up six scales: verbal, perceptual-performance, quantitative, memory, motor, general cognitive. The General Cognitive Scale is a composite of the Verbal, Perceptual-Performance, and Quantitative Scales. The test materials are attractive and help to facilitate the establishment and maintenance of rapport. The sequential organization of the McCarthy Scales is an important feature that also promotes the establishment of rapport. The test begins with manipulative items; gross motor tests appear midway when the child is becoming restless and interest is beginning to wane; and the final items require limited vocalizations in anticipation of the child's state of fatigue. The McCarthy Scales include several built-in precautions to promote optimum measurement of the child's ability in each task. Extra trials are permitted for many items to give a child a second chance; only the best performance is counted. To ensure that the child understands the task at hand, he is frequently given feedback on the easier items; on one subtest examples are given to get the child started. In addition, the inclusion of several multipoint items rewards the child for virtually any response approximating correct performance. The test can be administered to children ranging in age from 2½ to 8½ years.

Test Name: Marshalltown Behavioral Developmental Profile (Copyright pending)
Author(s): M. Donahue, A. F. Keiser, J. D. Montgomery, V. L. Roecker, L. I. Smith, and M. F. Walden
Publisher: The Marshalltown Project
Address: 507 East Anson Street, Marshalltown, IA 50158

Purpose/Description: The purpose of the profile is to facilitate individual prescriptive teaching of preschool children within the home setting. There are three developmental categories: communication, motor, and social. The behavioral items are grouped in age categories with 1 month of age, 3-month segments from 12 to 24 months, 6-month segments from 24 to 36 months, and 12-month segments from 36 to 72 months. A total of 327 items is provided. Each item is briefly stated in behavioral terms; however, no criteria examples are given. A direct test procedure is used; there is no allowance for parent report. An age-level score is obtained for the three developmental categories; also computed are an overall mean age and a developmental quotient. The profile is designed for use with children from birth to 6 years of age.

Test Name: Milani-Comparetti Developmental Scale (1973)
Author(s): A. Milani-Comparetti and E. A. Gidoni
Publisher: Meyer Children's Rehabilitation Institute
Address: University of Nebraska Medical Center, Omaha, NE 68131

Purpose/Description: The Milani-Comparetti Developmental Scale is a series of simple procedures designed to evaluate a child's physical development from birth to about 2 years. By using this test, a physician, therapist, or public health nurse can determine in a short period of time whether a child's physical development corresponds to that of a normal child's. The individually administered procedures are divided into two parts. The first half of the test evaluates the child's motor development. This series of procedures is called Spontaneous Behavior and assesses the child's ability to control the head and body, to move from one position to another, to stand up from a supine position, and to move about. It consists of nine procedures. The second half of the test assesses those reactions that are predictable, that is, those responses that a normal child automatically gives to specific stimuli. These responses appear in the normal child at fairly specific times in the child's development. This portion of the test is called Evoked Responses and consists of 18 different procedures. One characteristic of the Milani-Comparetti test is its simplicity. The test can be administered on a table with no special equipment. It may also be administered repeatedly. Repeated evaluations are often valuable as they assist in the detection of developmental delay. The test is not a substitute for standardized tests of infant behavior. Rather, it is a complement to such instruments. It is intended to be used with children in the age range of birth to 2 years.

Test Name: Miller Assessment for Preschoolers (MAP) (1982)
Author(s): L. J. Miller
Publisher: Kid Technology
Address: 11715 E. 51st Avenue, Denver, CO 80239

Purpose/Description: The MAP was developed to provide a statistically sound, short screening tool that could be used to identify children who exhibit moderate preacademic problems affecting one or more areas of development. In addition, it was developed to provide a comprehensive, structured clinical framework that would be helpful in defining strengths and weaknesses and would indicate possible avenues of remediation. It is an individually administered screening tool that provides a comprehensive overview of a child's developmental status with respect to other children the same age. Twenty-seven core items make up the MAP, but it is designed to be given as a unit only. The score is valued only if based upon performance of all the test items. The items can be grouped as follows:

1. Sensory and motor abilities: Sense of position and movement, sense of touch, basic components of movement and coordinaton.
2. Cognitive abilities: Verbal and nonverbal items examining memory, sequencing, comprehension, association, and expression.
3. Combined abilities: Items requiring the interpretation of visual-spatial information

The kit includes an examiner's manual, cue sheets, item score sheet/behavior during testing, record booklet, drawing booklet, scoring transparency, and scoring notebook. The materials are contained in a carrying case that also provides a shield, enabling the examiner to prepare test materials out of view of the child. The MAP is intended for use with children ranging in age from 2 years, 9 months to 5 years, 8 months.

Test Name: Minnesota Child Development Inventory (MCDI) (1972)
Author(s): H. Ireton and E. Thwing
Publisher: Behavior Science Systems, Inc.
Address: P.O. Box 1108, Minneapolis, MN 55440

Purpose/Description: The MCDI was devised to furnish pediatricians and other clinicians working with school-age children with means of evaluating a child's development without the expenditure of professional time. The MCDI is a standardized instrument that uses the mother's observations to measure the development of her child. The inventory consists of a booklet and an answer sheet for the mother, and a profile deduced from her replies. The booklet contains 320 statements that describe the behaviors of children in the first 6½ years of life. These statements were selected on the basis of (1) representation of real developmental skills, (2) observability by mothers in real life situations, (3) descriptive clarity, and (4) age-discriminating power. The mother indicates those statements referable to her child's behavior by marking Yes or No on the answer sheet. The 320 items have been grouped into eight scales: general development, gross motor, fine motor, expressive language, comprehension-conceptual, situation comprehension, self-help, and personal-social. The MCDI can be completed for children ranging in age from 6 months to 6 years. There is limited room for growth at the top of the inventory; it would be difficult to demonstrate a range of skills for children at the upper end of the age range.

Test Name: Minnesota Infant Development Inventory (MIDI) (1980)
Author(s): H. Ireton and E. Thwing
Publisher: Behavior Science Systems, Inc.
Address: P.O. Box 1108, Minneapolis, MN 55440

Purpose/Description: The MIDI was designed to obtain and summarize a mother's observations of her baby's current development. The MIDI measures development in five areas: gross motor, fine motor, language, comprehension, and personal-social. It provides an opportunity for the mother to describe her baby and report any problems or concerns about the child. The inventory consists of a test booklet of 75 statements that describe the developmental behaviors of children in the first 15 months of life. This is an individually administered instrument. It is designed for children ranging in age from 1 to 15 months.

Test Name: A Motor Development Checklist (1976)
Author(s): A. M. Doudlah
Publisher: Library Information Center
Address: Central Wisconsin Center for the Developmentally Disabled, 317 Knutson Drive, Madison, WI 53704

Purpose/Description: The purpose of the checklist is to assess the child's motor development in terms of spontaneous action patterns, which are stated to be the most representative of a child's status. The sequence of motor development can be used for planning and evaluating the effectiveness of therapy programs. The sequence of motor development is considered crucial; time and rate of development are not as important. The checklist is an observational record and consists of a videotape, *Motor Development Checklist,* and scoresheets. Observation is done monthly, and length of observation depends on the spontaneous motor movements of the child. The scoring can be done two ways: (1) indicate presence of motor behavior or (2) use the following scale: does not perform task, beginning to attempt task, performs task occasionally, or performs task skillfully. The second scoring method provides more time-related information about progress. The profile is for use with children from birth to the walking state (approximately 15 months).

Test Name: Portage Guide to Early Education (Revised) (1976)
Author(s): S. Bluma, M. Shearer, A. Frohman, and J. Hilliard
Publisher: The Portage Guide
Address: Cooperative Educational Service Agency 12, 412 East Slifer Street, Portage, WI 53901

Purpose/Description: The Portage Guide to Early Education (revised edition) was developed to serve as a guide to those who need to assess a child's behavior and plan realistic curriculum goals that lead to additional skills. The checklist and card file can aid in assessing present behavior, targeting emerging behavior, and providing suggested techniques to teach each behavior. The guide contains three parts: (1) a checklist of behaviors on which to record an individual child's developmental progress, (2) a card file listing possible methods of teaching these behaviors, and (3) a manual of directions for using the checklist and card file and methods for implementing activities. The checklist serves as a method of informal assessment. The checklist is color-coded and divided into six developmental areas: infant stimulation, socialization, language, self-help, cognitive, and motor. A checklist can be completed on each child upon entry into a program. The checklist can serve as an ongoing curriculum record for all of the preschool years; essentially, the same checklist can be used each year. The behaviors are listed sequentially, at 1-year intervals, for each category from birth to 6 years. The guide is designed to be a curriculum planning tool. The information derived from it is used to delineate those skills acquired and those yet to be taught. The skills listed on the checklist are behaviorally stated. No specific criteria are provided, although some items do include examples. The examiner might refer to the card file to determine specific activities that could be used to assess the skill. There is a total of 580 items (535 if the infant stimulation items are not used). The checklist as well as the entire Portage Guide to Early Education can be used with children between the mental ages of birth and 6 years of age; the materials can be used with normal preschool children or preschool children with handicaps.

Test Name: Preschool Attainment Record (PAR) (Research Edition) (1966)
Author(s): E. A. Doll
Publisher: American Guidance Service
Address: Publisher's Building, Circle Pines, MN 55014

Purpose/Description: The PAR is an expansion of the early age levels of the Vineland Social Maturity Scale and is designed to measure the physical, social, mental, and language attainments of young children. This individually administered record includes eight categories of development: ambulation, manipulation, rapport, communication, responsibility, information, ideation, and creativity. For each category there is one item per 6-month age interval. Item types, arrangement, and standardized interview procedures are the same as those of the Vineland Social Maturity Scale. The appraisal is conducted by means of an interview and observations. The record can be used with children ranging in age from birth to 7 years. It is well adapted for testing deaf, blind, or aphasic children; children with cerebral palsy, mental retardation, autism, or schizophrenia; and children whose development has been impaired by sensory or cultural deprivation or who do not speak English.

Test Name: Preschool Language Scale (1969)
Author(s): I. L. Zimmerman, V. G. Steiner, and R. L. Evatt
Publisher: Charles E. Merrill Publishing Co.
Address: 1300 Alum Creek Drive, Columbus, OH 43216

Purpose/Description: The Preschool Language Scale was designed to detect language strengths and deficiencies. It consists of two main sections: auditory comprehension and verbal ability. A supplementary articulation section is also included. Test materials include a manual, picture book, and a 16-page test scale form. The Auditory Comprehension Scale consists of subtests that require a nonverbal response such as pointing to a picture the examiner has named. The Verbal Ability Scale consists of items that require a child to name or explain. The articulation section requires the child to say words and sentences after the examiner. The scale is not a test, but an evaluation instrument, still in experimental form, to be used to detect language strengths and weaknesses. The scale can be used with children ranging in age from 18 months to 7 years. The authors claim that it can be used with children of all ages who are assumed to be functioning at a preschool or primary language level.

Test Name: Receptive-Expressive Emergent Language Scale (REEL) (1971)
Author(s): K. Bzoch and R. League
Publisher: University Park Press
Address: 233 East Redwood Street, Baltimore, MD 21202
Purpose/Description: The purpose of the REEL Scale is to identify very young children who may have specific handicaps requiring early habilitative and educational intervention. The REEL Scale is administered principally through a parent or informant interview. The instructions allow considerable license in probing for information on each item. The manual recommends but does not require direct observation of the child to confirm questionable parent responses. Beginning with the startle responses (birth to 1 month), the test extends to a 36-month level. Six items (three expressive, three receptive) are listed for each 1-month interval through the first year. The second year items span 2-month intervals; the third year, 3-month intervals. The scale is founded on two basic premises regarding language function: (1) the auditory modality is the primary means of acquiring language, (2) speech behavior and cognition are inseparably interconnected. The REEL Scale is intended for use with children of ages from birth to 36 months.

Test Name: Reflex Testing Methods for Evaluating CNS Development (2nd Ed.) (1979)
Author(s): M. R. Fiorentino
Publisher: Charles C. Thomas
Address: 301-327 East Lawrence Avenue, Springfield, IL 62717, (217) 789-8980

Purpose/Description: The purpose of the test is to determine neurophysiological reflexive maturation of the CNS at the spinal, brain stem, midbrain, and cortical levels. The manual presents a normative sequential development of reflexive maturation and possible abnormal responses found in individuals with CNS disorders, such as cerebral palsy. Photographs and explanations of reflex responses and test positions with normal and abnormal responses are illustrated. Each reflex tested can be rated on a reflex testing chart and resulting functional responses on a motor development chart. Testing takes approximately 20 to 30 minutes. The test can be administered to children of ages from birth through 6 years.

Test Name: Rockford Infant Developmental Evaluation Scales (RIDES) (1979)
Author(s): Project RHISE, Children's Development Center
Publisher: Scholastic Testing Service
Address: 480 Meyer Road, Bensenville, IL 60106

Purpose/Description: The RIDES provides an informal indication of a child's developmental status in five major skill areas. The RIDES checklist consists of 308 developmental behaviors for ages ranging from birth to 4 years. They represent the most commonly cited descriptors of normal development found in the professional literature. Items are placed within age ranges and skill areas. The five skill areas are: personal-social-self-help, fine motor/adaptive, receptive language, expressive language, and gross motor. The RIDES is designed for use with children from birth to 4 years of age.

Test Name: Sequenced Inventory of Communication Development (SICD) (1975)
Author(s): D. L. Hedrick, E. M. Prather, and A. R. Tobin
Publisher: Western Psychological Services
Address: 12031 Wilshire Boulevard, Los Angeles, CA 90023

Purpose/Description: The SICD attempts to systematically assess receptive and expressive communication development for children aged 4 months to 4 years. The ultimate purpose is to increase efficiency for remedial programming both in the home and in the educational setting. There are two major sections to the inventory: a Receptive Scale and an Expressive Scale. The factors assessed in the Receptive Scale are awareness, discrimination, and understanding. The Expressive Scale is intended to represent a cross section of linguistic and psychological paradigms. Five factors are presented. Three are representative of communicative behaviors: initiating, imitating, and responding behaviors. Two are representative of linguistic behaviors: verbal output and articulation. The initiating, imitating, and responding behaviors are further subdivided into three assumed levels of progression: motor response, vocal response, and verbal response. The items include a developmental range from 4 to 48 months.

Test Name: Standford-Binet Intelligence Scale, Form L-M (1916, 1937, 1960, 1973; new revision imminent)
Author(s): L. M. Terman and M. A. Merrill
Publisher: Riverside Publishing Co.
Address: 1919 South Highland Avenue, Lombard, IL 60148

Purpose/Description: The Standford-Binet Intelligence Scale assesses general intellectual ability. The authors emphasize that it is not suited to the measurement of differential aptitudes. The Standford-Binet is an individually administered intelligence test that can be given to individuals from age 2 years up through adulthood. All materials required for administering the test are included in a compact carrying case. Materials appear to be adequate in terms of their size, durability, and usefulness for a wide range. The picture materials are, for the most part, black-and-white line drawings. These drawings are clearly presented; they may have somewhat limited appeal for very young children who often respond more readily to colored illustrations. The manual for administering the test is included in the carrying case. The Standford-Binet can be administered to individuals ranging in age from 2 years to 18 years (adulthood).

Test Name: Uniform Performance Assessment System (UPAS) (1981)
Author(s): N.G.Haring,O.R.White,E.B.Edgar,J.Q.Afflick,and A.H.Hayden

Publisher: Charles E. Merrill Publishing Co.
Address: 1300 Alum Creek Drive, Columbus, OH 43216

Purpose/Description: The UPAS is an instrument designed to monitor the progress of individuals whose skills are normally acquired between birth and the sixth year. UPAS was developed specifically to assist teachers and parents in meeting the needs of handicapped individuals. UPAS is a curriculum-referenced test that helps teachers and parents select which skills and behavior should be targeted for instruction for young or low-functioning pupils. There are four major curricular areas addressed by UPAS and organized in separate sections: (1) preacademic/fine motor development, (2) communication, (3) social/self-help skills, and (4) gross motor development. An additional section focuses on specific problems dealing with inappropriate behaviors. The UPAS has approximately 250 items with between 45 and 76 items on a given subscale. The UPAS tutor needs to have the UPAS criterion tests manual, UPAS stimulus cards, and UPAS records forms to complete an assessment. The criterion tests manual describes each test item and how it should be assessed. Each criterion test defines skills in terms that are observed directly and easily tested and describes specific standards for acceptable performance. The criterion tests are labeled according to curricula area and item number within each of the four aforementioned areas. The skill needed, equipment and materials, test/observation procedure, and criteria for scoring are included on each criterion test card. The UPAS is designed for children of ages from birth to 6 years.

Test Name: Verbal Language Development Scale (VLDS) (1971)
Author(s): M. Mecham
Publisher: American Guidance Service
Address: Publisher's Building, Circle Pines, MN 55014

Purpose/Description: The author developed this informant-interview scale of verbal language development as a method of assessing what a child does in daily life communicative activities. The VLDS is an extension of the communication portion of the Vineland Social Maturity Scale. The instrument is a 50-item scale that is designed to be administered to an informant regarding a child's performance on tasks that are primarily verbal. The 50 items serve as a basis for obtaining language age equivalents. The scale is purported to be used with children ranging in age from birth to 15 years. It is interesting to note, however, that 37 items reflect child behavior prior to 6½ years; only 5 items reflect child behavior for ages 9 to 15 years.

Test Name: Vocabulary Comprehension Scale (1975)
Author(s): T. E. Bangs
Publisher: Teaching Resources
Address: 50 Pond Park Road, Hingham, MA 02043-4382

Purpose/Description: The purpose of the Vocabulary Comprehension Scale is to provide teachers of language or learning handicapped children with baseline information related to comprehension of pronouns and words of position, quality, quantity, and size. The author suggests that this baseline data will enable the teacher to plan classroom and home activities that will assist the child in developing a vocabulary that will be appropriate for entrance into kindergarten or first grade. The scale consists of 61 items. Objects rather than pictures are used, as the author felt this would increase the reliability of responses. Most of the words, with the exception of the pronouns, are paired opposites. Materials are provided to develop two different scenes for eliciting responses from the children. A tea set and a male and female doll are used to measure the child's comprehension of pronouns. A garage with trees, a fence, a ladder, cats, and a dog are used to elicit responses for most of the words of position, quality, quantity, and size. A few additional items are provided to measure the comprehension of words not included in the two scenes. All items are administered according to the directions on the scoring form. The child is asked to name or point to all of the objects before beginning the actual assessment. The items are arranged according to four categories: garage scene, tea party scene, buttons, and miscellaneous. The scale was standardized on a population of children ranging in age from 2 to 12 years.

Test Name: Vulpe Assessment Battery (VAB) (1969, revised 1979)
Author(s): S. G. Vulpe, E. I. Pollins, and J. Wilson
Publisher: Canadian Association for the Mentally Retarded
Address: Kinsmen NIMR Building, York University Campus, 4700 Keele Street, Downsview (Toronto), Ontario, Canada M3J 1P3, (416) 661-9611

Purpose/Description: The purpose of the VAB is to provide a test of competencies in various developmental areas and to provide a sequential teaching approach. The Vulpe Assessment Battery is an individually administered comprehensive test including items/activities in the areas of: (1) basic senses, developmental reflexes, postural mobility, balance, motor planning, and muscle strength; (2) environment (physical plan and caregiving personnel); (3) organizational behaviors, attention, motivation, response to environmental limits, dependence, independence; as well as the usual areas of gross motor, fine motor, expressive language, receptive language, and activity of daily living. There are many subsections under each of these areas. There is a total of 1,340 possible items on the test. The battery was designed for children developing atypically from birth through 6 years of age.

Test Name: Wechsler Preschool and Primary Scale of Intelligence (WPPSI) (1967)
Author(s): D. Wechsler
Publisher: The Psychological Corporation
Address: 7555 Caldwell Avenue, Chicago, IL 60648

Purpose/Description: The WPPSI provides a systematic appraisal that purports to measure the mental ability of young children. It continues the theoretical and methodological approaches to the measurement of mental ability that were the principles in the construction of the Wechsler Intelligence Scale for Children (WISC). The WPPSI is actually a downward extension of the Wechsler Adult Intelligence Scale (WAIS) and WISC. The WPPSI consists of a battery of subtests, each of which when treated separately may be considered as measuring a different ability and when combined into a composite score may be considered a measure of overall or global intellectual capacity. It consists of 11 subtests, 6 verbal (one is optional) and 5 performance. Eight of the subtests are similar to subtests of the WISC, although there are modifications. The directions for administering and scoring the WPPSI are clearly contained in the test manual. The materials are durable and are not ambiguous. Examiners trained in the process of individual test administration and psychology should have no trouble administering and interpreting the WPPSI. The WPPSI has been developed for use primarily with children 4 to 6½ years old. In general, the authors recommend that the WPPSI be used instead of the WISC at levels where the two scales overlap.

Test Name: Woodstock-Johnson Psycho-Educational Battery (WJPEB) (Parts 1–3, 1977; Part 4, 1984)
Author(s): R. W. Woodcock, M. B. Johnson, R. H. Bruininks (Parts 1–3); R. F. Weatherman, and B. K. Hill (Part 4)
Publisher: Teaching Resources
Address: P.O. Box 4000, One DLM Park, Allen, TX 75002

Purpose/Description: The WJPEB is a wide-range comprehensive set of tests for measuring cognitive ability, achievement, interests, and independent behavior. The authors state that the battery was designed as an overview rather than as a tool for in-depth diagnosis. This individually administered battery is organized into four parts. Part 1 is intended to provide information regarding a subject's cognitive functions and scholastic achievements: reading, mathematics, written language, science, social studies, and humanities. Part 3 measures a subject's level of preference for participating in various scholastic and nonscholastic forms of activity. Part 4 is intended to provide information regarding an individual's functional independence and adaptive behavior in motor skills, social and communicative skills, personal living skills, and community living skills. Norms are provided from the preschool (age 3 years) to the geriatric (age 80 years) level.

Author Index

Subject Index

Italic page numbers refer to figures and tables.

DATE			
OCT 1 9 1991			
MAY 1 9 1999			